D0040990

DemoCRIPS AND
ReBLOODlicans

DemoCRIPS AND ReBLOODlicans

NO MORE GANGS IN GOVERNMENT

JESSE VENTURA

with Dick Russell

SKYHORSE PUBLISHING

Copyright © 2012 by Jesse Ventura with Dick Russell

All Rights Reserved. No part of this book may be reproduced in any manner without the express written consent of the publisher, except in the case of brief excerpts in critical reviews or articles. All inquiries should be addressed to Skyhorse Publishing, 307 West 36th Street, 11th Floor, New York, NY 10018.

Skyhorse Publishing books may be purchased in bulk at special discounts for sales promotion, corporate gifts, fund-raising, or educational purposes. Special editions can also be created to specifications. For details, contact the Special Sales Department, Skyhorse Publishing, 307 West 36th Street, 11th Floor, New York, NY 10018 or info@skyhorsepublishing.com.

Skyhorse® and Skyhorse Publishing® are registered trademarks of Skyhorse Publishing, Inc.®, a Delaware corporation.

Visit our website at www.skyhorsepublishing.com.

10 9 8 7 6 5 4 3 2 1

Library of Congress Cataloging-in-Publication Data

Ventura, Jesse.
 DemoCRIPS and reBloodlicans : no more gangs in government / Jesse Ventura, with Dick Russell.
    p. cm.
 ISBN 978-1-61608-448-6 (hardcover : alk. paper)
 1. Business and politics--United States. 2. Corporations--Political activity--United States. 3. Lobbying--United States. 4. Campaign funds--United States. 5. Political parties--United States. 6. Two-party systems--United States. 7. United States--Politics and government. I. Russell, Dick. II. Title.
 JK467.V45 2012
 322'.30973--dc23
                                   2012015895

Printed in the United States of America

To
Hunter S. Thompson,

A real journalist and a man who warned us

CONTENTS

"*There is no nation on earth powerful enough to accomplish our overthrow. Our destruction, should it come at all, will be from another quarter. From the inattention of the people to the concerns of their government, from their carelessness and negligence. I must confess that I do apprehend some danger. I fear that they may place too implicit a confidence in their public servants and fail properly to scrutinize their conduct; that in this way they may be made the dupes of designing men and become the instruments of their own undoing. Make them intelligent, and they will be vigilant; give them the means of detecting the wrong, and they will apply the remedy.*"

—Daniel Webster

DemoCRIPS AND ReBLOODlicans

CHAPTER ONE

GANG WARFARE:
DEMOCRIPS VS. REBLOODLICANS

L et me start out by explaining the title of this book for those readers who might not be familiar with the Crips and the Bloods. The
Crips were a street gang founded in Southern California in 1969 and
were looking to unite local gang members in South Central Los Angeles to battle other street gangs.[1] According to Crips founder Stanley
Tookie Williams, blue eventually became the color associated with
the Crips after one of their first members, Buddha (who habitually
wore a blue bandana), was shot and killed in February 1973.

As time went on, the Crips became popular and were able to
incorporate other gangs into their ranks. With more than 35,000 estimated members, the Crips engaged in a whole slew of illegal activities, ranging from drug distribution and extortion to the general
spread of gang-related violence through the '70s and '80s.

The Bloods formed in reaction to the Crips in 1972. Initially
founded by members of the Pirus street gang, a faction that broke
off from the Crips, the Bloods set themselves apart by resorting to
extreme violence and the production of crack cocaine in the 1980s.
(They got some help with that from the federal government, which
used the proceeds to fund the Nicaraguan Contras.)[2] The color for
the Bloods, not too surprisingly, is red.

Okay, think about this for a moment. The color schemes, for example. Think "red states" and "blue states." Aren't the Republicans considered the "red state" party, and the Democrats "blue" like the Crips? Besides trying to kill each other off while building up their own coffers with funds-for-favors, don't the Republicans and the Democrats do everything they can to incorporate any "neighboring street gangs?"

The current state of political discourse and activity in our country is one that bears a close resemblance to gangland warfare. So in my view, it's highly appropriate to equate "DemoCrips" and "Re-Bloodlicans" with their street counterparts. The only difference is that the two parties (gangs) have just been at it longer. The two political gangs have their turf, and that's what they protect. They operate identically with street gangs: Dues are paid by members of the gang; all decisions are made within the gang; there's hierarchy within the gang. Gang members became the admired objects of rap songs, and the party (gang) members have become media celebrities.

And why do we allow them to use a fun word like *party*? When you say party, you think of a joyous occasion. My Webster's dictionary defines party as "a social gathering or assembly of persons for entertainment, amusement, or pleasure," as in partygoer, party time, party girl, party hearty, party on, and so forth. Everybody loves to party! Well, I guess our politics have pretty much become entertainment, but you'd think we might take governance more seriously than to just identify it with partying.

Besides, what these people are doing is hardly cause for joy. The reality is, they're stealing our country, and they're doing it in the same manner that any street gang does: by acquisition of turf. And right now, your candidate for president is not chosen by you the public—he or she is chosen by the two gangs.

So let's call a party a party and a gang a gang. I can also say that with a straight face because I was a member of the Mongol Motorcycle Club, South Bay California chapter. That was toward the end of my service as a Navy SEAL and after my discharge from active duty. Eventually, I became the sergeant-at-arms of my chapter before I left in 1974.

Of course, even in the outlaw motorcycle world, we don't call ourselves gangs. We're motorcycle clubs. That's what you see on the back of every jacket—MC for Motorcycle Club. Just like the gun club or the chess club—you pick a name to project the image that you want—whether it's true or not, such as the Democratic Party (gang) and the Republican Party (gang). Of course, nobody gets shot (generally speaking); they just get paid off and set up (think Monica Lewinsky and Clinton's impeachment). However, some of these gang members do go to jail like other gangsters, for instance Governor Good-Hair, Hot Rod Blagojevich, who got caught on tape saying what the other gang members say in private.

All right, time to get serious. There's another comparison to be drawn between political and street gangs, and that's collateral damage to innocent civilians. Think about it. When bikers fight in a bar, and occasionally guns get drawn, if somebody happens to get in the way, too bad. When politicians fight each other within our government and take their bribes from the lobbyists, we're the ones who always pay the price. It's not only about war, but also about collateral damage to people losing their homes and jobs.

So what is this book about, and what am I advocating? If the word "gang" offends you, then for this paragraph I'll use the term "cabal" for party leaders who are out to maintain their hegemony over our system of government (much to the detriment of most Americans, not to mention the ideals and intentions of the founding fathers).

Or I'll use another analogy: pro wrestling. I know that sounds kind of silly, but it's true. The two gangs pretend to be adversaries in front of the public—good-cop, bad-cop, depending on whether you're sitting in the high-priced seats or the bleachers—but ultimately, they're both working for the same things: maintaining their power, getting richer, and making sure their wealthy backers keep control of the ship-of-state.

I've often been asked what has gone so fundamentally wrong with our country. My response is that the Democrats and Republicans are equally responsible and equally guilty because they've been in charge for over 150 years. They've created a system based upon bribery. Today, Wall Street owns our politicians, no matter which party (gang) it is—their allegiance is to the corporations and big business. "We basically have two bankrupt parties bankrupting the country," is the way a Stanford political scientist, Larry Diamond, put it.[3]

The loose definition of fascism is when corporations take over government. And I think in the United States, we're right on the brink of that, if we're not there already.

Consider the following:

- Wall Street gets bailed out, while average homeowners who got bilked by the banks go broke.
- Not one Street-wise exec gets prosecuted for mega fraud, but if you get caught selling an ounce of marijuana, hasta la vista, baby.
- American Airlines declares bankruptcy so they won't have to pay their debts or renegotiate their labor contracts, but the law doesn't let a regular family declare personal bankruptcy to renegotiate their mortgage.
- We hear all the Rebloodlicans squawking about the budget deficit, but the true reason it's been growing is because of how big money has corrupted the government—including the thievery of our election process.

These are some of the things that the Occupy Wall Street (OWS) movement—which was born in Manhattan's Zucotti Park in the heart of Wall Street and has sprouted up around the world—are protesting about. They're not all opposed to capitalism. (I love Wall Street, I just don't like the crooks and conspirators who run it.) The occupiers are simply saying, "Stop it, Wall Street, stop buying the allegiance of our politicians!" They want leaders, not politicians, who are committed to the challenges of average people to put a roof over their head and food on their table. They want proof that their leaders are acting for the greater common good and not simply out of greed or lust for power. They want leaders who are accountable for their actions—like President Truman said, "the buck stops here."

Despite the media spin that the Occupiers are sex-crazed twenty-somethings with nothing better to do than loaf, party, and trash the parks, the facts bear out that the OWS movement is diverse, and its members are older than you think. For every young person, there is one in his or her forties. The occupiers are from all walks of life, and supporters are sending contributions from as many as thirty-seven countries.[4] Almost half the people polled by the New York Times/CBS News in October 2011 said they believed "the sentiment at the root of the Occupy movement generally reflects the views of most Americans." They want higher taxes for corporations and millionaires and a more even distribution of wealth. But full 89 percent of Americans say they "distrust government to do the right thing."[5]

So these demonstrations seem to be waking more people up. In Minnesota, I wanted to be the first political face in the country to come forward and support this movement. I went down there about half a dozen times. One night I made a trip to the hardware store and bought all the hand warmers they had, which I took down to the park in a big bag and set on their table. I said, "Hey I'm too old to spend the night, but for you young people doing this, these will help keep you warm."

Now get this: In Minnesota they wouldn't allow generators for the people to keep warm—they say no generators are permitted in the park—but there *was* a generator there, and it was running 24-7. You know what it was for? It had a camera on top of a pole, keeping all the protesters under surveillance. So it's okay for the government, but for people to keep warm exercising their First

Amendment rights, it's not allowed! One set of rules for one side, a different set for the other side. You'll read more about what's happening to the Bill of Rights in our supposed democracy as this book unfolds.

It's my hope that this book puts forward a step toward winning back our country. For the first time, I've taken a new position. From my perspective, I can't be an advocate anymore for third-party politics. I know this might stun some people, but I no longer support any third party. I happily wore that banner with pride for six or seven years. However, we've got to face the reality that the two parties control the system to such an extent that, to be viable, a third party would have to sell out and become just as bad.

Look at the Tea Party, it's already become corrupt! I'll spell out the details as we go along. When the major players are Glenn Beck and his ilk, I don't see that as a good alternative. It just adds another head to the already two-headed monster.

So I am in favor of abolishing *all* political parties within the system. To what level can we take that? Do we have the ability to remove them from ballots, to where people simply run by their names and are not identified by party? Wouldn't it then become incumbent upon us, the people, to know who these people *are*, rather than simply going out and voting for a specific party line?

The party line isn't what our country was supposed to be about. If we go back to our founding fathers, when they created these United States, it wasn't so that we would go vote for the political agenda of a particular group. They had in mind that we would vote for individuals and what each individual stood for. Now, could the individual be endorsed by a political party? Certainly that could happen, just the same as you could be endorsed by any other special interest group, the teacher's union or whatever. It still leaves that freedom in place. But the domination by these gangs has got to end! Hey, if competition is good for our economy, why isn't the same true for our politics?

I'll be laying out some heavy, maybe unpleasant, truths in this book. You'll learn about the money trail that leads from the rich and powerful and their lobbyists to the politicians and how that puts a stranglehold on our democracy. You'll get my take on the Obama administration and on the various rival Rebloodlican gang members challenging the Democrips in the 2012 election. You'll learn about the perils of computerized elections and how they take away our fundamental right to vote. You'll see how the politicians get "perks" that you can't and get away with shit that you'd go to jail for. You'll be chilled, as I have been, to learn about the police-state tactics that are undermining our freedoms and values, about the role of the media in maintaining "business as usual" when it comes to the politics in this country, and how the constitutional guarantee about separation of church and state is becoming a moot point. You'll learn about third-party politics, both historically and personally from my experience, and hopefully understand my call to get away from all that. And I'll be laying out something of a blueprint for how we might leave behind all the "party line" bullshit and in the process restore our country to what it used to stand for.

Let's first look at what the founders of our great country had to say about political parties. It might surprise you.

NOTES

1. Origin of Crips: Stanley Tookie Williams and Tavis Smiley, *Blue Rage, Black Redemption* (New York: Simon & Schuster, 2007).

2. Crips and Contras: Gary Webb, Dark Alliance: The CIA, the Contras and the Crack Cocaine Explosion, Seven Stories Press, 1999.

3. Larry Diamond quoted "Third Party Rising," by Thomas L. Friedman, op-ed in *New York Times*, October 31, 201.

4. "Who is Occupy Wall Street? After six weeks, a profile finally emerges," by Gloria Goodale, *The Christian Science Monitor*, November 1, 2011.

5. "New Poll Finds a Deep Distrust of Government," by Jeff Zeleny and Megan Thee-Brenan, *New York Times*, October 26, 2011.

CHAPTER TWO

WHAT THE FOUNDERS SAID (AND DID)

Our founding fathers created the Constitution and the Bill of Rights. What was their perception of political parties? Did they want them to have the power that we see so clearly today? Did they want them submitting the candidates you would vote for as president? Did they want platforms to come out of political parties and candidates to have the party next to their names?

These are all questions I've been wondering about, and going back to our beginnings seems like a good place to start—especially since so many politicians in both the Democratic and Republican Parties (gangs) are so fond of fabrications about the founders so as to justify their own actions.

George Washington, as it turns out, hated the whole idea of political parties that pitted one group of citizens against another. Here is what Washington had to say in his farewell speech in 1796:

> They [political parties] serve to organize faction, to give it an artificial and extraordinary force; to put, in the place of the delegated will of the nation, the will of a party, often a small but artful and enterprising minority of the community; and, according to the alternate triumphs of different parties, to make the public administration the mirror of the ill-concerted and incongruous projects of faction, rather than the organ of consistent and wholesome plans digested by common counsels, and modified by mutual interests.

However combinations or associations of the above description may now and then answer popular ends, they are likely, in the course of time and things, to become potent engines, by which cunning, ambitious, and unprincipled men will be enabled to subvert the power of the people, and to usurp for themselves the reins of government; destroying afterwards the very engines, which have lifted them to unjust dominion.

Was Washington farseeing or what?! We've become the United States of Usurpers, and, if I may continue the thought, based on Usury. Later in that same speech, Washington went on to warn about what political parties can ultimately lead to:

The alternate domination of one faction over another, sharpened by the spirit of revenge, natural to party dissension, which in different ages and countries has perpetrated the most horrid enormities, is itself a frightful despotism. But this leads at length to a more formal and permanent despotism. The disorders and miseries which result gradually incline the minds of men to seek security and repose in the absolute power of an individual; and sooner or later the chief of some prevailing faction, more able or more fortunate than his competitors, turns this disposition to the purposes of his own elevation, on the ruins of public liberty.[1]

There you have it, direct from the mouth of one of the fathers of our country. Keep in mind that, when the Constitutional Convention took place in 1787, there weren't yet any official political parties. The debate over the Republic's future did have two sides: The Federalists were in favor of a strong centralized government, while the anti-Federalists were worried that the position of the president could devolve into a monarchy, like the English one we'd just broken away from, and that the rights of the states and of individuals would be compromised.

The Federalist Party started off really and truly as a "faction" formed by Alexander Hamilton, the first Secretary of the Treasury under President Washington. A rival faction formed around

Thomas Jefferson who, as Secretary of State, opposed Hamilton's idea for a powerful federal government. Like the Bloods who built up their rival gang, the Crips, the divide between Hamilton and Jefferson, spawned two national parties: the Federalists, with Hamilton and John Adams, versus the Democratic-Republican Party, with Thomas Jefferson as well as James Madison, the "Father of the Constitution." That's the first time anything resembling partisan party politics occurred in our country, and it was during Washington's first term. But even though he was sympathetic to the Federalist Party, Washington was pretty much an independent—and he sure foresaw the pitfalls if the country partied on.

So did our second president, John Adams, who once said, "There is nothing I dread so much as a division of the Republic into two great parties, each arranged under its leader and converting measures into opposition to each other." Adams believed that political parties were to be feared as "the greatest political evil under our Constitution."[2]

Here's what a columnist for *USA Today* had to say recently about our second president:

> Adams feared big political parties for what they have become: polarizing institutions, rather than mediating ones. He did not trust concentration of power. He would wonder about states passing laws making it so difficult for other political organizations to get on ballots.[3]

Never mind the prophetic thinking of Washington and Adams, things were still shaping up along party lines early on. In 1796, the Federalists took the states in the North (except Pennsylvania), while the Democratic-Republicans took the South. Then, four years later, the Federalists got voted out, and Thomas Jefferson came into office. He'd been a huge supporter of including the Bill of Rights in the Constitution, and part of his argument was that it was needed to protect citizens against government monopolies. (With what's going on today, he must be turning over in his grave!)

Jefferson didn't feel as strongly as Washington and Adams did about the notion of parties. In 1798, Jefferson wrote, "In every free and deliberating society, there must, from the nature of man, be opposite parties, and violent dissensions and discords; and one of these, for the most part, must prevail over the other for a longer or shorter time." But Jefferson also had his doubts. "Were parties here divided merely by a greediness for office," he said, "to take a part with either would be unworthy of a reasonable or moral man." And after he became president, Jefferson said flat out, "The greatest good we can do our country is to heal its party divisions and make them one people."[4]

It might be that Jefferson had some pangs about what went down in 1800. He believed strongly that government had no right to trample on the rights of the individual. In his words, financiers, bankers, and industrialists make cities "the cesspools of corruption."[5] But getting elected meant bringing in some new tactics and techniques. One of these was the media, which was only newspapers at the time. Editorials slamming the opposition popped up everywhere, and some said that the newspapers "elected" Jefferson. "It was the good fortune of Republicans to have within their ranks a number of highly gifted political manipulators and propagandists," according to Fisher Ames, a one-time member of the House of Representatives and contemporary. Candidates were said to present their positions "to coin the compelling slogan and appeal to the electorate on any given issue in a language it could understand."[6] Sound familiar?

Maybe it's not too surprising that the famous gun duel where Aaron Burr shot Alexander Hamilton took place a few years later—a pretty specific indication of the gang-like quality at the foundational level of American politics, wouldn't you say? Burr coming on the scene really marked the beginning of party politics, and Hamilton believed that Burr's self-interested nature made him unfit to hold the highest office in the land. In an 1801 letter to his friend, John McHenry, who'd been Secretary of War under Washington and Adams, Hamilton wrote:

Nothing has given me so much chagrin as the Intelligence that the Federal party were thinking seriously of supporting Mr. Burr for president. I should consider the execution of the plan as devoting the country and signing their own death warrant. Mr. Burr will probably make stipulations, but he will laugh in his sleeve while he makes them and will break them the first moment it may serve his purpose.[7]

Sounds like Burr was the forefather of more than a few of today's politicians? Burr didn't have Goldman Sachs in his corner, but he's the guy who decided to enlist the Tammany Hall "social club" to fuel his machine, which developed the techniques for organizing the party in New York. All Burr believed in was political power, and he was America's first truly amoral candidate for higher office. (Maybe it's no accident that Burr was also the grandson of Jonathan Edwards, the Connecticut theologian who wrote the famous sermon about "sinners in the hands of an angry God." Hell was a real place, according to grandpa Edwards.)

What about our fourth president, James Madison, whom you might call a moral aristocrat? As a leading advocate for the limited role of government, believing the feds needed to be tightly restrained, Madison once put it like this: "In framing a government which is to be administered by men over men, the great difficulty lies in this: You must first enable the government to control the governed; and in the next place, oblige it to control itself."[8]

But Madison did need to help create party politics in order to get Jefferson elected against the Hamiltonians. And by 1812, when Madison was president, we find that politicians started looking to manipulate—dare I say, cheat—on elections. That year, the governor of Massachusetts, Elbridge Gerry, redrew the boundaries of legislative districts to corral voters into "blocs" that would support his Democratic-Republican Party over its rival, the Federalists. In one instance, Governor Gerry changed the district lines in such a way that it came to resemble that of a salamander. Hence, we have the term "Gerrymander," which still refers to the election-manipulation tactic of redrawing district lines to benefit the incumbent political party (gang).

In 1820 the Mason-Dixon Line was extended west to define the boundary between slave and free states, geographically emphasizing a rift that had been widening between the North and South for decades. As the national mood grew tenser over the issue of slavery, political parties lost traction for a brief period of time. By the 1820s, the Federalists had dissolved entirely, and the only party in existence (the Democratic-Republicans) was starting to splinter. In 1824, four different men ran for president—all independent of parties (gangs): Andrew Jackson, Henry Clay, William Crawford, and John Quincy Adams. Jackson got the most votes, both electoral and popular. But Clay cut a deal, and the House of Representatives "selected" Adams over the other candidates—not unlike the Supreme Court selecting George W. Bush over Al Gore (winner of the popular vote) in 2000. Then Adams made Clay his Secretary of State as a part of the deal—what Jackson called the "corrupt bargain."

"Old Hickory" was, not surprisingly, furious, and this was when our "modern [gangland] politics" truly began. Now, I'm a strong admirer of Jackson. Up until he came along, our presidents had been privileged citizens endowed with monetary wealth, at least in comparison to the people they were representing. But Jackson wasn't rich, and the common man could easily relate to him. He was a real everyday person and former military man who just happened to be running for office, a bit like somebody else I know (hint: a former wrestler).

A few of my favorite Jackson quotes are these:

- "I have always been afraid of banks."
- "It is to be regretted that the rich and powerful too often bend the acts of government to their own selfish purposes."
- "I weep for the liberty of my country when I see at this early day of its successful experiment that corruption has been

14

imputed to many members of the House of Representatives, and the rights of the people have been bartered for promises of office."

- "Unless you become more watchful in your states and check the spirit of monopoly and thirst for exclusive privileges you will in the end find that . . . the control over your dearest interests has passed into the hands of these corporations."
- "The people are the government, administering it by their agents; they are the government, the sovereign power."[9]

The irony is that Jackson, running again in 1828, marked the beginning of how money came to infect virtually every aspect of the electoral process. Because Jackson didn't have the cash to put together another bid for the White House, he organized a campaign staff to go out and raise money for his candidacy. You can hardly blame him, but that hadn't happened before, at least to this extent.

And guess who Jackson's "stage manager" was? A fellow named Martin Van Buren, who'd set up a political machine called the Bucktails in 1817 in New York. Their emphasis was on "party loyalty," and Van Buren was a New York protégé of Aaron Burr. Van Buren was so smart at manipulating the machine that he became known as the "Little Magician." Now he became the prime mover behind the Jacksonian Democrats in a nasty mudslinging campaign where you appeal to the people and tell them what they want to hear (and what *you* want them to hear).

Jackson accused Adams of gambling recklessly with taxpayer money. Adams responded by calling Jackson an adulterer and a bigamist. Some of the press referred to Jackson as a "jackass" (which was how the donkey became the symbol of the Democrats). When the results were announced, with Jackson the winner, he invited one and all of his supporters to attend the inaugural party at the White House—and they trashed the place, destroying lights and furniture and breaking punch bowls, acting a lot like an L.A. street gang. Jackson's wife, Rachel—after complaining about chest pains and other related aggravations due to Adams' personal attacks on her marriage—died suddenly in December 1828. Jackson later accused the Adams campaign of causing her death. And, lo and behold, the two-party system was born: Jackson and his Secretary of State Van Buren with the Democrats, and Adams and Clay opposing them eventually as the Whigs. Van Buren soon became president himself in 1837. From 1833 onward, those two parties had a stranglehold over elections in the United States until the Civil War.

The Republicans originally came into being as a third party. That's what Abraham Lincoln was, lest we forget amidst the bozos that pass for Republicans today. And since the Whigs fell apart around that time, we've seen those other two parties dominate our politics for the past 150 years. That's getting a little stale, wouldn't you say?

I can't end this chapter without a quote from one of our "founding mothers," for lack of a better term. I just found out recently that the lyrics to our grand anthem, "America the Beautiful," were written in 1894 by a Massachusetts poet named Katharine Lee Bates. She turns out to have been a passionate feminist, who was also extremely upset about the Gilded Age of greed that the country was then experiencing. The third verse that we don't hear today—but *should* hear, now more than ever—said this:

> *America! America!*
> *God shed his grace on thee*
> *Till selfish gain no longer stain*
> *The banner of the free!*[10]

So would our forefathers and mothers be comfortable with the system that we see today? Sure, they talked against parties and factions, but they also were the ones that created them. But I have to believe they would not be happy with what our system has evolved into. They never could have realized how powerful these parties would become in a time of mass politics and excessive wealth.

It's time for the New Revolution, the re-founding of the country.

NOTES

1. Washington's 1796 farewell speech: http://avalon.law.yale.edu/18th_century/Washing.asp.

2. Adams on political parties: Chuck Raasch, "John Adams would be surprised by today's politics," *USA Today*, www.usatoday.com/news/opinion/columnist/raasch/2004-07-29-raasch_x.htm.

3. "Adams feared big political parties . . .": Ibid.

4. Jefferson on parties: "Thomas Jefferson on Politics & Government," http://extext.virginia.edu/jefferson/quotations/jeff0800.htm.

5. Cities "the cesspools of corruption": Lance Banning, *The Jeffersonian Persuasion: Evolution of Party Ideology* (New York: Cornell University Press, 1978).

6. "To coin the compelling slogan . . .": Harry M. Tinkcom, *The Republicans and the Federalists in Pennsylvania 1790–1801: A Study In National Stimulus and Local Response* (Pennsylvania Historical & Museum Commission, 1950).

7. Bernard C. Steiner and James McHenry, *The life and correspondence of James McHenry* (Cleveland: Burrows Brothers Col, 1907), p. 484.

8. Madison quote: Robert Allen Rutland, *James Madison: The Founding Father* (Columbia, MO: University of Missouri Press, 1987), p. 33.

9. Andrew Jackson quotes: www.brainz.org/50-best-andrew-jackson-quotes.

10. Paul Krugman, "Beautifying America," *New York Times*, January 4, 2011, www.readersupportednews.org.

CHAPTER THREE

"THE NATURAL ORDER OF THINGS TODAY"

In 1976, I was just starting out as Jesse "The Body" Ventura when the film *Network* was released, but I remember like it was yesterday the speech Mr. Jensen gives to Mr. Beale where he lays out "the natural order of things today":

> There is no America. There is no democracy. There is only IBM and ITT and AT&T, and DuPont, Dow, Union Carbide and Exxon. Those are the nations of the world today. . . . We no longer live in a world of nations and ideologies, Mr. Beale. The world is a college of corporations, inexorably determined by the immutable by-laws of business.

Mr. Jensen concludes that our children will live to see "one vast and ecumenical holding company for which all men will work to serve a common profit. In which all men will hold a share of stock. All necessities provided. All anxieties tranquilized. All boredom amused."[1]

It was one of those electric movie moments that, in hindsight, can only be called prophetic. I wish it was sci-fi, believe me. Not that we weren't warned; Abraham Lincoln had this to tell America back in 1864: "Corporations have been enthroned and an era of corruption in high places will follow, and the money power of the country will endeavor to prolong its reign by working upon the prejudices of the people until all wealth is aggregated in a few hands and the Republic is destroyed." That was more than a hundred years before *Network*, folks!

After that, we had our Robber Baron era—that of über-rich industrialists like John Jacob Astor, Andrew Mellon, J. P. Morgan, John D. Rockefeller—our Gilded Age, and then Theodore Roosevelt busting the trusts and FDR taking on the big bankers during the Great Depression. Then came the Sixties and the Vietnam War . . . followed by Nixon and Watergate. A lot of government secrets began coming out—like how the CIA assassinated foreign leaders (domestic, too, but that never got admitted) and experimented with mind control, using human beings as unwitting guinea pigs to test experimental drugs. You can read about much of this history in two of my earlier books, *American Conspiracies* and *63 Documents the Government Doesn't Want You to Read*.

However, before we examine the result of all this in today's political world, I want to stay with some recent history—because it's important to understand the background and to realize that what's come to a head with the "marriage" of corporations and politics has been getting worse and worse for more than thirty years. Probably no historian has spelled this out more clearly than the late Howard Zinn, in his book *A People's History of the United States*, and that's the book I'm going to draw on for the facts and figures you'll be reading here.

In 1960, the year John F. Kennedy squeaked out a narrow victory over Richard Nixon, 63 percent of the eligible voters exercised their right. By 1976, the year *Network* came out, that number had dropped to 53 percent. "More and more they [the people] declared, if only by nonparticipation, their alienation from the political system."[2] Politicians were no longer inspiring "because it seemed that behind the bombast, the rhetoric, the promises, their major concern was their own political power."

Back then, the parties were already devolving into the gangs they are today. At a turning point, Democrip Jimmy Carter's tax "reforms" mainly benefited the corporations and their CEOs. The scale of wealth was the only major difference between then and now. At that time, multinationals, as they were known, were a group that "constituted the third-largest economy in the world," right behind the United States and the Soviet Union. While Exxon Oil's "net income rose 56 percent to more than $4 billion, 3,000 small independent gasoline stations went out of business" in 1979. A portent of things to come.[3]

Along came Ronald Reagan, who was followed by George H. W. Bush. "By the fall of 1991, Reagan and Bush had filled more than half of the 837 federal judgeships, and appointed enough right-wing justices to transform the Supreme Court."[4] (Remember the awarding of the 2000 election to George Bush, and the Court's recent decision declaring that corporations are legal persons.) In the '80s, the big oil company bosses "contributed $270,000 to redecorate the White House living quarters."[5] I guess they figured that they owned it. Soon after, Reagan turned mandatory enforcement of our environmental laws into a "voluntary" approach by big businesses.

His eight years in office were the start of a familiar litany: cut social programs, increase spending on defense, cut taxes on the wealthy, and watch unemployment increase (thirty million people in 1982). With the help of Democrats in Congress, Reagan's administration lowered the tax rate on the richest people to 50 percent. Remember that during World War II, anybody making over $400,000 a year paid 91 percent of that to taxes. That was a time— maybe the last—when there was a sense that everybody was in this together . . . it had taken both officers and troops fighting together to win the war—so naturally what followed was the GI Bill for education to help out everyone who had fought for our country. There was far more equality in society, and there were attempts to create even more. And when Eisenhower was President through most of the '50s, the top tax rate was still around 90 percent and not much lower under Kennedy after that in the early '60s. And guess what—this was when the middle class was the most prosperous, with lots of good jobs. Seems like those high taxes didn't really destroy jobs, as the gangsters keep telling us these days.

But the times had changed by the late '70s. From 1978 under a Crip to 1990 under two Bloods, the top 1 percent gained a trillion dollars! Corporate CEOs who made forty times as much salary as the average factory worker in 1980 were earning ninety-three times as much by the end of the decade.[6] (Now the difference is over 300 times as much!)[7] "Less and less wealth was going to people who produced something," as Kevin Phillips said.[8] And when the savings-and-loan scandal hit, bilking people out of billions, in the '88 campaign, Michael Dukakis didn't point fingers at the Republicans "because the Democrats in Congress were heavily involved in bringing about and then covering up the situation."[9]

No matter which party (gang) was in power, since World War II the military budgets had continued to escalate, and "Democrats and Republicans had long been joined in a 'bipartisan foreign policy'"—what Eisenhower had called the "military-industrial complex" in his farewell speech. During the Reagan-Bush years, we started getting more aggressive, "either directly in invasions, or through both overt and covert support of right-wing tyrannies that cooperated with the United States."[10] Remember the Iran-Contra deal and Ollie North, guns for drugs, and all that? Later came Panama, where we took out dictator Manuel Noriega before he could snitch on how involved he was with our drug-dealing spies, and then the Desert Storm operation where we invaded Iraq.

Today, the military budget is about one-third of our total U.S. budget, and we spend more on military (and related matters) than *all* the other countries in the world combined. There might be some who argue that point depending on what you include, but if you count veterans benefits, there's no doubt about it.

Through it all, as Howard Zinn put it, there was a "political consensus of Democrats and Republicans in Washington, which set limits on American reform, making sure that capitalism was in place, that national military strength was maintained, that wealth and power remained in the hands of a few."[11] By the 1988 election, when Poppa Bush ran against Dukakis, only 27 percent of eligible voters turned out. If you polled the people, 84 percent in 1990 wanted a surtax on millionaires. A majority also wanted a single-payer health care system. "Clearly, there was something amiss with a political system, supposed to be democratic, in which the desires of the voters were repeatedly ignored." We were a class society where the top 1 percent by the '90s owned 33 percent of the wealth, while thirty to forty million people lived in poverty.[12]

Did Bill Clinton bring the change he promised in the '90s? During his terms in office, big corporations started giving money to the Democratic Party (gang) "on an unprecedented scale." In paving the Democrip's way for Obama, "his key appointments to the Treasury and Commerce Departments were wealthy corporate lawyers, and his foreign policy staff—the Secretary of Defense, the Director of the CIA, the National Security Adviser—were traditional players on the bipartisan cold war team."[13] He didn't go for any new federal job programs and "continued to spend at least $250 billion a year to maintain the military machine." In '99, the United States "sold over $11 billion of arms, one-third of all weapons sold worldwide."[14] "Clinton's foreign economic policy was in keeping with . . . both major parties [being] more concerned for corporate interests than for the rights of working people, here or abroad, and saw foreign aid as a political and economic tool more than as a humanitarian act."[15] (And people wonder why Ron Paul wants to cut off foreign aid!)

While Clinton talked tough on law and order, the FBI's assault on the Branch Davidian compound in Waco, Texas, resulted in the deaths by fire of at least eighty-six men, women, and children. The 1996 Crime Bill, voted for overwhelmingly by both parties (gangs) and endorsed with enthusiasm by Clinton, "extended the death penalty to a whole range of criminal offenses, and provided $8 billion for the building of new prisons."[16] And the "Anti-Terrorism and Effective Death Penalty Act" in '96 allowed the "deportation of any immigrant ever convicted of a crime, no matter how long ago or how serious."[17]

Did you know that we incarcerate more of our people—both total and per capita— than any other country in the world? And that the rate of incarceration, starting in 1980, tracks completely with the increase in wealth inequality? And that we have the fifth highest rate of executions—only exceeded by those fine democracies China, Iran, Iraq, and Saudi Arabia?[18] Do you think that might hint at being a measure of failure in our society?

We'll get to today's figures in the next chapter, but consider the precedents:

> The 400 richest families owned $92 billion in 1982, but thirteen years later this had jumped to $480 billion. In the nineties, the wealth of the 500 corporations of the Standard and Poor's Index had increased by 335 percent. The Dow Jones average of stock prices had gone up 400 percent between 1980 and 1995, while the average wage of workers had declined in purchasing power by 15 percent . . . in 1998, one of every three working people in the United States had jobs paying at or below the federal poverty level.[19]

For the 2000 election, the Bush campaign raised $220 million and the Al Gore campaign $170 million.[20] You'll be amazed to compare this with today's figures (coming attraction advertisement). It was often hard to tell the difference between where the candidates stood on issues (yes for death penalty and big military spending, for example). Only Ralph Nader's third-party effort emphasized things like education, environment, and health care—but they wouldn't let him take part in the debates. As soon as the Supreme Court handed Bush the presidency, "he pushed tax cuts for the wealthy, opposed strict environmental regulations that would cost money for the business interests, and planned to 'privatize' Social Security by having the retirement funds of citizens depend on the stock market."[21] The way was being paved for today's crusaders.

Then came September 11, about which I continue to believe we've not been told the full truth. When a lie that big can be perpetrated on the people, you know it's just about game over. I've covered my thoughts about this in *American Conspiracies* and more than once on my television show, *Conspiracy Theory with Jesse Ventura*. But let me pause to refresh your memory about the USA PATRIOT Act that passed in Congress with one dissenting vote, an Act:

> Which gave the Department of Justice the power to detain non-citizens simply on suspicion, without charges, without the procedural rights provided in the Constitution. It said the Secretary of State could designate any group as "terrorist," and any person who was a member of or raised funds for such an organization could be arrested and held until deported.[22]

Nine/eleven, and the subsequent invasion of Iraq and toppling of Saddam, swept under the rug further inquiry about Enron, WorldCom, or Bush's banking regulators taking a chainsaw to thousands of pages of things that Wall Street took exception to—decisions "that allowed the free market to operate as a barroom brawl." Goldman Sachs' CEO, Hank Paulson, (before he became Treasury Secretary) went to the Securities and Exchange Commission to get lending restrictions relaxed for the five big investment banks. After that, Goldman went "berserk with lending lust. By the peak of the housing boom in 2006, Goldman was underwriting $76.5 billion worth of mortgage-backed securities—a third of which were subprime—much of it to institutional investors like pensions and insurance companies. And in those massive issues of real estate were vast swamps of crap."[23]

Considering all this, recall the words of Thomas Jefferson from 1774 in *Rights of British America*, two years before the Revolution began:

> Single acts of tyranny may be ascribed to the accidental opinion of a day; but a series of oppressions, begun at a distinguished period

and pursued unalterably through every change of ministers, too plainly prove a deliberate, systematic plan of reducing [a people] to slavery.[24]

Near the end of his *People's History*, Howard Zinn also said something prophetic, anticipating the OWS movement that he didn't live to see take shape in our country.

These struggles would involve all the tactics used at various times in the past by people's movements: demonstrations, marches, civil disobedience; strikes and boycotts and general strikes; direct action to redistribute wealth, to reconstruct institutions, to revamp relationships; creating . . . a new joy in the collaboration of people. . . . There would be many defeats. But when such a movement took hold in hundreds of thousands of places all over the country it would be impossible to suppress, because the very guards the system depends on to crush such a movement would be among the rebels. It would be a new kind of revolution, the only kind that could happen, I believe, in a country like the United States. It would take enormous energy, sacrifice, commitment, patience. But because it would be a process over time, starting without delay, there would be the immediate satisfactions that people have always found in the affectionate ties of groups striving together for a common goal.[25]

NOTES

1. Quotes from *Network*: http://majorityrights.com/weblog/com ments/the_world_is_a_business_mr_beale/.

2. "More and more they declared . . .": Howard Zinn, *A People's History of the United States*, paperback edition (New York: HarperPerennial Modern Classics, 2005), p. 564.

3. Multinationals and Exxon Oil/small stations: Zinn, pp. 568 and 571.

4. Reagan and Bush, judges: Zinn, p. 574.

5. Oil bosses and White House: Zinn, p. 577.

6. Figures on corporations: Zinn, pp. 580–581.

7. 300 times as much: "Executive Excess 2011," Institute for Policy Studies, August 31, 2011.

8. Kevin Phillips: Zinn, p. 582.

9. Dukakis: Zinn, p. 583.

10. "Bipartisan foreign policy . . . tyrannies that cooperated . . .": Zinn, pp. 584–585.

11. "Political consensus of Democrats and Republicans . . .": Zinn, p. 601.

12. Figures on wealth: Zinn, p. 612.

13. Corporations and appointments: Zinn, pp. 644–645.

14. Miitary spending/arms sales: Zinn, pp. 651 and 653.

15. "Clinton's foreign economic policy . . .": Zinn, p. 657.

16. Waco and 1996 Crime Bill Zinn, pp. 646–647.

17. "Anti-Terrorism and Effective Death Penalty Act": Zinn, p. 649.

18. Fifth highest rate of executions: "Death Sentences and Executions, 2011," report by Amnesty International.

19. Figures: Zinn, p. 662.

20. 2000 campaign spending: Zinn, p. 675.

21. Bush "pushed tax cuts for the wealthy . . .": Zinn, p. 677.

22. USA PATRIOT Act: Zinn, p. 680.

23. Goldman Sachs' "lending lust": Matt Taibbi, "It's time to enshrine Hank Paulson as national hero," *The Smirking Chimp*, June 8, 2009.

24. Thomas Jefferson quotes, www.thinkexist.com.

25. "These struggles would involve all the tactics . . .": Zinn, pp. 639–640.

CHAPTER FOUR

THE RICH GET RICHER AND THE POOR GET POORER

Before I get to some astounding facts about the famed top 1 percent or 0.01 percent, here's a new one for you: A recent analysis of the relationships between 43,000 transnational corporations has identified a "super-entity" of 147 closely knit firms whose ownership was all held by others *within the same group*. What does that amount to? "In effect, less than 1 percent of the companies were able to control 40 percent of the entire network," according to one of the systems analysts, James Glattfelder. These "super-connectors" were mainly banks. The top twenty were led by Barclays at the top of the list, followed by a few I'd never heard of—maybe because they've found new ways to put big initialed names to mask the companies' identities. I'm talking about Capital Group Companies, Inc., and FMR Corporation (formerly Fidelity Investments), AXA (once called Equitable Insurance), and State Street Corporation (Boston's State Street bank), followed by JP Morgan Chase at #6.[1]

Now, here in the richest country on earth, let's dive down to examine what's happening on the bottom of the pile. I know this chapter has a lot of statistics to take in, but they're important to digest, though you may need to take some Tums:

- In mid-December 2011, the latest census data showed that a record number of Americans—almost one out of two—are either in poverty or barely getting by on earnings that categorize them as low income.[2]
- The Census Bureau had earlier reported that our country's poverty rate spiked to 15.1 percent in 2010, the fourth straight year of increase. That comes out to about 46.2 million Americans, and one out of every five American kids. In 2010, one out of seven households (17.2 million) didn't have enough food to put on the table.
- The total number of people living below the poverty line (an income of $22,314 for a family of four in 2010) is now at the highest level in the fifty-two years officials have been gathering these statistics. Meanwhile, the median household income fell by 2.3 percent to $49,445 between '09 and '10—with the worst-off 10 percent seeing a decline of 12.1 percent.[3]
- If you think this is an urban or isolated rural phenomenon, you're wrong. Poverty is increasing faster in the suburbs than anywhere else in the country. For the first time ever, the Bureau of Labor Statistics says that there were 2.7 million more suburban households below the poverty line than city households. And over the previous decade, the suburbs had seen a 53 percent increase in poverty![4]
- There are 18.5 million vacant homes in this country—banks have foreclosed approximately 8 million since 2007 (and it's likely that millions more are to come).
- There are about 3.5 million homeless Americans, many of them veterans of our misguided wars.[5] That figure includes about 1.6 million kids, most of them under the age of seven.[6]

Doesn't it start to make you mad reading all of this, about what is happening to our kids and families and vets? Remember when this was the country where we were all in the same boat—and now it is looking like the Titanic, with the rich folks still dancing on the upper decks.

A record forty-five million Americans are now living on food stamps, a weekly stipend to help them make ends meet. That's nearly one out of six, and it's continuing to rise. According to the mayors in twenty-nine cities, more than one out of four people who need emergency food assistance didn't get it.[7] It's all run by a program out of the Department of Agriculture called the Supplemental Nutrition Assistance Program. That's right, SNAP for short.[8] They haven't released the figures on how many people have "snapped," but it's sure not decreasing. The food stamp numbers actually started rising in 2008, when Bush's recession began. With more and more people out of work, the numbers have soared since then— one reason Newt Gingrich calls Obama "the food stamp president." Seems to me like it was Bush and his bankster friends who started the rush to food stamps when they crashed our economy.

For 90 percent of Americans, wages are steadily declining. Of course, that's for the ones who still hold jobs. "Of 13.3 million unemployed Americans now searching for work, 5.7 million have been looking for more than six months, while millions more have given up altogether."[9]

At the same time, U.S. millionaire households hold at least $45.9 trillion in wealth. And the majority of that money belongs to the *upper one-tenth of 1 percent* of our population. My mind boggles—I honestly can't comprehend how much $1 trillion is, let alone $45.9 trillion. One trillion, so I've read, is equal to one thousand billion. So if you multiply that by $45.9 . . . my calculator just crashed.

I'm taking this figure from a report that came out in August 2011, by David DeGraw, aptly titled "Analysis of Financial Terrorism in America."[10] By comparison, he notes that the entire cost of food stamps for Americans in 2010 was a "mere" $65 billion. Of course, that $45.9 trillion figure includes about $6.3 trillion that's been stashed away in offshore accounts, so I guess the greediest don't have *everything* over the neediest. (Since that money doesn't get declared, the result is a tax revenue loss to the Treasury of about $337 billion a year.)[11]

This report is mind blowing, even for those of us who've heard the figure about the top 1 percent owning 40 percent of all the wealth.

- Overall, the richest 400 people in America (all of them billionaires!) possess as much money as the bottom 50 percent of Americans combined (some 154 million people!).
- The top tax bracket for annual income starts at $50 million and up . . . there are only 74 Americans in that group. Now get this: Back in 2008, before things really went south for the economy, their average income was $91.2 million. The next year, 2009, that soared to $518.8 million each, which means that while everybody else was mired in the recession, the richest 74 increased their income by over five times in the space of a year.
- They were making more bucks than 19 million workers combined! On the scale of about $10 million a week! Today, the average CEO pay is 350 times what the average American worker makes. In 2010, Fortune 500 CEOs saw their average pay escalate by 36.5 percent.

So, as Butch Cassidy once said to the Sundance Kid, "Who *are* those guys?" Or, if you prefer a line from the movie version of *The Grapes of Wrath*, "Who *do* we shoot?" In fairness to Wall Street, it must be pointed out that no less than six Walton kids—heirs to the Wal-Mart fortune—are on the top 400 list. Their combined worth is almost $70 billion, which calculates out to the total wealth of the entire bottom 30 percent of Americans. They spend a portion of that fortune lobbying to cut their estate taxes, which President Obama agreed to do for all those rich Americans saddled so unfairly with a "death tax."[12] The CEO of Wal-Mart earns, if you can believe this,

$19,000 an hour. At the same time, his million-or-so employees have to work on holidays for between eight to ten dollars an hour.[13] This is aided and abetted by the fact that Wal-Mart imports more than $20 billion a year in products from sweatshops in China.[14]

For corporate CEOs, 2010 was a record year on Wall Street, their compensation going up by more than 30 percent. They pulled in about $149 billion that year. Topping the heap was Jamie Dimon, CEO of JP Morgan Chase, at $90 million in take-home pay. Vikram Pandit, CEO of Citigroup, wasn't far behind with $80 million, even though he might hit over $200 million in added compensation and bonuses. **These are the guys we bailed out with our taxes after they crashed the economy.**

Lest we forget, there's Goldman Sachs, or "Government Sachs" as they're nicknamed around the Washington Beltway. As David DeGraw put it:

> Former Goldman Sachs CEO and Bush Treasury Secretary Hank Paulson had already amassed at least $700 million prior to moving to the US Treasury in 2006. Current Goldman Sachs CEO Lloyd Blankfein and a few other top executives at Goldman Sachs just received $111.3 million in bonuses. Blankfein just took home $24.3 million, as part of a $67.9 million bonus he was awarded. Goldman's President Gary Cohn took home $24 million, as part of a $66.9 million bonus he was awarded. Goldman's CFO David Viniar and former co-president Jon Winkelried both took home over $20 million in bonuses.[15]

Too big to wail? Not when it came to getting government bailout money for their companies in 2008–09. A report issued January 2011 by the special inspector general's office keeping tabs on where the money went says that U.S. taxpayers are still owed $132.9 billion that the companies haven't repaid. This is going to go on for years.[16] We'll get to more on the bailout beneficiaries in due course.

I propose a new episode of *Let's Make A Deal*. Between 2000 and 2011, in the mergers and acquisitions department among the "top financial advisers," Goldman Sachs ranks numero uno with 396 deals worth a cool $640 billion. Next comes Morgan Stanley (308 deals worth $498 billion), followed by JPMorgan Chase, Credit Suisse, and Bank of America/Merrill Lynch. As for the top legal advisers, leading the field with 135 deals worth $401 billion is none other than Sullivan & Cromwell,[17] the law firm that gave the Dulles brothers (CIA's Allen and State's John Foster) their start in the 1920s and went on to notoriety in the rise of Nazi Germany.

But if the profiteering of the big banks might seem a bit abstract, the health care story will most certainly hit home for you, dear reader. We Americans happen to pay more in medical expenses than any other country on the planet—in fact, twice as much as most! And generally with worse results! Without health insurance, we're sunk—but more than 50 million Americans can't afford the escalating costs of the premiums. Think about this: "Over 60 percent of all personal bankruptcies are the result of medical bills."[18]

So how are the health insurance CEOs making out? Almost as good as the Wall Street titans. According to a story in the *Los Angeles Times*, "Leaders of Cigna, Humana, UnitedHealth, WellPoint, and Aetna received nearly $200 million in compensation in 2009 . . . while the companies sought rate increases as high as 39%." Prime example: Cigna paid CEO H. Edward Hanway and his successor, David Cordani, $136.3 million in 2009.[19]

And let's not leave out the Big Oil companies. While the rest of us have seen prices soaring at the pump, the top five companies r﹍ed in $101 billion in profits during the first nine months of 2011. ExxonMobil, Chevron, Shell, BP, and ConocoPhilips were on track to surpass their record-setting profits of 2007 and 2008 before the recession hit. Meanwhile, their chief lobbyist, the American Petroleum Institute, is fighting hard to keep those tax breaks that stand to be worth another $40 billion over the next decade. Once a gusher, always a gusher: That's our Congress's motto, apparently.[20] And every time the gas prices go up at the pump, Big Oil rakes in even more money. Heads they win, tails we lose.

When it comes to taxes, if I may be so bold, I find the reality rather "revolt"-ing. A comprehensive new study released in November 2011 revealed that seventy-eight out of America's 280 most profitable Fortune 500 companies paid *zero* federal income taxes in at least one of the last three years. At the same time, those 280 companies were making almost $1.4 trillion in pre-tax profits. Oh, and receiving almost $223 billion in tax subsidies from the government. Topping the list of those recipients was Wells Fargo ($18 billion over three years), followed by AT&T ($14.5 billion), Verizon ($12.3 billion), General Electric ($8.4 billion), IBM ($8.3 billion), ExxonMobil ($4.1 billion) and Boeing ($3.6 billion).[21] Another study found that 265 big corporations avoided $42.7 billion in taxes from 2008 to 2010—for comparison's sake, that's enough money to hire more than a million teachers, instead of laying them off because state budgets can't afford them.[22]

Another report looked at 100 publicly-traded U.S. corporations with the highest paid CEOs. It turns out that twenty-five of those guys made more in salary and other compensation in 2010 than their companies paid in federal income taxes on the annual financial statements. Those same companies averaged global profits of $1.9 billion. Since we're naming names, among the top beneficiaries were Verizon CEO Ivan Seidenberg, Cablevision's James Dolan, and eBay's John J. Donahoe.[23] Donahoe got a compensation package worth over $12 million, while eBay received a federal refund of $113 million.[24]

Good old Verizon. Over the past three years, the company earned $21.5 billion in pre-tax U.S. profits and gave its top five execs $181 million. At the same time, Verizon dumped 40,000 workers and is demanding a billion dollars from 45,000 more who are union-represented (a $22,000 cut per worker).[25]

And good old Countrywide Financial, the fraud-riddled mortgage lender that got picked up for chump change by Bank of America in '08. Eileen Foster, who used to be a top executive there, told *60 Minutes* that loan officers "were compensated regardless of the quality of the loan" and that the company's recycle bins were full of "signatures that had been cut off of one document and put onto another and then photocopied, you know, or faxed"[26] before putting a heavy-duty black mark on the word "recycling." In plain language, that's called "fraud." Wonder if any of these banksters will see the inside of a jail? Somehow I doubt it.

The "Analysis of Financial Terrorism in America" report also takes a look at the taxation trail. A total of 1,470 Americans earned more than a million dollars in 2009 and didn't pay *any* taxes. Not so long ago, in 1970, millionaires were accustomed to paying about 70 percent of their annual income to taxes. By 1995, the wealthiest 400 Americans were paying 30 percent. In 2009, it was 22.4 percent. Today, that's dropped to 18 percent.

Note that this is income tax only. The rate is even lower if you take into account 15 percent capital gains rate—meaning that the super rich in our superpower are paying fewer taxes overall than your average secretary.[27] It's all structured so that the very wealthy don't earn their income from pulling down a salary. That's what stock options are all about—cash it out and pay capital gains tax as opposed to the income tax rate. Among politicians, Mitt Romney admits to paying about 13 percent of his mega-bucks in taxes, though with capital gains it's likely less than that. There are other ways you can dodge the tax code—like Romney's offshore accounts in Bermuda and the Cayman Islands.

With unemployment still at more than 8 percent, if an average American worker is lucky enough to get a regular paycheck, he's sure not likely to get much of a raise. Compare that to what's happening with the top exec CEOs at 200 big companies analyzed by Equilar, an executive compensation data firm. Their median pay was $10.8 million in 2010—a 23 percent gain from the year before.[28]

One windfall write-off for both the corporations and their execs has to do with stock options. Some CEOs take token salaries and live off their ownership stakes. "These stock riches don't show up on the current pay lists, but they can be huge," according to the *New York*

Times. "Warren E. Buffett, for instance, saw his stock holdings rise last year by 16 percent to $46 billion. Other longtime chief executives or founders who are sitting on billions of paper profits include Jeffrey P. Bezos of Amazon.com and Michael S. Dell, the founder of Dell."[29]

After the market collapsed in '08, hundreds of CEOs got granted "unusually large packages of stock options" from their companies. And through a loophole in our tax code, the same companies can claim huge deductions in future years for having granted those options—much more in write-offs than the options were worth. Which, more than incidentally, "will deprive the federal government of tens of billions of dollars in revenue over the next decade."[30] This is patently absurd, especially at a time when the deficit is spiraling out of control and the big talk in D.C. is about cutting social programs like Medicare.

So the good times for CEOs and their companies just keep on keepin' on. Don't get me wrong, I know a lot of good people who happen to have money, and of course I've made my share. But we're talking about not only a huge gap between the rich and the poor, but a monumental scam that Bill Moyers recently called "perversion of democracy." He added, "Our politicians are little more than money launderers in the trafficking of power and policy—fewer than six degrees of separation from the spirit and tactics of Tony Soprano."[31]

Pretty strong words from LBJ's former Press Secretary. This all reminds me of some lyrics from "Pretty Boy Floyd," written by Woody Guthrie (it's his 100th birthday in 2012):

> Yes, as through this world I've wandered
> I've seen lots of funny men;
> Some will rob you with a six-gun,
> And some with a fountain pen.
>
> And as through your life you travel,
> Yes, as through your life you roam,
> You won't never see an outlaw
> Drive a family from their home.[32]

Reminds me, too, of Gordon Gekko's "greed is good" speech from the movie *Wall Street*. "I create nothing. I own," he said and at another point wondered aloud, "Now you're not naïve enough to think we're living in a democracy, are you, buddy?"[33]

Before we take a long look at how money in politics has corrupted our system, and to borrow another line from the movie *Network*, when will we the people rise up and shout that they're "mad as hell and not gonna take it anymore?!" All Occupy All the Time!

NOTES

1. Coghlan, Andy and Debora MacKenzie. "The Capitalist Network That Runs the World." *New Scientist*, October 20, 2011.

2. "Census data: Half of U.S. poor or low income," www.cbs.news. com, on newsfromunderground.

3. American poverty: Fletcher, Michael A. "U.S. poverty rate reaches 15.1 percent." Received from News from Underground, September 13, 2011.

4. Hirsch, Michelle. "America's Best Kept Secret: Rising Suburban Poverty." *The Fiscal Times*, December 28, 2011.

5. Loha, Tanuka. "American Paradox: 18.5 Million Vacant Homes and 3.5 Million Homeless." *Human Rights Now*, January 1, 2012.

6. Homeless kids: "8 Stories Buried by the Corporate Media That You Need to Know About." December 16, 2011, www.alternet.org.

7. Mayors on emergency food: Ibid.

8. Americans on food stamps: "Food stamp 'challenge' lays bare hard times in US," September 30, 2011, www.alternet.org.

9. Unemployment figures: "The Middle-Class Agenda," *New York Times*, December 20, 2011.

10. McGraw, David. "Meet the Global Financial Elites Controlling $46 Trillion in Wealth." August 11, 2001, www.alternet.org.

11. $337 billion a year: November 2011 report, Tax Justice Network.

12. Walton family figures: Garofalo, Pat. "Walmart Heirs' Net Worth Equals Bottom 30% of Americans." *ThinkProgress*, December 10, 2011, citing a study by the Center on Wage and Employment Dynamics.

13. CEO of Wal-Mart: Gibson, Carly. "America Has Become a Fascist Police State." November 26, 2011, www.readersupportednews.org.

14. Wal-Mart and China: Nadar, Ralph. "Time to Topple Corporate Dictators." February 20, 2011, www.opednews.com.

15. Goldman Sachs: McGraw, David. "Meet the Global Financial Elites Controlling $46 Trillion in Wealth." August 11, 2001, www.alternet.org.

16. "Taxpayers still owed $132.9B from bailout: report," *Associated Press*, January 26, 2012.

17. "Mergers and Acquisitions," *New York Times*, January 3, 2012.

18. Health care statistics: McGraw article.

19. Insurance company earnings: Article by Noam N. Levey, *Los Angeles Times*, August 11, 2010.

20. Oil company profits: "Big-five oil companies: $101 billion in profits for 2011," October 28, 2011, www.dailykos.com.

21. Taxes and Fortune 500 companies report: Citizens for Tax Justice and the Institute on Taxation and Economic Policy, "Corporate Taxpayers and Corporate Tax Dodgers, 2008–2010," www.thestand.org /?p=6846.

22. Avoiding taxes/teachers comparison: Leopold, Les. "How can the world's richest country let children go hungry? 6 tricks corporate elites use to hoard all the wealth." December 21, 2011, www.alternet.org.

23. CEOs and company taxes: Zajac, Andrew. "CEOs Earned More Than Companies' Tax Bills." August 31, 2011, www.bloomberg.com.

24. Donahoe compensation; Kocieniewski, David. "Where Pay For Chiefs Outstrips U.S. Taxes." *New York Times*, August 31, 2011.

25. Verizon: Peres, Kenneth R. "Modern-Day Scrooges Must Learn the Lesson of 'A Christmas Carol." *The Progressive*, December 25, 2011.

26. La Roche, Julie. "Ex-Countrywide Exec Blows the Lid off the systematic Fraud at the Company." December 5, 2011, www.businessinsider.com.

27. Millionaire tax rates: Ibid.

28. CEO compensation: Joshi, Pradnya. "We Knew They Got Raises. But this?" *New York Times*, July 2, 2011.

29. CEOs and ownership stakes: Ibid.

30. Kocieniewski, David. "Tax Benefits From Options As Windfall for Businesses." *New York Times*, Deember 30, 2011.

31. "Our politicians are little more than money launderers . . .": Moyers, Bill. "How Wall Street Occupied America." *The Nation*, November 21, 2011.

32. "Pretty Boy Floyd," http://woodyguthrie.org.

33. *Wall Street* film quotes: Krugman, Paul. "All The G.O.P.'s Gekkos." *New York Times*, December 9, 2011.

CHAPTER FIVE

WHAT THE TWO GANGS DO FOR THE RICH

Let me return to our founders for a moment. What John Adams feared in America's future was what he called "an aristocratic despotism"—the possibility of "the rich, the well born and the able acquir[ing] an influence among the people that will soon be too much for simple honesty and plain sense." He wrote about "the weakness, the folly, the pride, the vanity, the selfishness, the artifice, the unbounded ambition, the unfeeling cruelty of a majority of those (in all nations) who are allowed an aristocratical influence."[1]

No wonder there was a lively debate in the newborn Congress about what to call the new head of state. "His Excellency" and "His Elective Highness" were both suggested, strangely enough by Vice President Adams, despite his worry about "aristocratical influence." (Maybe in response, Adams' opponents called him "His Rotundity.") Both "excellency" and "highness" were rejected as sounding too royal. Congress went with the straightforward, no nonsense suggestion of James Madison, "Mr. President."

Madison was also afraid that the "spirit of speculation" would result in "a government operating by corrupt influence, substituting the motive of private interest in place of public duty."[2] And Thomas Jefferson expressed the hope that "we shall crush in its birth the aristocracy of our monied corporations which dare already to challenge our government to a trial of strength and [to] bid defiance to the laws of our country."

Theodore Roosevelt spoke in 1907 about "certain malefactors of great wealth" who "combine to bring about as much financial stress as possible, in order to discredit the policy of the government and secure a reversal of that policy, so that they may enjoy unmolested the fruits of their own evil-doing. . . . I regard this contest as one to determine who shall rule this free country—the people through their governmental agents, or a few ruthless and domineering men whose wealth makes them peculiarly formidable because they hide behind the breastworks of corporate organization."[3]

Of course, the founders didn't all see eye to eye. John Jay, who became the first Chief Justice of the United States, is quoted by his brother as having said, "Those who own the country ought to govern it."[4] I'm sure the majority of today's justices would be nodding their heads in unison to that one, but we'll get to that in due course.

According to my *Merriam-Webster's Dictionary*, corporatism is defined as the "organization of a society into industrial and professional corporations serving as organs of political representation and exercising control over person and activities within their jurisdiction." Now let's expand that a little bit to what Italian dictator Benito Mussolini once said: "Fascism should more appropriately be called Corporatism because it is a merger of state and corporate power."

Today in America, we're living in a corporatocracy, or a plutocracy, or if you prefer, an oligarchy. In this chapter, I want to delve into how the rich buy influence from their ever-willing partners in politics to the point where Spencer Bachus,chairman of the House Financial Services Committee, has said: "My view is that Washington and the regulators are there to serve the banks."[5] The result being complete impotence by the government, when it pretends to address the various financial issues plaguing our country.

It's not just federal but at the state level too. I can speak from personal experience. People from both parties went public in the last governor's race in Minnesota and said that a major mistake was made when we overturned mybudget in '03. What they did to me, they did feeling that the economy would rebound back big. They gambled, threw the dice, and craps came up. We've fallen a long way in less than a decade. Through most of my term, we'd had a budget *surplus*, and I was able to provide citizens the largest tax rebate any state had ever given. In July 2011, my home state was facing a $5 billion budget gap. When the entire biannual budget is only $32 billion, that's a substantial chunk. You're looking at about 20 percent of your budget that has to be fixed either with taxes raised or services cut. All because the two parties did what they always do—made political decisions without caring about people, just their parties.

Tim Pawlenty, who became governor after I decided not to run again, wouldn't increase taxes on the wealthy, but he cut $2.7 billion from health care and the University of Minnesota under a declared "emergency." The State Supreme Court, in 2010, ruled that his unilateral cuts had violated our Minnesota constitution. In 2011, the solution to the budget gap from the Rebloodlicans in the Minnesota legislature ended up shutting down the state government because they wouldn't raise taxes on the 7,700 people in Minnesota who make over $1 million a year. More than forty state agencies closed down, including the state parks during the Fourth of July! Some 22,000 workers were placed on furlough. We became a national example of political dysfunction. By the time an agreement was reached—without any tax increases, but with the state delaying more aid to our schools—and the shutdown ended after twenty days. Lost revenues were in the millions.[6]

Minnesota held a mirror up to the bigger picture. For several years now, federal government officials have said time and again that we had to shoot hundreds of billions to big banks in order to save our financial system, and supposedly also to benefit Main

Street. Yeah, well, I liked this summation by Edward J. Kane, a finance professor at Boston College, when he appeared before a Senate banking panel in August 2011: "Our representative democracy espouses the principle that all men and women are equal under the law. During the housing bubble and the economic meltdown that the bursting bubble brought about, the interests of domestic and foreign financial institutions were much better represented than the interests of society as a whole."[7]

Robert Reich, the secretary of labor under President Clinton, wrote recently: "Everyone knows the biggest banks are too big to fail—and yet, despite this, Congress won't put a cap on the size of the banks. The assets of the four biggest—J.P. Morgan Chase, Bank of America, Citigroup, and Wells Fargo—now equal sixty-two percent of total commercial bank assets. That's up from fifty-four percent five years ago. Throw in Goldman Sachs and Morgan Stanley, and these six leviathans preside over the American economy like Roman emperors."[8]

Representative democracy? Roman emperors? I'm glad some people are laying it out in those terms. How do they get away with it? Their Daddy Warbucks in government is the Federal Reserve, our sinful—I mean central—bank that controls U.S. monetary policy and has for almost one hundred years. So just how unaccountable are they? In August 2011, the first-ever audit of the Federal Reserve showed they'd provided over a trillion dollars in "emergency" loans between late 2007 and mid-2010 to the financial sector. Then it came out in November 2011 that, while Congress was debating whether to bail out the banksters back in 2008 with a $700-billion blank check, the Fed was already giving the six biggest banks under-the-table, no-strings-attached loans of $7.77 trillion. The banks then used the low interest rates charged by the Fed to bring in another $13 billion in income. The Fed gave Morgan Stanley $107 billion in September 2008, Citigroup almost $100 billion in January 2009, and Bear Stearns $30 billion "to see it through its 2008 shotgun marriage with J. P. Morgan."[9]

A later analysis by a Ford Foundation project of all the various "liquidity swaps," "mortgage-backed security purchases," and the like showed that the total "emergency assistance" from the Fed to both domestic *and* foreign entities is no less than $29.616 trillion. That mind-blowing number is more than twice the U.S. GDP for 2010.[10]

All this thanks to the Federal Reserve Board of Governors, who aren't elected by anybody but are really more powerful than the government. The current president of the Federal Reserve Bank of New York, William Dudley, kept his investments in AIG and General Electric while the Fed was simultaneously giving bailout funds to both companies. And nobody but Bernie Sanders, the independent U.S. senator from Vermont, raised the conflict-of-interest card.

The former New York Fed president Tim Geithner was connected to Goldman Sachs through a series of hedge funds; he went on to run Obama's Treasury Department. "The main problem," said Randall Wray, an economics professor from the University of Missouri-Kansas City, "is the lack of congressional oversight, and the way the Fed seemed to pick winners who would be protected at any cost."[11] (Remember Fannie and Freddie, the mortgage honchos which got about $150 billion in bailout money and exist today thanks to the largesse of future taxpayers.)

On his website, Ron Paul has this quote from none other than Henry Ford: "It is well that the people of the nation do not understand our banking and monetary system, for if they did, I believe there would be a revolution before tomorrow morning."[12] Paul pulls no punches about the Federal Reserve, which, he wrote in the *Wall Street Journal*, "has caused every single boom and bust that has occurred in this country since the bank's creation in 1913. . . . The Fed's actions have had one aim—to keep prices elevated at bubble levels,thus ensuring that bad debt remains on the books and failing firms remain in business, albatrosses around the market's neck. . . . If the Fed would stop intervening and distorting the market, and would allow the functioning of a truly free market that deals with profit and loss, our economy could recover. The continued existence of an organization that can create trillions of dollars out of thin air to purchase financial assets and prop up a fundamentally insolvent banking system is a black mark on an economy that professes to be free."[13]

In late January 2011, the Financial Crisis Inquiry Commission finally released its awaited report on the debt crisis of a few years earlier. It was called "a confusing and contradictory mess . . . as impenetrable as the collateralized debt obligations at the core of the crisis. . . . This commission's investigation was spiritless and sometimes plain wrong." Unbelievably, the Rebloodicans proposed removing the term "Wall Street" from the report altogether.[14]

As it turns out, thirty big U.S. corporations spent more money lobbying than they paid in federal taxes from 2008 to 2010. In fact, twenty-nine of these companies managed to pay no federal income taxes at all! That's because they're "job creators," right? Keep in mind that the tax code calls for thirty-five percent of corporate profits to go toward taxes. But those same twenty-nine companies got tax *rebates* instead—in General Electric's case, nearly $5 billion, on top of a $140 billion bailout on the way to global 2010 profits of $14 billion![15] The combined profits of those twenty-nine outfits hit $164 billion, and the rebates almost $11 billion.

"How can this be?" you ask. Well, the most blatant recent example I know, in terms of what goes on inside the revolving door between financial bigwigs and politicians, is the case of Jon S. Corzine. He'd been a lot of things to a lot of people in the past. He'd joined Goldman Sachs as a young bond trader back in 1975 and eventually ascended to the top with a rep as a big-risk, big-profit guy. After Corzine lost out in a Goldman power struggle in 1999 with Hank Paulson (soon to be W's Treasury secretary), Corzine went on to become a U.S. senator from New Jersey and then the state's governor. And after he lost a reelection race in 2010, he ended up the CEO of a little-known brokerage house called MF Global.

There, Corzine succeeded in stopping a new federal regulation that would have put a crimp in risky trades using customer's money. Just like the one he set out to make.

Never one to shy from a challenge, Corzine placed a $6.3 billion bet on the sovereign debt of five European countries. Bad timing, Jon. It wasn't long before MF Global was up for sale and then filing for bankruptcy in the fall of 2011. When Corzine was subpoenaed to testify before a congressional committee, he said he was "stunned" to find out that about a billion dollars of customer money couldn't be found. You read right, a *billion dollars* somehow misplaced! What was more than a little embarrassing was when a subsequent witness said that MF Global "had used $175 million in customer funds to lend from one arm of the firm to another" and that Corzine knew about it.[16]

Here's how they worked it: Four days before the company fell apart, MF Global "unloaded hundreds of millions of dollars' worth of securities to Goldman Sachs"—the behemoth that Corzine previously headed up. According to some ex-MF Global employees, the deal was cleared by JPMorgan Chase, which was letting the company draw down a $1.2 billion revolving line of credit at the time. It all happened lickety-split in the realm of the titans. While "it is unclear what type of assets Goldman bought from MF Global," Global customers "have not yet received an estimated $900 million from their accounts, which remain frozen as regulators search for missing funds."[17]

But don't bet on good ol' boy Jon Corzine ending up in the hoosegow any time soon. Columnist Frank Rich puts it like this: "The Obama administration seems not to have a prosecutorial gene. It's shy about calling a fraud a fraud when it occurs in high finance."[18] Corporations too big to prosecute became the order of the day under George W. Bush, but it's ongoing. There's a veritable "who's who" that's never been called to account for illegal activities ranging from bribery to tax evasion to just about everything in between. Among others, deferred prosecution has benefited Boeing,

AIG, AOL, Halliburton, BP, Health South, Daimler Chrysler, Wachovia, Merrill Lynch, Pfizer, UBS, and Barclays Bank.[19]

Remember the savings and loan crisis in the 1980s? Well, more than eight hundred bank officials went to jail then for criminal activity. Not this time, bay-bee. As early as 2008, before the public had any idea what had been going on, the FBI had scaled back a plan to investigate mortgage fraud. One of the worst offenders was Angelo R. Mozilo, the CEO of Countrywide Financial, based in L.A. The U.S. attorney there dropped an investigation of Mozilo after he cut a deal with the Securities Exchange Commission (SEC). Mozilo paid $22.5 million in penalties "without admitting or denying the accusations" against him.[20]

The SEC is notorious for lack of enforcement. So much so that a federal judge who's overseeing a $285 million settlement between Citigroup and the SEC—a deal that would close the book on the fact "that the bank deceived investors in the sale of mortgage securities" for over a billion dollars—wondered aloud whether the SEC has "an interest in what the truth is." An analysis by the The New York Times of SEC "investigations over the last decade found nearly 350 instances where the agency has given big Wall Street institutions and other financial companies a pass" and also grants waivers whereby "the companies continue to use rules that let them instantly raise money publicly, without waiting weeks for government approvals."[21]

The SEC had all its teeth extracted some time ago, and those few slaps it metes out are pretty damn limp-wristed. The same federal judge mentioned above, Jed S. Rakoff, tossed out an earlier paltry settlement between the SEC and Bank of America over how the company acquired Merrill Lynch.[22] Almost all the biggest financial corporations—including Goldman Sachs, Morgan Stanley, JP Morgan Chase, and Bank of America—"have settled fraud cases by promising that they would never again violate an antifraud law, only to have the SEC conclude they did it again a few years later." But the SEC hasn't brought a single contempt charge against these guys for a decade.[23] You can "take it to the bank" that punishment ain't gonna happen. A warning, maybe, but no citation. And any executives named as defendants? No way, José. The days when the fellows running Enron and WorldCom got called on the carpet are pretty much over. Solomon L. Wisenberg, once in charge of a financial institutions fraud unit at the Justice Department, sums it up: "Traditionally, a bank would tell the Department of Justice when an employee engaged in crimes, but what do you do when the bank itself is run by a criminal enterprise?"[24]

Keep in mind that the SEC is the government agency that's supposed to make sure the street gangs keep and retain records on their activities, and a number of enforcement cases have been brought when they didn't. Except it turns out to be a pot-calling-the-kettle-black situation, because it's come out that the SEC "illegally destroyed files and documents related to thousands of early-stage investigations over the last 20 years"—against the likes of Bernie Madoff, Goldman Sachs, Citigroup, B of A, and Lehman Brothers; you don't need a scorecard to list the players. The SEC claims they saw the light and changed the no-search-but-destroy policy in 2010.[25]

Elizabeth Warren, now a candidate for the Senate against Scott Brown in Massachusetts, and a rare people's advocate, wrote recently: "The big banks and their allies followed a now-familiar game plan: Launch an offensive against anyone trying to enforce the law with rigor; work overtime to block serious investigation of illegal activity; and persuade the government to accept a slap-on-the-wrist settlement to absolve their violations of the law."[26]

Instead, the Street is suing, via their big lobbyists, to overturn whatever government rules it doesn't like. In December, they filed one against the Commodites Futures Trading Commission because the new Dodd-Frank law authorizes it to put limits on their speculative trading. But Wall Street is claiming the commission's cost-benefit analysis was inadequate. Translation: Don't touch my profits, buddy. A year earlier, Wall Street sued the SEC on the same grounds after the SEC tried making it easier for shareholders to nominate directors to their companies. This is despite the Dodd-Frank bill being "filled with loopholes big enough for Wall Street executive and traders to drive their Ferrari's through," as Robert Reich wrote.[27]

AIG is the insurance giant that made reckless bets on mortgage-backed securities that went south. But they're also one of a handful of bailed-out big companies that got granted a special waiver by the Treasury in 2008, which allows their net operating losses to offset any taxes owed to the government. That waiver, to a company that claimed more than $19 billion in profits for only the last three months of 2011, will most likely let them avoid paying anything in taxes for a decade! But in a lawsuit that really takes the cake, the former head of AIG, Maurice "Hank" Greenberg, has filed a $25-billion case against the federal government for taking an eighty percent interest in his insurance behemoth during the financial crisis without "due process or just compensation," in alleged violation of the Fifth Amendment. So the government, which bailed out AIG to the tune of $182.3 billion, is now being demanded to pay the company's shareholders since AIG's stock price has dropped ninety-eight percent since mid-2007. But if corporations are people, why the fuck not?[28]

But if these lawsuits are bass-ackwards unless you're the best "double-thinker" on the planet (remember Orwell's 1984: "War is Peace"), the corporatists in Congress are right there cheer-leading. After a "bipartisan supercommittee" was established to deal with the deficit, the Rebloodlicans refused to hike taxes on the wealthiest Americans; in fact, they "wanted to cut them even below their current bargain-basement level." (I mean, you'd think their clients shopped at Wal-Mart or Target.) How far do Obama and the other Democrips have to cave? The original "grand bargain" that the Bloods rejected "would have cut $1 trillion in domestic and defense spending, and $650 billion from Medicare, Medicaid, and Social Security, all because it would have raised tax revenues by

$1.2 trillion."[29] When three million people were set to lose their unemployment insurance—and were plenty pissed off about it—the Rebloodlicans ultimately quit stonewalling in December.

Things have come to such a dastardly pass that there's been a bill introduced in the House with more than two hundred cosigners, as of last December, called the Regulations from the Executive in Need of Scrutiny Act (REINS, for short, which I suppose is their play-on-words for "reining in" the government). What this bill would do is "stop any major regulation issued by a federal agency and costing more than $100 million from taking effect unless it received approval from both houses of Congress and the president. Many such rules are issued every year involving everything from food safety to efficiency standards for cars." In a wipeout of the legislative process, one house "can effectively undo a law by killing off regulations that carry out the law without the consent of the other parties involved in its creation." Wow, remember when Congress used to enact the laws and then the executive branch would "negotiate with stakeholders and write detailed regulations?"[30] "REINS would delay product-safety rules affecting family products like toys and cribs, complicate the FDA's regulation of food and prescription drugs, and slow delivery of Social Security and Medicare."

There's another bill called the Regulatory Accountability Act, which "would subject agencies to nearly boundless inquiries into the cost of new regulations and give corporations numerous opportunities to delay rule-making indefinitely. Few major rules would ever see the light of day."[31] Government Sachs spent $4.6 million in 2010 lobbying Congress to water down the Dodd-Frank law, which tries to exert a wee bit of control over the $600 trillion derivatives market, much of it "on hired guns from major Washington lobbying firms, including former Senate majority leader Trent Lott (R-Miss.) and former House minority leader Richard A Gephardt (D-Mo.)."[32] Always an equal opportunity employer.

As for corporate whistleblowers, few as they may be, they pretty much get the silent treatment from Washington. Of 1,273 complaints filed between 2002 and 2008 by employees who spoke out and were retaliated against by their companies, only seventeen times did the government rule for the whistleblower; 841 of the complaints were dismissed without even being heard. Eileen Foster was a senior exec at Countrywide Financial who uncovered massive fraud and talked about it on *60 Minutes*. But nobody in government saw fit to contact her afterward.

The Dodd-Frank Wall Street Reform and Consumer Protection Act is supposed to encourage reporting violations to the SEC and even providing rewards to Wall Street whistleblowers. But a bill introduced by New York Blood Rep. Michael Grimm called, get this, the Whistleblower Improvement Act, would require these "do-gooders" to first report the problems to their employers before even thinking about tattling to the government. "This would be like requiring police officers to tip off suspects before they begin an investigation," as the Project on Government Oversight puts it. Watch for the Grimm Act to resurface in Congress's near future.

Then there's the story of Leyla Wydler, who, in 2003, sent a letter to the SEC about the Stanford Financial Group, her former employer that she alleged was involved in "a lingering corporate fraud scandal perpetrated as a 'massive Ponzi scheme' that will destroy the life savings of many, damage the reputation of all associated parties, ridicule securities and banking authorities, and shame the United States of America." She sent copies to the trade group supposedly responsible for enforcing the regs, along with media including the *Washington Post* and *Wall Street Journal*. Nobody responded. Over four years later, it came out that Stanford had indeed "orchestrated a $7 billion Ponzi scheme which cost thousands of defrauded investors their savings."[33]

In March 2012, Texas financier Robert Allen Stanford finally wast convicted in a Houston federal court after being charged with defrauding almost 30,000 investors in 113 countries, by way of dishing out $7 billion in false high-interest certificates of deposit at his Caribbean-based bank on the island of Antigua. The media trumpeted about Stanford's private yachts and the castle he bought a girlfriend in Florida. But they didn't say a word about what *Bill Moyers' Journal* first revealed several years back:

"He bankrolled junkets to [Antigua's] balmy shores for several members of Congress including Texas Republican senator John Cornyn and New York Democratic congressman Charlie Rangel, [then] chair of the powerful House Ways and Means Committee. Stanford partied with Nancy Pelosi and Bill Clinton at the Democratic National Convention [in 2008]. And when Tom DeLay was still House majority leader, he flew the friendly skies in Stanford's private jet sixteen times in three years, including a trip to Houston for DeLay's arraignment on money-laundering charges. . . .

"Sir Allen also showered millions of dollars on political campaigns; much of it in the very year Congress was debating a bill to curb financial fraud. Two of the biggest recipients were Democratic Senator Bill Nelson and Republican John McCain, one of the original Keating Five. Three key Democrats on the Senate Banking Committee got checks from Stanford, too. Surprise, surprise: The reform bill never got out of the Senate."

Barack Obama, John Boehner, and Harry Reid, along with the national fundraising committees for both gangs, also were blessed with Stanford's largesse. Even though some have returned their contributions to a court-appointed receiver that's supposed to be refunding the defrauded investors, "roughly $154,000 recovered from elected officials is a fraction of the $1.8 million missing." And, in a bit of hypocrisy that takes the cake, the two gangs' national campaign committees are appealing to a higher court about having to return what Stanford gave them![34]

While tax rates are at a sixty-year low, our budget deficit keeps right on growing. (During the summer '11, battle over the debt ceiling, Rebloodlicans tried to sneak in riders that "would essentially have blocked the E.P.A. and the Interior Department from doing their jobs.")[35] No less a personage than the "Oracle of Omaha," mega-billionaire Warren Buffett came right out and told Congress's supercommittee on reducing the deficit to quit "coddling" him and his rich buddies. Buffett pointed out that he paid a lesser tax rate (17%) than anybody else in his office, and he didn't think that was right. He called for rolling back the millionaire tax cuts.[36] Maybe some in the government could listen up—if they weren't so busy raking it in.

Like Illinois senator Richard Durbin said in a rare moment of congressional candor back in '09, the big financial groups around Capitol Hill "frankly own the place." Generally speaking, you don't hear many donkeys braying or elephants trumpeting, unless it's to toot their own horns. No, it's all about knowing who's gonna add the most sweetener to your honey pot.

Has there been any legislation to put the brakes on the high-finance racketeers?

None of the so-called legislative efforts—Dodd-Frank or you-name-it—have come close to pushing the kind of regulation that's needed. Obama, in his 2008 campaign for presidency, took a huge amount of money from the financial industry; so, you think he's gonna tie their hands in a real way? Otherwise, why wouldn't he have given that interim appointment to Elizabeth Warren to run the new consumer protection agency that supposedly was gonna cut some nuts off. Nope, Obama's backers didn't want Mrs. Oversight to get any real power.

These behemoth corporations are still too big to fail, let alone jail, and you can bet that if another JPMorgan or Goldman Sachs starts to go under, they'll get saved for fear of crashing the economy. Nothing that really caused our dilemma has changed. These two gangs are definitely "equal opportunity pushers"—and I use that term the same way it refers to the cartels.

Protecting the rights of corporations to pollute is another big-ticket item. In 2011, the Rebloodlican House voted 191 times "to undercut clean air and water laws while blocking efforts to limit global warming, protect public lands, and guard against future oil spills" and to reject attempts to strengthen the regulations. After all, the mantra goes, "regulations cost jobs and all they're out to do is help the working guy."[37]

In December 2011, a study from Germany called "Bankrolling Climate Change" identified the top twenty banks who financially support the coal industry. A typical sized six hundred-megawatt coal-fired power plant costs over $2 billion, and, since 2005, this report found $308 billion in coal financing. The biggest offenders? Round up the usual suspects, the bailed-out boys: JPMorgan, Citibank, and Bank of America. And the "doublespeak" is staggering. "JPMorgan claims they are helping the world transition to a low-carbon economy. Citi calls itself, on its website, the most innovative bank in climate change. Bank of America calls global climate change the most formidable challenge we are facing."[38] One thing you gotta say for BP, at least they're honest about it—they shut down their solar business in December, saying they "can't make any money" selling panels while they're still spending $20 billion a year developing oil and gas.[39]

As Robert F. Kennedy, Jr. put it recently: "The same DOE [Department of Energy] loan guarantee program that supported [new] solar projects gave an astonishing $8.3 billion loan guarantee—many times the size of the solar projects—to Southern Company to build two nuclear power plants. Nuclear power is an industry with a product so expensive it cannot compete in any version of free market capitalism. Big nuke is totally dependent on massive, monstrous public and government subsidies at every stage of its life. Oil is a close second. A comprehensive inventory of oil subsidies by former California EPA chief Terry Tamminen, in his acclaimed book *Lives Per Gallon*, calculates U.S. subsidies to the oil industry at upward of one trillion dollars annually!"[40]

In 2009, the American Clean Energy and Security Act was introduced in the House. It would have established an emissions trading plan similar to the European Union's, aimed at limiting the amount of greenhouse gases. But the Heritage Foundation and the American Petroleum Institute (API) came out against the bill, claiming it would raise taxes (!) and thus the price of gasoline and related energy expenses. Bad for the bottom line. The API spent millions greasing the lawmakers who eventually killed the bill in the Senate. PACs from Big Oil and Big Gas gushed-and-flatulated $6.6 million to federal candidates from January '09 until June '10—about sixty percent going to the Bloods and the other forty percent to the Crips.[41]

One thing both gangs agree on is keeping the military budget intact. Over this past decade, our military spending has gone from $300 billion to $700 billion. During the same time period, we've spent over $7.6 trillion on military and homeland security. And we're trying to find someplace to reduce the deficit? The majority of Americans, according to a poll taken by *Reuters*, are in favor of cutting defense spending, which now exceeds that of *all other countries in the world combined* and consumes more than one-third of the federal budget. And part of that involves what the Government Accountability Office has said are "staggering" cost over-runs by the Pentagon. Their contractors are getting away with fraud on a scale bigger than Wall Street, if that's possible! It seems that eighty percent of the three- and four-star officers who retired from 2004 to 2008 went to work as either consultants or defense industry execs.[42]

I'm sixty years old, and my country has been at war more than half of my life. If we hadn't fought all these wars, do you think our economics would be as bad as they are today? Another lie that the government is perpetrating is that when you join the military, it's to protect *us*, the average U.S. citizens. No, you're the muscle arm of the corporations when you put on that uniform. I challenge the government, on all the wars since World War Two, to give me one example where the United States was in danger of being invaded and having our lifestyles being changed. The domino effect of communism proved not to be true. That was what they sold us for awhile. Today they're selling us patriotism, and that's false. The military today is there to push corporate interests throughout the world. When corporations are threatened, the U.S. military goes in to quell the threat.

In some ways, things haven't changed all that much since the 1930s, when Major General Smedley Butler, the most decorated Marine in American history, put out this message in a speech to the American Legion: "I spent thirty-three years being a high-class muscle man for Big Business, for Wall Street and the bankers. In short, I was a racketeer for capitalism." He listed having "helped purify Nicaragua for the international banking house of Brown Brothers," and helping make Mexico "safe for American oil interests" and the Dominican Republic "for American sugar interests," among others. Butler came right out and told veterans that war was "largely a matter of money. Bankers lend money to foreign countries and when they cannot repay, the President sends Marines to get it. I know—I've been in eleven of these expeditions."[43]

But more and more, our foreign wars now involve the use of private contractors. In 2007, when the Iraq War was at its peak, there were more than 180,000 civilians (American and foreign, including Iraqi) being paid by we, the taxpayers, compared to 160,000 regular soldiers.[44] And that didn't even count the private security companies (PSCs) like Blackwater, Dyncorp International, and Triple Canopy, which basically comprised a mercenary force. "Some twenty different PSCs, employing ten thousand people, are working directly for the U.S. government, primarily for [the Department of Defense] and the Department of State," according to a Congressional Research Service Report in 2008. "The total direct cost to the U.S. government for acquiring security services in Iraq is not known. The U.S. Congressional Budget Office recently estimated that between 2003–2007 the U.S. government obligated between $3 billion and $4 billion to PSCs to acquire security services." Pay scale ranged as high as $1,500 a day, way beyond what our troops get.[45] During that same '03–'07 time frame, there were more than three hundred reported cases of contracting mistakes. Not one employee got fired or denied promotion. "In a stunning confession, the

Pentagon itself acknowledged that $8.2 billion of taxpayer money flowed through contracts into Iraq, some in stacks or pallets of cash, without appropriate recordkeeping or oversight."[46] And these guys were also unaccountable in terms of what actions they took, including the killing of civilians.

Iraq and Afghanistan are our first contractors' wars, but this is just part of an escalating trend that's outlined in Allison Stanger's book, *One Nation Under Contract*, for those who want to pursue the story further. "Democrats and Republicans alike embraced outsourcing the work of government to the private sector whenever possible," she says. In 2000, the Defense Department spent $133.2 billion on contracts. By 2008, it was $391.9 billion, an almost three-fold increase. State Department spending on contracting soared 431 percent from 2000–2008, while contracting at US AID grew "a whopping 690 percent."[47]

Of course, contracting and paid mercenaries are what happen when the government wants to run its wars without the involvement of the citizens. When we had a draft, the gangs couldn't just get us into a war without some kind of sacrifice from the people of the country. The gangs like it better this way, using volunteers, mercenaries, and contractors, and never including the costs in the Federal Budget. Most Americans are pretty far removed from these wars we are waging, and so the gangs can do whatever they want without Americans protesting much. And the only politician who is speaking out against all this is Ron Paul, who is standing with integrity against both the Bloods and the Crips.

Then there's the prison industry. Ever heard of the Corrections Corporation of America (CCA)? They're our country's biggest operator of for-profit prisons, a trend that's been rapidly growing. As of the end of 2009, about 129,000 people in the U.S. were being held in privately managed correctional facilities. That's 16.4 percent of federal, and 6.8 percent of state, inmate populations. The CCA, which operates sixty-six of these places, has seen its revenues expand more than five-fold since the mid-1990s, since first the "war on drugs," and now the business of locking up undocumented immigrants has "blossomed." They and the GEO Group, its biggest competitor, generated more than $2.9 billion in 2010.

What's in it for them? Long before this latest development, as of 2008 "at least thirty-seven states have legalized the contracting of prison labor by private corporations that mount their operations inside state prisons. The list of such companies contains the cream of U.S. corporate society: IBM, Boeing, Motorola, Microsoft, AT&T, Wireless, Texas Instruments, Dell, Compaq, Honeywell, Hewlett-Packard, Nortel, Lucent Technologies, 3Com, Intel, Northern Telecom, TWA, Nordstrom's, Revlon, Macy's, Pierre Cardin, Target Stores, and many more. . . . Just between 1980 and 1994, profits went up from $392 million to $1.31 billion." The inmates in state pens do get paid, generally minimum wage.

"Thanks to prison labor, the United States is once again an attractive location for investment in work that was designed for third world labor markets. A company that operated a maquiladora (assembly plant in Mexico, near the border) closed down its operations there and relocated to San Quentin State Prison in California. In Texas, a factory fired its 150 workers and contracted the services of prisoner-workers from the private Lockhart Texas prison, where circuit boards are assembled for companies like IBM and Compaq."[48]

Now we have a prison-industrial complex right alongside our military-industrial complex, all in pursuit of profits. And it's all intertwined with partners-in-politics. A 2011 report titled "Gaming the System" by the nonprofit D.C. group Justice Policy Institute describes how CCA had spent $17 million on federal lobbying efforts since 2000, along with doling out more than $1.2 million through their Political Action Committee to federal politicians. These same corporations have contributed over $7.2 million to state candidates and parties. Here's how the game works:

"After serving eighteen years in the U.S. House of Representatives [Ohio's] John Kasich retired in 2000 and took a managing director position in Ohio with Lehman Brothers. Lehman Brothers has a long standing history with private prison companies, spending most of the late 1990s and 2000s before their collapse underwriting bonds for managing credit for both CCA and Cornell [Corrections]. After winning the governorship of Ohio in 2010, Kasich laid out his plans for privatizing state prison operations, along with appointing a former CCA employee to head the Ohio Department of Rehabilitation and Correction. Rounding out Kasich's connections to CCA is his close friend and former congressional chief of staff whose lobbying firm was hired to represent CCA in January 2011."[49]

This past February, CCA sent letters out to forty-eight states offering to buy up their prisons to help out with "challenging corrections budgets." All they're asking in return for that outlay of $250 million are a twenty-year management contract and a guarantee that the prison will remain at least ninety percent of capacity. Harley Lappin, CCA's chief corrections officer (and ex-director of the Federal Bureau of Prisons), wrote that he hoped the states "will share our belief in the benefits of the purchase-and-manage model." Up until 2011, when Ohio peddled one of its biggest to CCA, the sale of a state prison to a private company had never happened.[50]

So, did you ever consider that one reason we're in these wars and keeping more people in prison is to feed the corporate maw and political trough? I think I'll take a ride down to my local post office while it still exists. Did you know the U.S. Postal Service (at age 236) is older than our Constitution? Not only the strongest union and second biggest employer (after Wal-Mart) in our country, but our most venerable institution. But now a good number of both Bloods and Crips are telling us that it's broke, and so Saturday mail service and mail processing centers and lots of local post offices need to be shut down, and about 120,000 workers laid off.

Want a clue as to the origin of the post office's financial crisis? It's not because of email or FedEx or UPS, for starters. Back in 2006, Congress passed something called the Postal Accountability Enhancement Act, which basically demanded that the agency give universal health care coverage to their current and future employees by paying $5.5 billion into the Treasury every year. No other entity in the country, public or private, ever had to do something like that. Does anybody else smell a conspiracy here? Universal health care coverage so somebody can privatize the post office?![51] This is the ugly pass we've come to, folks. Stamp me ready for a revolution.

NOTES

1. Adams on "aristocratic despotism": "Politics in America: Only the Rich Need Apply," by Andrew Trees, www.latimes.com, December 12, 2010.

2. Jefferson and Madison quotes: "Why 'We the People' Must Triumph Over Corporate Power," by Bill Moyers, www.alternet.org, December 11, 2011. (Foreword to *Corporations Are Not People: Why They Have More Rights Than You Do and What You Can Do About It*, by Jeffrey Clements).

3. Theodore Roosevelt quote: http://boatagainstthecurrent.blogspot, com/2008/10/quote-of-day-theodore-roosevelt-on.html.

4. "Those who own the country ought to govern it": en.wikiquote. org/wik/John_Jay

5. Spencer Bachus quote: "The Bipartisanship Racket," by Frank Rich, *New York Times*, December 19, 2010.

6. Minnesota shutdown: "Antitax Extremism in Minnesota," editorial, *New York Times*, July 6, 2011; "Amid Minnesota Crisis, Pawlenty Faces Scrutiny," by Trip Gabriel, *New York Times*, July 14, 2011; "Minnesota Government Shutdown 2011 Ends," www.huffingtonpost.com, July 20, 2011.

7. Edward J. Kane: "The Rescue that Missed Main Street," by Gretchen Morgenson, *New York Times*, August 28, 2022.

8. Robert Reich on the big banks: "The Remarkable Stupidity of the Street," Robert Reich's Blog, December 10, 2011, www.readersupported-news.org.

9. $7.77 trillion to banks from fed: "Secrets of the Bailout, Now Told," by Gretchen Morgenson, *New York Times*, December 4, 2011; "$7.7 Trillion to Wall Street—Anything to Keep the Banksters Happy!," by Thom Hartmann, *Truthout*, December 3, 2011, both citing *Bloomberg News* analysis.

10. "Bail-out Bombshell: Fed 'Emergency' Bank Rescue Totaled $29 Trillion Over Three Years," by J. Andrew Felkerson, www.alternet.org, December 15, 2011, citing Ford Foundation, *A Research and Policy Dialogue Project on*

Improving Governance of the Government Safety Net in Financial Crisis.

11. William Dudley, qutoe from Wray: "First Federal Reserve Audit Reveals Trillions in Secret Bailouts," August 29, 2011, citing GAO report, newsfromunderground.com.

12. Quote from Henry Ford: www.ronpaul.com, "Honest Money."

13. "Blame the Fed for the Financial Crisis," by Ron Paul, October 20, 2011, http://online.wsj.com

14. Financial Crisis Inquiry Commission report: "Washington's Financial Disaster," by Frank Partnoy, *New York Times*, January 30, 2011.

15. GE bailout and profits: "Corporate Tax Holiday in Debt Ceiling Deal: Where's the Uproar," by Matt Taibbi, www.rollingstone.com, July 22, 2011.

16. *New York Times* articles: "As Regulators Pressed Changes, Corzine Pushed Back and Won," November 4, 2011;"Corzine Defends Actions at MF Global," December 9, 2011; "A Romance With Risk That Brought n a Panic," December 12, 2011; "Confusion Follows a Claim that Corzine Knew of a Funds Transfer," December 14, 2011.

17. "MF Global sold assets to Goldman before collapse: sources," by Lauren Tara Laapra and Matthew Goldstein, www.reuters.com, January 3, 2012.

18. "The Obama administration seems not to have a prosecutorial gene . . .": "What Happened to Change We Can Believe In?", by Frank Rich, *New York Times*, October 24, 2010.

19. Deferred prosecution and corporations: "How Wall Street Crooks Get Out of Jail Free," by William Greider, *The Nation*, April 11, 2011.

20. Savings-and-loan prosecutions, FBI and mortgage fraud, Angelo Mozilo: "A Financial Crisis with Little Guilt," *New York Times*, April 14, 2011.

21. "The SEC Is Letting Large Banks Off," by Edward Wyatt, *New York Times*, February 3, 2012.

22. "Judge in Citigroup Mortgage Settlement Criticizes S.E.C.'s Enforcement," by Peter Lattman, *New York Times*, November 10, 2011.

23. Financial promises and no contempt: "Promises Made, and Remade, by Firms in S.E.C. Fraud Cases," by Edward Wyatt, *New York Times*, November 8, 2011.

24. Solomon L. Wisenberg quote: "Behind the Gentler Approach to Banks by U.S.," by Gretchen Morgenson and Louise Story, *New York Times*, July 8, 2011.

25. "S.E.C. Files Illegally Destroyed, Lawyer Says," by Edward Wyatt,

New York Times, August 18, 2011.

26. Elizabeth Warren: "Where is Wall Street accountability?," by Elizabeth Warren, *Politico*, December 8, 2011.

27. Wall Street suing government: "The Remarkable Political Stupidity of the Street," *Robert Reich's Blog*, December 10, 2011.

28. AIG: "Greenberg sues U.S. for $25 billion over AIG takeover," by Jonathan Stempel, www.reuters.com, November 21, 2011.

29. Deficit deal: "The supercommittee collapses," editorial in the *New York Times*, November 22, 2011.

30. REINS: "Undermining the Executive Branch," editorial in the *New York Times*, December 5, 2011.

31. "REINS would delay . . ."; Regulatory Accountability Act: "The GOP's Deregulation Obsession," by Robert Weissman, *The Nation*, October 31, 2011.

32. Government Sachs lobbying: "The Tea Party and Goldman Sachs: A Love Story," by Robert Scheer, *Truthdig* (quoting *LA Times*), July 6, 2011.

33. "Why No One Would Listen: Corporate Whistleblowers Get the Silent Treament from Washington," by Eyal Press, www.tomdispatch.com, March 6, 2012.

34. "Politicians Won't Return Ponzi Payoffs," by Michael Winship, Moyers & Co., March 10, 2012.

35. Debt ceiling riders: ""Springtime For Toxics," by Paul Krugman, *New York Times*, December 26, 2011.

36. "Looking Closer at Taxes on the Rich," by David Kocieniewski, *New York Times*, August 16, 2011.

37. "G.O.P. vs. the Environment," editorial, *New York Times*, October 15, 2011; "Where the Real Jobs Are," editorial, *New York Times*, January 2, 2012.

38. "The Wall Street-climate change connection," by Justin Elliott, www.salon.com, citing new study by Urgewald, a German environmental organization, December 10, 2011.

39. "BP Axes Solar Power Business," by Terry Macalister, www.guardian.co.uk, December 21, 2011.

40. DOE loans to nuclear, and oil subsidies: "Big Carbon's Sock Puppets Declare War," by Robert F. Kennedy, Jr., www.readersupportednews.org, November 25, 2011.

41. Big Oil and Dirty Coal: "Big Oil and Corporate Polluters Spent Over $500 Million to Kill Climate Bill and Push Offshore Drilling," by Daniel J.

Weiss, Rebecca Lefton and Susan Lyon; National Wildlife Federation and Audubon Society websites.

42. Pentagon and spending: "Why is the Most Wasteful Government Agency Not Part of the Deficit Discussion?", by David Morris, *On the Commons*, July 12, 2011.

43. Smedley Butler: Jules Archer, *The Plot to Seize the White House*, New York: Hawthorne Books, 1973.

44. "Contractors outnumber troops in Iraq," by T. Christian Miller, *Los Angeles Times*, July 4, 2007.

45. "CRS Report for Congress: Private Security Contractors in Iraq," August 25, 2008, found online.

46. Allison Stanger, *One Nation Under Contract*, Yale University Press, 2009.

47. *"One Nation Under Contract*—Six Questions for Allison Stanger," by Scott Horton, www.harpers.org, April 2011.

48. "At least 37 states . . .": "The prisonindustry in the United States? Big business or a new form of slavery?", by Vicky Pelaez, www.globalresearch.ca, March 10, 2008.

49. "Gaming the System": report by Justice Policy Institute, October 2011 (found online).

50. "Private Prison Corporation Offers Cash In Exchange For State Prisons," by Chris Kirkham, www.huffingtonpost.com, February 14, 2012.

51. "Postal Workers: The Last Union," by Allison Kilkenny, www.truthout.org, September 8, 2011.

CHAPTER SIX

LUCRATIVE LOBBYING: WHAT THE RICH CAN DO FOR THE GANGS

You gotta hand it to Jack Abramoff. Back in 2006, the super-lobbyist pled guilty to fraud, tax evasion, and conspiracy to bribe public officials in what some called the biggest congressional scandal in more than a century. Two Bush White House officials got convicted in the scandal, along with U.S. Rep. Bob Ney and nine more lobbyists and staffers in Congress. Now Abramoff is out of jail. He just came out with a book called *Capitol Punishment* and is making the rounds of the talk shows and even visiting Ralph Nader's office to take questions from campaign finance reform activists!

Casino Jack, whistleblower? Well, he certainly seems willing to give some inside information on how the lobbying looters operate. I use that term for good reason because Abramoff himself has coined the phrase "lobbyist safecracker method." He described in one interview how he was working for a big D.C. law firm, Greenberg Traurig, which got hired by special interest groups to push for or against specific legislation. (That's what lobbying is, though it's often called "government relations." But then again you could also call it legalized bribery.) One of Abramoff's clients was the multinational Tyco International Corporation, which in 2003 gave his firm $1.3 million to twist arms in Congress.

"They were fighting to stay out of the tax bill that year, which would have retroactively taxed them to the tune of about $4 billion," Abramoff recalled. The bill, introduced by Iowa's Rebloodlican Senator Charles Grassley, had a provision that targeted outfits like Tyco, which claimed an offshore tax status. So Abramoff got everybody and their brother to make contributions to Grassley's reelection campaign. "That's the lobbyist safecracker method, is raise money and become a big donor." One of his team members started doing some morning jogging with the senator. Abramoff's company held a fundraising event for him. Eventually, although Grassley himself wasn't the culprit, the provision Tyco was worried about got dumped from the bill.[1]

What lobbying was really all about, Abramoff recalls, was "becoming friends" with our legislative gang members and giving them "a stream of goodies that led to an ability to ask them back for stream of goodies the other way." Those offered goodies included stock tips, skybox tickets to pro football games, lavish restaurant meals, and "featherbedding," which is defined as making lucrative job offers to chiefs of staff in Congress. "I started to notice pretty quickly that the second I said that to them, they were so incredibly complimented, that from then on anything I asked was just absolutely granted." As the word got out, "it seemed 90 percent of the people I dealt with up there wanted to come work for me . . . in a year or six months but from that entire period of time they really worked with me anyway. . . . That was an incredible way to control a congressional office."

Abramoff told the crowd at Nader's Public Citizen organization:

> I was involved deeply in a system of bribery—legalized bribery for the most part; illegal bribery, unfortunately for me, somewhat. And that system, which I took advantage of, which I also took for granted as do many who are still in it, still to a large part exists today.[2]

In case anyone's interested in asking, Eye to Eye Strategies is helping Casino Jack book speaking engagements at a going rate of between $15,000 and $25,000 per event. Like he says, that's necessary because "I owe $44 million in restitution." Besides which, he says he'd really like to change the system and "none of the candidates, including Obama, is talking about real reform anymore"[3]

When you've got Jack Abramoff as the voice of reform, do you think maybe it's time to think about changing the game? For lobbying all told, thirty big corporations spent almost half a billion dollars over a three-year period between 2008 and 2010. That's "about $400,000 each day, including weekends." Those same companies had combined profits of $164 billion and tax rebates of nearly $11 billion. They paid more to lobby Congress than they paid in federal income taxes.[4] Think there's any tie-in there?

Like Abramoff, a few Congress-folk do get caught with their fingers in the cookie jar. The most notorious in recent years was Randy "Duke" Cunningham, a Rebloodlican Representative from the San Diego area. He served on the House subcommittee that provided the funding for the Pentagon. On a note card in his office, "starkly framed" under the congressional seal, the Duke had a "bribe menu." It listed "an escalating scale for bribes, starting at $140,000 and a luxury yacht for a $16 million Defense Department contract. Each additional $1 million in contract value required a $50,000 bribe. The rate dropped to $25,000 per additional million once the contract went above $20 million. At one point, Cunningham was living on a yacht named after him, 'The Dukester,' docked near Capitol Hill, courtesy of a defense company president." (One outfit alone, MZM Inc., gave Cunningham over $1 million in cash, cars, and antiques in exchange for $150 million-plus in business.) The Dukester ended up in the dumper—he's still serving out a 100-month jail sentence and has become an advocate for prison reform.[5]

On the other side of the aisle, Louisiana Democrip Rep. William Jefferson got sentenced to thirteen years in 2009 after being charged with bribery, racketeering, and money laundering. Over a five-year period, Jefferson had gone to a dozen mostly African companies involved in oil, sugar, communications, and more—saying he'd promote their ventures through the trade subcommittee in exchange for millions in his pocket. He turned out to be a fan of veggie burgers: The FBI found $90,000 of cold cash inside veggie burger boxes in Jefferson's home freezer, all neatly wrapped inside aluminum foil. Just call him the where's-the-beef-bandit.[6]

"This sentence should be a clear signal that our society will not tolerate bribery; it's not just another cost of doing business in government," said U.S. Attorney Neil H. MacBride after the verdict.[7] Uh huh.

❖ ❖ ❖

We've come a long way from John Adams' pointing out that paying a reasonable salary to our elected officials was "one of the best securities of liberty and equality." Today, we're a government of the rich, by the rich, and for the rich.

Consider this: If you're elected today to the U.S. House or Senate, the job itself pays $174,000 a year. More than most people make, but still not outrageous. But a 2009 study by the Center for Responsive Politics (would that we had such!) uncovered that 261 of the 535 members of Congress were millionaires—and that's without being required to report their homes as assets. The median income of our legislators was $911,000, and in the Senate alone was $2.38 million. As one op-ed writer put it, "This is not too shabby when the median household income in America is roughly $50,000."[8] In short, our federal lawmakers are nine times richer than the other Americans.

At the top of the heap is Rebloodlican Representative Darrell Issa from Southern California, with a net worth that's topped out at $700,850,000. He's chairman of the House Oversight and Government Reform Committee, the dude who asked 150 businesses and trade groups to identify "overly burdensome" regulations that he could try to kill. Since he got elected to Congress in 2000, an exposé in the *New York Times* revealed that he's "bought up office buildings, split a holding company into separate multibillion-dollar businesses, started an insurance company, traded hundreds of millions of dollars in securities, invested in overseas funds, retained an interest in his auto-alarm company and built up a family foundation. . . . He has secured millions of dollars in Congressional earmarks for road work and public works projects that promise improved traffic and other benefits to the many commercial properties he owns north of San Diego . . . it is sometimes difficult to separate the business of Congress from the business of Darrell Issa."[9] What's that panel he chairs again? Of course, the House Overload and Government Refill Committee.

Coming in second behind Issa in the Richest-Person-in-Congress sweepstakes is Michael McCaul of Texas (Rebloodlican, $502,205,003), followed by Jane Harman (Democrip, $493,604,000), Mark Warner (Democrip, $309,088,999), and John Kerry (Democrip, $281,976,067).[10]

What about the candidates for president? The richest, by far, is Mitt Romney, whose fortune is around a quarter of a billion dollars. Among the other early Rebloodlican contenders, Jon Huntsman, Jr. (whose daddy owns a global chemical company) is worth $70.3 million and Newt Gingrich $30.6 million. Also, solidly in the top 1 percent is Herman Cain, with earnings of over $1.2 million a year, and Rick Santorum, at more than $700,000 in 2010. Of course, Barack Obama's right up there too, thanks mostly to sales of his books, with $11.8 million in assets.[11]

But even if you're not among the top 1 percent while "serving" your gang—I mean country—there's plenty of opportunity later on. A study released in September 2011 found that close to 400 of our ex-lawmakers have made the jump to nearby K Street, where the lobby lizards await.[12] I mean, they don't have to actually make new friends, right? Influence Peddlers United could be their slogan.

"A former member of the House or Senate with even modest seniority can now expect to walk into a job paying up to $1 million or more a year—and much more when bonuses were paid for bringing in new clients," writes Thomas B. Edsall, author of *The Age of Austerity*. The record setter for ex-members was Louisiana's Rebloodlican Representative Billy Tauzin, who made over $11.5 million in 2010 running the big lobbying arm for the drug industry, the Pharmaceutical Research and Manufacturers of America.

But it turns out that the top four lobbying buckaroos on a list of the most influential are all former Democrips.[13] John Breaux of Louisiana, who served in Congress from 1972 to 2005, has a company called the Breaux Lott Leadership Group (a subsidiary of Patton Boggs LLP law firm), which raked in billings of $11.83 million in 2010 "from such clients as Citigroup, Goldman Sachs, General Electric, AT&T, Tyson Foods and the Pharmaceutical Research and Manufacturers of America." (Breaux once famously said to reporters, "My vote can't be bought, but it can be rented.")[14]

Another case in point: Dick Gephardt, who represented a "working class" district in Missouri for years and rose to become House Majority Leader, started the Gephardt Government Affairs Group in 2007. With clients that include Boeing (paying them $440,000), Waste Management ($320,000), Visa ($200,000), Goldman Sachs ($200,000), and Ameren Corporation ($200,000), his lobbying company earned nearly $7 million in revenues in 2010. "What matters is what the Senate is doing on the payroll tax, not whether some old members of Congress do lobbying," said ex-Rep. Tom Downey with a straight face, while his Downey McGrath Group "reported lobbying income of $3.32 million from such clients as Time Warner Cable, FedEx, the National Association of Chain Drugstores and the investment bank Lazard Ltd."[15]

Two more senators joined the lobbying club early in 2011—Rebloodlican Robert Bennett and Democrip Bryan Dorgan—both becoming part of the Arent Fox LLP. "Rules in Congress prohibit former House members from lobbying their ex-colleagues for a year and senators have a two-year waiting period. But former members can immediately advise clients on how to maneuver the halls of Congress and influence policy before actually registering as lobbyists."[16]

Like boss, like employee. A 2011 report by LegiStorm, an online disclosure site, found that almost 5,400 ex-congressional staffers moved on from Capitol Hill to be federal lobbyists over the past decade. "Twenty-five powerhouse firms and organizations employ 10 or more former Hill workers. The largest number are at the Podesta Group, followed by the U.S. Chamber of Commerce, which employs at least 21."[17]

Altogether, about 14,000 people work up there on the Hill, and about 11,700 more are registered to lobby there. It's the old familiar revolving door. In 2010, the London School of Economics reported that 1,113 of those lobbyists used to work in the personal office of one legislator or another.[18] Remember the congressional supercommittee debt panel that got established in the summer of 2011 to figure out how to make those huge cuts in federal programs? Well, that supposedly sent K Street into a panic; but not to worry:

> Nearly 100 registered lobbyists who used to work for members of the supercommittee are now representing defense companies, health-care conglomerates, Wall Street banks and others with a vested interest in the outcome of the panel's work, according to a *Washington Post* analysis of disclosure data. Three Democrats and three Republicans on the panel also employ former lobbyists on their staffs.[19]

(Two-thirds of the lobbyists with ties to the supercommittee are Democrips.)

Since the Rebloodlicans gained control of the House in 2010, almost a hundred members of Congress have hired lobbyists as their chiefs of staff or legislative directors—more than ever before.[20] Obama made it a point that his administration wasn't going to hire lobbyists, but it turns out there's a "waiver process" if you haven't engaged in the practice for two years. So Vice President Joe Biden was free to bring on a new counselor, Steve Ricchetti of the lobby firm bearing his name, because he stopped doing it in 2008 and since had "advised clients on public policy, communications strategy and grassroots efforts."[21] Where that fine line is, who can say?

It's not just politicos at the top who do the revolving-door waltz. Walter Lukken, in the later years of Bush's administration, was chief regulator of the commodities markets. He was supposed "to spot and combat speculative abuses and manipulations that might have led to artificial price hikes and other disruptions." In 2008, "Lukken presided over some of the worst chaos in the commodities markets in recent history." The huge spike in commodity index speculation—which "had grown from $13 billion in 2003 to more than $260 billion as of March 2008"—was, in Lukken's mind-set, "not a result of manipulative forces." He's since reaped his reward. Early in 2010, Lukken got named to head the Futures Industry Association, the top lobby group for futures investors. One expert said of the appointment: "It's not the revolving door. It's the express elevator."[22]

Perhaps no corporation plays this switching partners game better than the agrichemical/biotech giant, Monsanto. When their artificial bovine growth hormone (BGH) first got approved for going into milk, Margaret Miller was their person in charge of preparing the report. By the time the report needed government evaluation, she was Deputy Director of Human Safety and Consultative Services in charge of overseeing the process. Then there's Michael R. Taylor. He began as a law partner representing Monsanto on BGH issues. Then he became the FDA's deputy commissioner for policy and wrote the labeling guidelines claiming "there was no difference between rGBH and regular milk." He returned to the Monsanto fold for a time, and today, Taylor is the Obama administration's food safety issues head honcho. Clarence Thomas used to work for Monsanto but, when the Supreme Court made a recent ruling in favor of their genetically modified alfalfa, Thomas voted aye without a blink. And there's Linda J. Fisher, who was once at the EPA heading their Office of Pollution, Prevention, Pesticides, and Toxic Substances. Monsanto brought her onboard to run their lobbying operation, after which she returned to EPA as its number two administrator under George W. Bush.[23]

❖ ❖ ❖

Last year wasn't a banner one for the lobby shops. Due to "the lingering slow economy and preoccupation with the debt ceiling discussions [that] really slowed down traditional legislative work to a crawl," according to the chairman of the Patton Boggs lobbying outfit, Nick Allard, his company was alone in seeing double-digit growth. They had $24.7 million in revenues for the first six months of 2011, after their big merger with John Breaux's shop.[24]

The figures for the clients of these firms are pretty staggering. In 1998, the total spending on lobbying was $1.44 billion. By 2011, that had soared to $3.3 billion. So, who's forking out the most cash in terms of influencing our "public policy?" At the top of the heap among lobbying clients is the U.S. Chamber of Commerce, which during those thirteen years shelled out more than $800 million.[25] The Chamber is the trade association that represents, among others, ExxonMobil and AIG. Their main issues are "job-killing regulations," going after "government-run" health care, and attacking any federal efforts to rein in domestic energy production. And Chamber CEO Tom Donohue is a master at raising funds from the energy, insurance, and pharmaceutical industries and Wall Street firms.

The Chamber was created in 1911, a year before the Federal Reserve and, since it's a tax-exempt group, by law it's allowed to keep its donors undisclosed. But some of these have since leaked out: Prudential Financial providing $2 million "to weaken the historic rewrite of the nation's financial regulations"; Dow Chemical, $1.7 million "fighting proposed rules that would impose tighter security requirements on chemical facilities"; Rupert Murdoch's NewsCorp,

$1 million "to support the chamber's political efforts" in 2010; un-named health insurance providers who "funneled at least $10 million" in 2009, "all of it anonymously, to oppose President Obama's health care legislation." Other donors to the Chamber include Goldman Sachs, Chevron Texaco, and Aegon, a multinational insurance company based in Europe.[26]

The Chamber geared up for the 2012 election year by running "advocacy [attack] ads" in a number of states, primarily targeting Democrips. They are, according to Scott Reed, a Rebloodlican operative who is now a senior political strategist for the Chamber— "engaged in presidential policies and issues as part of our voter education."[27] They use the lobbying firm Hunton and Williams, one of whose attorneys "solicited a set of private security firms . . . collectively called Team Themis—to develop tactics for damaging progressive groups and labor unions." The hacktivist group Anonymous posted emails about this, including a company entrapment project calling for creating a "false document perhaps highlighting periodical financial information" that would get passed on to a group opposing the Chamber, which would then be exposed as fake and undermine the group's credibility.[28]

Coming in second among the big lobbying spenders was General Electric ($282 million). Over the past decade, GE was awarded almost $32 billion in federal contracts, the majority going to their defense and health-care subsidiaries. At least eight GE lobbyists used to work for members of the debt-ceiling supercommittee,[29] so I wonder what budget cuts they're planning to recommend? Following GE on the client list were the American Medical Association ($254 million), American Hospital Association ($214 million), and Pharmaceutical Research & Manufacturers of America ($214 million). The pharma trade group also gave $15 million to the Chamber of Commerce in 2008.[30]

In 2011, commercial banks spent a record $62 million on lobbying (as a whole, the financial sector spent $472 million). Wells Fargo led the way, followed by Bank of America. Those two had close to a hundred meetings with federal agencies over the course of the year. There's also a Financial Services Roundtable, which has been flooding regulators with comment letters on the Dodd-Frank financial reform law that passed in the summer of 2010. Out of 225 rules that were supposed to have taken effect from the legislation so far, more than 70 percent have missed their deadlines. "One of the ways they [the financial industry] win the battle is by attrition, by ensuring that there's so much activity things get delayed," says Nancy Watzman, a consultant with the watchdog Sunlight Foundation.[31]

"Corporations don't lobby Congress for fun," said NPR's Planet Money Blog in 2012. "They lobby because it helps their bottom line. Getting a regulation gutted or a tax loophole created means extra cash for the corporation. But getting laws changed can be very expensive. How much money does a corporation get back from investing in a good lobbyist?"

Economists tracked the return on investment (ROI) from the American Jobs Creation Act that passed Congress back in 2005. This "benefited hundreds of multinational corporations with a huge, one-time tax break. Without the law, companies that brought profits earned abroad back to the U.S. had to pay a tax rate of 35 percent. With the law, that rate dropped to just over 5 percent. It saved those companies billions of dollars."

All told, companies spent $282 million lobbying for that bill to pass and saved a combined $88.6 billion in taxes.[32] The ROI was 22,000 percent. For every lobbying buck spent, the corporations got $220 in tax benefits.[33] Sure is hard to find a better investment than that.

House Speaker John Boehner is a big favorite of these guys. On his way to that position in 2010, he maintained "especially tight ties with a circle of lobbyists and former aides representing some of the nation's biggest businesses, including Goldman Sachs, Google, Citigroup, R.J. Reynolds, Miller-Coors, and UPS. They have contributed hundreds of thousands of dollars to his campaigns, provided him with rides on their corporate jets, socialized with him at luxury golf resorts and waterfront bashes, and are now leading fund-raising efforts for his Boehner for Speaker campaign, which is soliciting checks of up to $37,8000 each, the maximum allowed." That campaign offered donors giving the maximum some special perks, like "meetings with Leader Boehner and much much more."[34] Yummmmm . . .

Is anybody minding the store or even calling a time-out? Here's the thing: The Rebloodlican candidates for office flat-out place no restrictions whatsoever on taking money from lobbyists. Since the day he announced he was running for president, Obama hasn't accepted a dime from registered lobbyists, says his press secretary. But Democrips under Obama do their courting of lobbyists off-site, for example, at coffee-house meetings that don't appear on the official White House visitor logs. The Lobbying Disclosure Act, a rather complex piece of legislation as you might imagine, has rules specifying whether contacts intended to influence a public official are "active" or "direct," rather than "routine" information-gathering sessions.

Lobbying isn't just about getting tax breaks for businesses, though. Foreign countries get into the act as well. Making no bones about what it's after—and pulling out all stops to try to get it—is the American Israel Public Affairs Committee, AIPAC for short. It employs about a hundred people at its headquarters a couple blocks from the Capitol. These guys have been around a long time, and right now, they're pushing like hell for an invasion of Iran. One of this lobbying group's sham charities is the nonprofit American Israel Education Foundation (AIEF), housed in the same building, which in 2011, gave all-expenses-paid trips to Israel for eighty-one members of Congress during the summer recess. That's right, nearly one-fifth of the entire House taking junkets that included "a round-trip flight in business class for lawmakers and their spouses (that alone is worth about $8,000), fine hotels and meals, side trips, and transportation and guides." The AIEF spent more than $2 million on these junkets, which did *not* include a look-see at Israeli problem areas such as the West Bank or the Gaza Strip.[35]

In exchange for all the fun and games, the Congress members are expected "to sing for their lavish dinners by honoring President Bush's 2007 pledge to provide the Israeli military with $30 billion of taxpayer-funded weapons between 2009 and 2018." It's interesting because, according to the post-Abramoff ethics reform legislation that took effect in 2007—excuse me for gagging, it was called the Honest Leadership and Open Government Act—travel junkets by nonprofits "that are controlled and directed by a lobbying entity" are supposed to be illegal. AIPAC in 2009 "generously contributed more than $3.2 million of employee salaries to cover the staff costs of AIEF." But, amazingly enough, AEIF, which "raked in more than $26 million in 2009," has no paid employees. Not a single one.[36] In 2009, AIEF transferred $13.5 million in tax deductible funding to AIPAC. The two organizations directorates are basically interlocking.[37]

But wait—there's more: AIPAC, through AIEF, has also been paying Sheldon Adelson, the casino tycoon who's worth almost $25 billion, "to help ferry lawmakers and their staff on luxury trips to Tel Aviv, Jerusalem, and other locations. In addition to well-known Vegas casinos like the Venetian and Palazzo, Adelson still owns a travel company that operates several private planes." The company is GMV Travel, which received $738,572 in compensation as the travel agent for a number of Congress members in 2005. Adelson, by the way, thinks Palestinians are an "invented people" and we should consider military force against Iran.[38]

AIPAC has come up with the notion of "asks," whereby they go to Capitol Hill basically demanding fealty to Adelson's friend, Israeli Prime Minister Benjamin Netanyahu, on Palestine or Hamas or Iran or whatever. Congress typically then introduces legislation saying yea to the "asks" (almost rhymes with "ass-kiss"). Woe be to those who don't go along. Rep. Betty McCollum, a Maine Democrat, wouldn't support a bill "that would have essentially banned all U.S. contacts with Palestinians." An AIPAC official from her district then called her a supporter of terrorism and warned that her behavior "would not be tolerated." [39] I guess "Don't ask, just tell" is the motto.

Besides the freebies doled out by their "educational" arm, AIPAC excels in the game of political contributions to the two gangs. According to Joel Beinin, a Middle East history professor at Stanford, in the 1970s and 1980s, AIPAC "was able to unseat representatives and senators who could not be counted on to support Israel without qualification, such as Senator Charles Percy (R-IL), Rep Paul Findley (R-OH) and Representative Pete McCloskey (R-CA)." In 2002, they successfully targeted African American Reps. Earl Hilliard and Cynthia McKinney for defeat in Democratic primaries.[40]

AIPAC's staff "analyzes congressional voting records and shares the results with its members, who can then contribute money to candidates directly or to a network of pro-Israel political-action committees . . . between 1990 and 2004, these PACs gave candidates and parties more than twenty million dollars." The AIPAC PACs had cutely innocuous names like Citizens Concerned for the National Interest.[41]

And the bottom line is that the United States gives Israel about $3 billion a year in military and economic aid. That comes out to something over $2,000 per U.S. taxpayer. Not a bad return on investment. . . . Except, for us, it's also about propelling us into another insane war in the Middle East. Just change the last letter of the country name, from Iraq to Iran.

Like Watergate's Deep Throat once said, "Follow the money." Sheldon Adelson, the eighth richest person in America, single-handedly kept Newt Gingrich in the Rebloodlican race for president by contributing $16.5 million to Newt's Super PAC.[42] "I'm against very wealthy people attempting to or influencing elections," Adelson said recently. "But as long as it's doable I'm going to do it." In fact, he says he might even give $100 million to Gingrich or some other Bloody kinsman.[43]

Wouldn't you agree that it's time for a little investigation into what Super PACs are all about, when it comes to the *Our Gang* miniseries that's playing out in our living rooms?

NOTES

1. Blumberg, Alex. "Jack Abramoff Explains the 'Lobbyist Safecracker Method.'" January 27, 2012, www.npr.org/blogs/money.

2. Milbank, Dana. "Jack Abramoff's Atonement." February 6, 2012, www.washingtonpost.com.

3. "Jack Abramoff's Road to Redemption and Paying $44 Million in Restitution." December 2, 2011, www.huffingtonpost.com.

4. www.publiccampaign.org, December 7, 2011.

5. Ross, Brian. "Froim Cash to Yachts: Congressman's Bribe Menu." February 27, 2006, http://abcnews.com.

6. Stout, David. "Ex-Rep. Jefferson Convicted in Bribery Scheme." August 6, 2009, www.nytimes.com.

7. U.S. Attorney: Press release, November 13, 2009, www.justice.gov.

8. Income in U.S. Congress: Tree, Andrew. "Politics in America: Only the rich need apply." December 12, 2010, www.latimes.com,.

9. Darrell Issa: Lichtblau, Eric. "Helping His District, and Himself." *New York Times*, August 15, 2011.

10. Top five wealthiest in Congress: www.opensecrets.org, December 27, 2011.

11. Dewan, Shaila. "Presidential Candidates? Few Are the 99 Percent." *New York Times*, October 29, 2011.

12. Farnam, T. W. "Revolving door of employment between Congress, lobbying firms, study shows." September 12, 2011, www.washingtonpost.com.

13. The list was compiled by "First Street," a Washington D.C. newsletter.

14. Breaux quote: Edall, Thomas B. "The Trouble with the Revolving Door." *The New York Times*, December 18, 2011.

15. Breaux, Gephardt, Downey: Ibid. Edall, Thomas B. "The Trouble with the Revolving Door." *New York Times*, December 18, 2011.

16. "Two ex-senators join major lobbying firm," January 11, 2011, www.usatoday.com.

17. "Revolving door of employment . . ."

18. Hill workers and lobbyist numbers: Ibid.

19. Eggen, Dan. "Members of debt panel have ties to lobbyists." September 5, 2011, www.washingtonpost.com.

20. Lobbyists being hired by Congress: "Cutting Out the Middleman." Editorial in *The New York Times*, April 3, 2011.

21. Bogardus, Kevin. "Ex-lobbyist won't need a waiver to work for Vice President Biden." March 5, 2012, http://thehill.com.

22. Walter Lukken: Taibbi, Matt. "Revolving Door: From Top Futures Regulator to Top Futures Lobbyist." January 12, 2012, www.rollingstone.com.

23. Bloom, Jeremy. "Monsanto employees in the halls of government." February 9, 2011, http://redgreenandblue.org.

24. Ho, Catherine. "Revenue drops for many leading lobby shops." July 31, 2011, www.washingtonpost.com.

25. Lobbying figures: www.opensecrets.org.

26. U.S. Chamber of Commerce: Lipton, Eric, Mike McIntire, and Don Van Natta, Jr. "Large Donations Aid U.S. Chamber in Election Drive; Democrats Top Targets." *The New York Times*, October 22, 2010.

27. Stone, Peter. "Big-Money Chamber of Commerce to Impact Elections, Mostly for GOP." McClatchy Newspapers, March 9, 2012.

28. Fang, Lee. "U.S. Chamber's Lobbyists Solicited Hackers to Sabotage Unions, Smear Chamber's Political Opponents," February 10, 2011, http://thinkprogress.org.

29. GE awards/lobbyists: "Member of debt panel have ties to lobbyists."

30. "Big-Money Chamber . . ."

31. Dunn, Andrew. "Commercial Banks Spent Record $62 Million on Lobbying in 2011." February 16, 2012, www.nationofchange.org.

32. Money spent and saved: "Repatriation Tax Holiday." January 16, 2012., www.dailykos.com.

33. Blumberg, Alex. "Forget Stocks or Bonds, Invest in a Lobbyist." January 6, 2012, www.npr.org.

34. John Boehner: Lipton, Eric. "G.O.P. Leader Tightly Bound to Lobbyists." *The New York Times*, September 12, 2010.

35. AIEF expense: "Bending Foreign Policy: Hawkish AIPAC's Education Arm Spent $2 Million on One-Sided Congressional Trips to Israel in 2011." March 5, 2012, www.republicreport.org.

36. AIEF and Congress junkets: Ruebner, Josh. "Robbing Peter to Pay Israel." www.informationalcearinghouse.info/article28829.htm.

37. AIEF funds to AIPAC: www.prnewswire.com/news-releases/aipac-congressional-lobbying-junkets-to-israel-illegal-charges-irs-and-doj-filing-immep-129535868.html.

38. Fang, Lee. "AIPAC Used Casino Magnate Sheldon Adelson's Private Jet Company to Ferry Members of Congress to Israel." March 7, 2012, www.republicreport.org.

39. Rosenberg, MJ. "Iran War: What Is AIPAC Planning?" February 28, 2012, www.huffingtonpost.com,.

40. AIPAC targeting politicians: "American Israel Public Affairs Committee." www.sourcewatch.org.

41. Staff analyses/PACs: Ibid.

42. $16.5 million to Gingrich: www.lasvegassun.com/news/2012/mar/26/millions-gingrich-adelsons-money-could-have-been-b/.

43. Bertoni, Steven. "Billionaire Sheldon Adelson Says He Might Give $100M to Newt Gingrich or Other Republican." February 21, 2012, www.forbes.com.

CHAPTER SEVEN

RUNNING FOR OFFICE: SUPER PACMEN

The great corporations which we have grown to speak of rather loosely as trusts are the creatures of the State, and the State not only has the right to control them, but it is duty bound to control them wherever the need of such control is shown.

—Theodore Roosevelt[1]

Back in 1907, Teddy Roosevelt asked Congress in two annual messages to initiate campaign finance reform, saying: "All contributions by corporations to any political committee or for any political purpose should be forbidden by law." The Tillman Act then passed in 1907 and included this statement: "It shall be unlawful for any national bank, or any corporation organized by authority of any laws of Congress, to make a money contribution in connection with any election to any political office."[2]

Almost a hundred years later, we've turned that law around by 180 degrees. In 2010, the Supreme Court declared corporations to be legally just like people (the infamous *Citizens United* decision). Since then, it's now become a free-for-all in terms of buying favors from the two gangs. And in this year's presidential election, it's a fire sale for Super PACmen.

I don't know how much you know about the video game, but players steer Pac-Man through a maze, which is roamed by four enemies trying to catch him. Near the corners of the maze are flashing dots called power pellets, which Pac-Man can use to eat his enemies. They then turn deep blue, but they can still reverse direction and come at him more slowly. The enemies are called ghosts and monsters. Does this remind anybody of the maze that the candidates can now use to avoid real scrutiny of who's buying them off, while the "power pellets" keep pouring in and the attack ads they fund keep spewing venom on more enemies?

Even though the politicians were always busy looking for loopholes to get more funds for their campaigns, until recently, there were some regulatory restraints in place. In terms of context, Political Action Committees, or PACs, are intended to function as organizations aimed at getting a particular candidate elected or advancing some form of policy or legislation. Each state has different laws governing the fundraising capabilities of a PAC, and a PAC supposedly can't be used to finance a run for president. If the PAC functions at the federal level, it can't directly take money from corporations and unions—but if a PAC functions at the state level, and provided that the particular state has laws favorable to these types of donations, then anyone can donate any sum of money to any PAC for any reason.

Mitt Romney, for example, received over $100,000 in campaign donations via various state-level PACs, allowing his campaign to skirt around federal campaign finance limits. Individuals have given Romney's "personal" PAC—Free and Strong America—large sums of money. Richard and Donna Marriott (of Marriott hotels) have spread at least $225,000 across PACs located in five different states. Edward Conrad, an executive at Bain Capital, a Boston-based private equity firm founded in 1984 by Romney and two others, donated $100,000. Hushang Ansary, former finance minister of

Iran under the Shah and current chairman of Stewart and Stevenson, a private oil-and-gas manufacturer based in Texas, contributed $95,000 to Romney's state-level PAC. Beyond that, Romney has also cozied up to David Koch, vice president of Koch Industries, a private conglomerate involved in energy and energy-related manufacturing/industry (and underwriter for a variety of conservative causes, including the Tea Party—we'll get to that in a bit).

But those sums pale in comparison to what we're seeing now that we've gone from PACs to Super PACs. Basically, what the Supreme Court did in 2010 "stripped away virtually all the constraints on the activities of corporations, unions, and wealthy individuals with respect to federal elections." The 5-4 decision in *Citizens United v. Federal Election Commission* used the First Amendment to claim that all limits on expenditures by candidates and independent groups were violations of "free speech." A subsequent ruling, by a D.C. District Court of Appeals, said that all limits on contributions to the groups making these expenditures should be null and void.[3] Mitt Romney summed it up at one of his early campaign stops at the Iowa State Fair: "Corporations are people, my friend . . . of course they are. Everything corporations earn ultimately goes to the people. Where do you think it goes? Whose pockets? Whose pockets? People's pockets. Human beings, my friend."[4] Since corporations are now people, isn't it natural they should have their "free speech" rights?

"Our . . . elections, the ones our government has modeled for the world, are a hoax. What other word should we use to describe this year's presidential election, whose outcome will turn on which party's super PACs gets the most generous bribes from billionaires?" asks columnist Robert Scheer.[5]

Consider this: Before *Citizens United*, the most money a single individual could give to a candidate was $2,500; to a PAC, $5,000; to a political party committee, $30,800.[6] With those kinds of rules in place, Howard Dean shocked the world back in 2003 by raising $828,000 in one day over the Internet, averaging $112 per contribution. Dean got 38 percent of his presidential campaign funds from donations of $200 or less. Four years later, Barack Obama raised one-third of his record-breaking $745 million from small donors. (Of course, the majority of his money came from big contributors at corporations like Goldman Sachs, Citigroup, and JP Morgan Chase.) This year, Ron Paul has stayed true to what Dean pioneered, raising 39 percent from small donors.[7]

Now the sky's the limit. It's a jungle out there, one that now includes Federal PACs and Leadership PACs, Super PACS aligned with issues and parties and candidates, and so-called nonprofit groups that give freely to Super PACs.

Super PACs are basically a beefed-up version of candidate campaign committees but don't have to abide by the same rules. Besides the Democrips' Priorities USA and Mitt Romney's Restore Our Future, they've got catchy names like Make Us Great Again (on behalf of Rick Perry), Our Destiny (for Jon Huntsman, Jr.), Citizens for a Working America (for Michele Bachmann).[8] The plain old PACs were at least monitored in terms of their fundraising and spending. But Super PACs raise and spend whatever they choose, with an unlimited ability to lie in order for their candidate to get elected.

Technically, the new Super PACs aren't supposed to directly coordinate with a candidate in terms of how they spend the money raised from their donors. But come on, they're pretty much run by the candidates' former staffers and consultants. The Restore Our Future backers of Romney by the end of January had raised $36.8 million, a lot of that in seven and six figure gifts from multi-millionaires and billionaires.[9] These "outside groups" are raising way more than the candidates directly.

In 2000, total campaign contributions to all politicians was $3 billion dollars. Four years after that, it had reached $4 billion. In the 2008 election, it went up to $5 billion.[10] That was the most expensive election in American history, but 2012 is going to make 2008 seem like chump change.

So who are the top honchos among the Super PAC givers?[11]

- As of the end of January 2012, in the lead was a Dallas magnate named Harold Simmons, with a net worth of $9.3 billion, $11.2 million of which he'd donated to candidates in the 2012 race. He started out backing Rick Perry, since the Texas governor had signed legislation that allowed Simmons' company, Waste Control Specialists, to accept "low-level" radioactive waste for his $500 million site from outside the state. Perry's Restoring Prosperity Fund got $100,000, as did Romney's Restore Our Future. (Whole lotta restoration goin' on . . .) The Super PAC behind Newt Gingrich, Winning Our Future, received a million bucks. Sounds more like Buying Our Future. . . .

- Sheldon Adelson and his wife Miriam (net worth: $21.5 billion) came out fully behind Newt, with $10 million going to his campaign, fully 84 percent of the funds for the Gingrich Super PAC. Another "substantial" contribution was said to have been made in February, which would catapult Adelson into the No. 1 spot. Gingrich, when asked what Adelson will get in return for his largesse, said: "Well, he knows I'm very pro-Israel." We looked into Adelson's AIPAC connection in the previous chapter, which Gingrich has since been channeling.

- Houston homebuilder Bob Perry (net worth: unknown) has put in $3.5 million. Of that, $2.5 million went to Karl Rove's American Crossroads Super PAC ($7 million more came from Perry in 2010) and another mil to Romney's. Back in 2004, Perry was a major funder of the Swift Boat ads that smeared John Kerry. He started out backing his namesake Rick Perry (no relation) and over time had given the governor $2.5 million. Bob Perry's in-house lawyer sits on the Texas Residential Construction Commission (TRCC) that the governor pushed through the legislative process. The TRCC has been dubbed the "homebuilder protection agency."[12]

- Jon Huntsman Sr. (net worth: $1 billion) was involved in a bit of nepotism. He gave $2.2 million to Our Destiny, the Super PAC supporting his son, Jon Jr. Huntsman the elder founded a huge corporation that makes and markets chemicals.
- Jeffrey Katzenberg (net worth: $1 billion in 2005) is a film producer and the CEO of DreamWorks Animation. He's forked over $2 million to Priorities USA, the Super PAC supporting President Obama.
- Julian Robertson (net worth: $2.4 billion) is considered the "godfather of the hedge-fund industry" (founder of Tiger Management) who's donated $1.25 million to Romney's Restore Our Future.
- Foster Friess, a mutual fund billionaire, has contributed $1 million to the Rick Santorum Super PAC, the Red, White and Blue Fund.

According to the *New York Times*, "A few of the megadonors gave through limited liability companies, shielding their identity. One $1 million donation to Restore Our Future came from F8 LLC, a company whose listed address in Utah leads to an accounting firm. A charitable foundation linked to Sandra N. Tillotson, co-founder of the skin care company Nu Skin, uses the same address. Ms. Tillotson was reimbursed by Restore Our Future in July [2011] for what appeared to be costs associated with a fundraiser at her New York apartment."[13]

The Supreme Court decision allows corporations to finance political ads "that directly support or oppose political candidates" and maintain complete anonymity.[14] According to the nonprofit organizations Center for Responsive Politics and Public Citizen, 46 percent of the outside groups in 2010 didn't disclose any info about their funding, and 66 percent of donors didn't disclose anything about their campaign ads.[15]

The candidate's hands stay clean, while the Super PACs do almost all the spending on the attack ads. Mitt Romney did this before the Iowa caucuses, spending a million bucks out of his up-front

PAC to talk about "his work in the private sector, his long marriage, and his devotion to his wife." In the meantime, he outsourced his slams against his then-main rival Newt Gingrich to Super PAC supporters from which he could wipe his fingerprints.[16]

There's also a whole bumper crop of nonprofit 501(c)(4) "social welfare groups," as they prefer to call themselves, set up to donate freely to Super PACs. They've got names like Freedom's Watch. Supposedly they're planning to pour about $240 million into the political arena in 2012. For example, Crossroads GPS is the nonprofit part of the American Crossroads Super PAC started by Karl Rove, and it's the nonprofit that raised $32.6 million in 2011, which was way more than American Crossroads' $18.4 million. (Rove's "nonprofit" has set a goal of raising $300 million this year.) The Democrips have Priorities USA and American Bridge 21st Century Foundation as the nonprofits in their apparatus, which raised $5.1 million (to the Super PACs' $8.1 million).

Bill Moyers recently wrote:

> According to the Sunlight Foundation, corporate front groups spent $126 million in the fall of 2010 while hiding the identities of the donors. Another corporate cover group—the American Action Network—spent more than $26 million of undisclosed corporate money in just six Senate races and twenty-six House elections. And Karl Rove's groups, American Crossroads and Crossroads GPS, seized on *Citizens United* to raise and spend at least $38 million, which NBC News said came from 'a small circle of extremely wealthy Wall Street hedge fund and private equity moguls'—all determined to water down financial reforms that might prevent another collapse of the financial system.[17]

As of August 2011, over 80 percent of the money in Super PACs that back Rebloodlican candidates had sprung from a mere 35 people who wrote six- or seven-figure checks.[18] This was all pioneered by a guy described as "Karl Rove's Karl Rove," the Republican strategist Carl Forti who co-founded the Black Rock Group. There haven't been too many bad days at Black Rock, which advises various outside spending groups on how to win friends and influence politicians.

It helps that the Federal Election Commission (FEC)—composed of three Rebloodlicans and three Democrips—issued a ruling not long ago "that outside-spending groups don't have to reveal their donors unless those donors earmark their contributions for specific ads."[19] So these "social welfare" nonprofits aren't required to tell the FEC where the bucks are stopping. Some of these haven't even filed their taxes for 2010 yet, so the IRS is clueless about their revenues and expenses. When the IRS came out and threatened to make five donors to these kind of groups pay gift taxes, Rebloodlican Senator Orrin Hatch wrote a letter questioning whether this action might be politically motivated and violate the First Amendment. So, in July 2011, the IRS dropped the audit idea, saying that "this is a difficult area, with significant legal, administrative and policy implications with respect to which we have little enforcement authority."[20]

So the gift horses are finding ever more clever ways to break through the starting gate, without any accountability. Nobody even knows who wrote the million-dollar check to Romney's Super PAC from a company called W Spann LLC, which sprang up in March 2011 "and dissolved in July with no listed officers or directors on record." The story on this was headlined, "Perhaps it was the campaign tooth fairy." Supposedly, it's illegal to be a straw donor— "people who cover their tracks by giving political money in the name of someone else."[21]

It works the other way around. "Restore Our Future, for example, has paid TargetPoint Consulting nearly $350,000 for survey research. Meanwhile, the Romney campaign has paid TargetPoint nearly $200,000 for direct mail consulting. In one instance, the campaign and the super PAC paid TargetPoint on the same day."[22]

At first, President Obama had called the Supreme Court's decision "a major victory for big oil, Wall Street banks, health insurance companies, and the other powerful interests that marshal their power every day in Washington to drown out the voices of everyday Americans."[23] But it wasn't long before Obama's then-Press Secretary Bill Burton announced his intention to start a group to raise "unlimited money from undisclosed sources" to aid the president's reelection campaign in 2012. After all, they didn't want to "cede the advantage to the Republican Party," since Karl Rove and the Koch brothers had formed their own groups to do the same.[24]

Last February, the Obama campaign staff sent out an email announcing that they were going to actively solicit as much as they could get for their Super PAC, Priorities USA Action. The president has let his campaign manager, Jim Messina, and even members of his cabinet speak at Super PAC events. "With so much at stake," Messina wrote on the campaign's blog, Obama couldn't afford to "unilaterally disarm."[25] So much for principles, eh?

David Pflouffe, Obama's chief political adviser, warned a dozen rich Democrips out in Silicon Valley that the president was threatened by hundreds of millions pledged to defeat him from the Koch brothers and other Blood Super PACs.[26] Time to shit or get off the pot, was the message.

So Obama has his "club of bundlers." No, I didn't say "bunglers" or "burglars," I said "bundlers." In case you haven't heard the term before, let me explain. Bundlers—and Obama has 445 of these, whom his campaign calls "volunteer fundraisers"—gather up the bucks from their rich friends and package it for Obama.[27] Bundlers are not registered as lobbyists, which on paper is a good thing because Obama publicly prohibited lobbyists from contributing to his campaign or holding jobs in his administration. But, just like he calls bankers "fat cats" and then has some of them join him for dinner at a New York restaurant where the tasting menu is $195 apiece (a few cats must have gotten a little fatter that night), there's a difference between what's said and what's done. [28]

Bundlers are major fund-raisers who both contribute their own money and seek money from others. There is even an exclusive "bundling club," the members of which have raised at least $500,000 each. Obama's 2012 campaign has a network of more than 300 of these folks. At least fifteen of those bundlers have strong ties to the lobbying industry and had raised more than $5 million for him by the fall of 2011. The *New York Times* gave the example of Sally Susman, who leads the powerful lobbying shop for the Pfizer drugmaker. A visitor to the White House on four occasions (two of those to talk about export issues), she was a "bundling clubber" who helped put together a $35,800-a-ticket dinner for the prez in New York. There's also David L. Cohen, overseer of lobbying at Comcast, a "clubber" who hosted 120 people paying $10,000 apiece to barbecue with Obama.

So I can't help but point out the hypocrisy here. It's certainly true that Obama built an amazing small-donor grassroots base for his 2008 campaign. They had a database of almost four million supporters, and added 260,000 new donors the first six months of 2011. But that March, when Obama brought a bunch of "players" from the Street to the White House to talk informally about financial regulation and the economy, seventeen of the thirty guests ended up among his bundler contingent. As Ellen Miller, executive director of the government watchdog Sunlight Foundation, said, "It's high-priced access to closed policy discussions with deep-pocketed individuals, just like it's always been."[29]

So, by the end of June 2011, three months after Obama formally declared he would seek a second term, over half a million people had contributed a record-breaking $86 million to his campaign or his joint fund with the Democratic National Committee. The bundlers accounted for at least 40 percent of that total.[30] By the end of September, another $42 million had been raised from 766,000 donations.[31]

Do you think it's just coincidental that one bundling club member, Marc Benioff, chairs a company called Salesforce.com, "whose software the Obama administration has adopted for wide use in federal agencies"?[32]

Here's another way to get around whatever rules and regulations still exist. Ever heard of RGA? That's the Republican Governors Association, based in Washington, D.C. During the 2010 midterm elections, the RGA spent $132 million—"more than the five biggest conservative super-PACs and 501(c) groups combined"—and helped bring in such "stellar" new governors as union-buster Scott Walker in Wisconsin. Since 2008, "the RGA has used a network of at least 15 state-level PACs to shuffle campaign cash around the country."[33]

In Michigan, for example, the Chamber of Commerce "officially didn't spend a dime on ads in 2010" (usually it coughed up over a million dollars), but it gave over $5 million to the RGA to put out an even *bigger* outlay. RGA Michigan 2010 suddenly sprang up and brought in bucks from Koch Industries' David Koch, Texas homebuilder Bob Perry, and a hedge fund CEO named Paul Singer, while "it had also funneled $3 million into the campaign coffers of Texas Gov. Rick Perry."[34] All in the name of democracy, folks.

Remember now, as Mitt Romney said, corporations are people. Since 1990, campaign contributions from the finance, real estate, and insurance sectors of our economy have increased around eight times. Opensecrets.org added up that $2.3 billion was spent by those companies between 1990 and 2010. "Our Congress today is a forum for legalized bribery," columnist Thomas L. Friedman summed it up. "Why are there 61 members on the House Committee on Financial Services? So many congressmen want to be in a position to sell votes to Wall Street."[35]

For the 2010 midterms, a whopping $73.8 million went to Democrips and $119.2 million for Rebloodlicans.[36] Here are some specific examples of how the bribery scheme worked then:

- Scott Brown, the freshman Republican Senator who took over Ted Kennedy's seat in Massachusetts in 2010, took huge amounts of money from the finance industry while working to stymie a financial regulatory bill.

- According to the website OpenSecrets.org, General Electric donated around $500,000 to the Obama campaign in 2008. Claiming all profits it reaped were overseas, as I mentioned before, GE didn't pay any taxes in 2010.

- In the lead-up to the 2010 midterm elections, Ernst & Young held a fundraiser for a little-known Michigan Republican named Dave Camp. He was running virtually unopposed in his district, yet the financial industry showered him with campaign contributions simply because he was expected to take over the House Ways and Means Committee if elected. He won, and did.

- Military contractors, weapons makers such as Lockheed Martin and Boeing, poured hundreds of thousands of dollars into the campaign for Howard McKeon, a Republican from California. McKeon later became Chairman of the House Armed Services Committee.

- The Pharmaceutical Research and Manufacturers of America (PhRMA) went the nonprofit route. They're the drug lobby's trade group, and they doled out $9.4 million to "social welfare" outfits like the American Action Network, a conservative group that poured big bucks into thirty-some races and spent over $26 million on political ads—more than anybody else except the Chamber of Commerce. Former Minnesota Senator Norm Coleman, whom I defeated for governor in 1998, was a co-founder of the American Action Network. Today, Coleman is a "senior government adviser" at Hogan Lovells, one of the lobby shops retained by PhRMA.[37]

- Doc Hastings, a Rebloodlican from Washington State, received big money from the oil and gas companies in the lead-up to midterm 2010 elections. He was successfully reelected and became Chairman of the Natural Resources Committee, the one that deals with petroleum conservation. Prior to the election, Hastings blocked a Democrip-sponsored bill that would have enhanced safety standards for offshore drilling in light of the BP oil rig disaster in the Gulf of Mexico.[38]

But in case you think BP is getting squelched by the Democrips for having polluted much of the Gulf coastline in the biggest off-shore oil spill in American history, it turns out BP is the Pentagon's biggest fuel supplier, their contracts having escalated 33 percent to hit $1.35 billion in the fiscal 2011 year. That ought to be more than enough to cover the violations of the Clean Water Act, I would think.[39] If not, oh well—BP's total profit in 2011 was $26 billion, a 114 percent jump from the previous year. They're currently spending millions lobbying the government to speed up more offshore drilling and leases.[40]

Before I run out of energy here, let's look deeper at Big Oil and Dirty Coal. Since the 1990 election cycle, individuals and PACs affiliated with oil and gas companies have donated $238.7 million to candidates—75 percent of that to Rebloodlicans. In 2008, Obama received $884,000 from the industry during the presidential campaign, more than anybody else in politics except his opponent, John McCain. In 2011–12, the top three oil-and-gas givers were ExxonMobil ($841,644), Koch Industries ($619,900), and Chevron ($445,546).[41]

As for nuclear, the Nuclear Energy Institute, the industry's big-daddy lobbyist in D.C., spent $3.76 million to lobby the federal government during the last election cycle. Exelon, which owns America's biggest nuclear fleet, contributed almost $515,000 more to Democrips (58%) than Rebloodlicans. The day after the election, both President Obama and House Speaker John Boehner said the importance of nuclear power was one thing they could agree on.[42]

What we've got today is a gang of super-rich Democrips fighting another gang of super-rich Rebloodlicans. Would you still call this a democracy? Shouldn't we come right out and admit we're a plutocracy? And shouldn't we call out the two gangs for showing their colors, once and for all? And those colors aren't the blue and red of the Crips and Bloods, but rather the green of all our money they are stealing.

NOTES

1. Theodore Roosevelt quote: www.goodreads.com/quotes/show /47025.

2. Tillman Act: Hartmann, Thom, *Unequal Protection*, Berrett-Koehler (2010), pp. 124–125.

3. Court decisions: Drew, Elizabeth. "Can We Have a Democratic Election?" *New York Review of Books*, February 23, 2012.

4. Romney defined corporations as people on August 11, 2011, in Iowa.

5. Scheer, Robert. "Elections Are For Suckers." February 9, 2012, www. truthdig.com.

6. Pre-*Citizens United* giving: Berman, Ari. "The .0000063 Percent Election." TomDispatch, Febuary 16, 2012.

7. Dean, Obama, and Paul: Ibid.

8. Catchy names for Super PACs: Confessore, Nicholas. "Lines Blur Between Candidates And PACs With Unlimited Cash." *New York Times*, August 28, 2011.

9. Stone, Peter H. "Top Fundraiser for Romney Super PAC Gets a $1.9 Million Payday." www.nationofchange.org/1330094683.

10. Campaign contributions to politicians: Nocera, Joe. "Boycott Campaign Donations!" *New York Times*, August 13, 2011.

11. Wittenberg, Ariel. "Super Donors: Our Reading Guide to the Top 10 Super PAC Givers." March 4, 2012, www.nationofchange.org.

12. Perry donors: Harkinson, Josh. "Rick Perry's Friends with Benefits." *Mother Jones*, November/December 2011.

13. "In G.O.P. Race, a New Breed of Superdonor." *New York Times*, February 22, 2012.

14. Supreme Court's *Citizens United* decision: Abramson, Jill. "Return of the Secret Donors." *New York Times*, October 17, 2010.

15. Contributions and non-disclosure: Bauerlein, Monika and Clara Jeffery. "Occupied Washington." *Mother Jones*, January/February 2012.

16. Romney and Gingrich: "The Slush Funds of Iowa." Editorial in the *New York Times*, January 3, 2012.

17. Corporate front groups: Moyers, Bill. "How Wall Street Occupied America." *The Nation*, November 21, 2011.

18. Super-PACs: Hightower, Jim. "The Corporate Takeover of the 2012 Presidential Election." *Other Words*, September 26, 2011, www.truth-out. org.

19. Carl Forti and Black Rock: Kroll, Andy. "Rove's Brain." *Mother Jones*, January/February 2012.

20. Strom, Stephanie. "I.R.S. Drops Audits of Political Donors." *New York Times*, July 8, 2011.

21. Million dollar check to Romney: "Perhaps It Was the Campaign Tooth Fairy." Editorial in the *New York Times*, August 9, 2011.

22. McIntire, Mike, and Michael Luo. "Fine Line Between 'Super PACs' and Campaigns." *New York Times*, February 26, 2012.

23. Obama on Supreme Court decision: "Supreme Court Blocks Ban on Corporate Political Spending." *New York Times*, January 21, 2010.

24. Priorities USA: "Democrats, Seduced by Secret Dollars." *New York Times*, May 8, 2011.

25. Reich, Robert. "The Sad Spectacle of Obama's Super PAC." February 20, 2012, www.nationofchange.org.

26. Confessore, Nicholas and Michael Luo. "Obama Allies Feel Pressure to Raise Cash." *New York Times*, March 14, 2012.

27. 445 bundlers: "The .0000063 Percent Election."

28. "Fat cats" and $195/plate: Confessore, Nicholas. "Obama Seeks To Win Back Wall St. Cash." *New York Times*, June 13, 2011.

29. Ellen Miller; Confessore, Nicholas. "Obama Has Early Fund-raisingLead for 2012 Elections," *New York Times*, July 16, 2011.

30. Obama and the bundlers: Confessore, Nicholas. "New Stable of Wealthy Donors Fueled Obama Campaign's Record Fun-Raising Quarter." *New York Times*, July 17, 2011; Lichtblau, Eric. "Obama Backers Tied to Lobbies Raise Millions." *New York Times*, October 28, 2011.

31. Confessore, Nicholas and Michael D. Shear. "Obama's Fund-Raising Outpaces G.O.P. Rivals'." *New York Times*, October 14, 2011.

32. Marc Benioff: Confessore, Nicholas. "Obama Has Early Fund-Raising Lead for 2012 Elections," *New York Times*, July 16, 2011.

33. RGA Network: Kroll, Andy. "The Governors' Three-PAC Monte." *Mother Jones*, January/February 2012.

34. The RGA: Ibid.

35. "Our Congress today . . .": Friedman, Thomas L. "Did You Hear the One About the Bankers?" *New York Times*, October 30, 2011.

36. Money to candidates in 2010: Corn, David. "And 2010's Biggest Winner Is . . . ," November 2, 2010, www.motherjones.com.

37. Beckel, Michael. "Drug Lobby Gave $9.4 Million to Nonprofits that Spent Big on 2010 Election." www.nationofchange.org-1330451337.

38. Ernst & Young, McKeon, Hastings campaigns: Lipton, Eric and David M. Herszenhorn. "Lobbyists Court Potential Stars of House Panel; Eyeing GOP Takeover." *New York Times*, October 27, 2010.

39. Ivory, Danielle. "BP Wins Most Pentagon Fuel Awards in Year after Gulf Explosion." February 24, 2012, www.bloomberg.com.

40. Leber, Rebecca. "BP Made $3 Million an Hour in 2011, While Spill Victims Continued to Suffer." February 20, 2012, www.nationofchange .org.

41. Oil and gas contributions: "Oil & Gas" section, www.opensecrets. org.

42. Nuclear industry contributions: Samuelson, Darren. "Nuclear lobbyists' clout felt on Hill." March 16, 2011, http://dyn.politico.com.

CHAPTER EIGHT

WHAT THE POLITICIANS GET AND GET AWAY WITH THAT YOU CAN'T

In this chapter, I want to look at the government health care and re-tirement benefits politicians get but we don't. I also want to focus on how many laws the two parties make that we have to comply with, but they don't. Should elected officials have more "perks" than the populace they govern? Shouldn't they abide by the same laws we're supposed to? I'll let you be the judge of that.

I'll start with this: Imagine what it would be like if everybody at the company you work for could vote himself or herself an an-nual raise in pay. Wouldn't that be a gas? Not that the management would like it much. Anyway, your U.S. Congress is quite free to do that for themselves, and most years they do. Since 1990, annual cost-of-living adjustments have been calculated through a formula that's based on changes in private sector wages and salaries, and Congress has accepted a pay raise thirteen times.

In 2009, the last time they went for this, each of the 535 members of the House and Senate combined got increases of $4,700 apiece, which cost us taxpayers about $2.5 million. The base pay for law-makers in the two houses is $174,000, and higher for the leaders. With their approval ratings in the dumper, they decided to forego the pay raises for both of the last two years. (The law requires them to vote against it, otherwise the increase becomes automatic.[1])

Have you ever heard of the Federal Employees Health Benefits Program (FEHB)?[2] That's where Congress members and other government employees obtain health insurance for themselves and their families. The FEHB's is the biggest employer-provided health insurance program in the country, with more than eight million members. Insurers who want to take part have to provide a full gamut of benefits. Congress members can choose "from an array of plans that have limits on how much they must spend out of pocket. The most popular of these plans has an out-of-pocket maximum for families of $7,000 in 2011."[3]

Everyone elected to Congress receives a subsidy equal to about three-quarters of their health insurance premiums—at the taxpayer's expense. All members of Congress (plus their family members) have guaranteed access to coverage—even if they have a pre-existing condition like cancer or diabetes. And they pay the same amount for coverage whether they're healthy or sick.

There's a "comprehensive package of health benefits that includes coverage for physician services, preventive care, hospital care, emergency care, mental health services, and prescription drugs. . . . Unlike what has happened to thousands of consumers in the individual market, when members of Congress get sick, their insurance company doesn't suddenly revoke their coverage."[4] All the plans offered to members of Congress have benefits covering prescription drug needs for the entire year, no gaps.

Their coverage also includes regular checkups and screenings, and if they pay a "nominal annual fee," for routine checkups and acute care services, they can get free care from clinics run by the Office of the Attending Physician on Capitol Hill. "Lawmakers can also utilize taxpayer-subsidized care at Walter Reed Army Medical Center in Washington, D.C. and the National Naval Medical Center in Bethesda, MD."[5] And anyone in Congress who's served a minimum amount of time in office is eligible for retiree health coverage—even if he or she retires early.

For appealing any claims that get denied, the U.S. Office of Personnel Management—overseer of the health insurance outfits offering the coverage—offers a clear process to do so. The OPM also prints an annual guide with all the private insurance plans to select from, and "OPM negotiates with insurers . . . to secure the lowest premiums possible and to prevent drastic rate hikes from year to year." According to the OPM, the most popular provider for all federal employees is Blue Cross Blue Shield.[6]

Pretty good deal, eh? Now let's open the window on pension plans. There's the Civil Service Retirement System, which anyone elected to Congress before 1984 generally participates in. Or, if you entered the arena after that, there's the Federal Employees Retirement System (FERS). Members do put in a percentage of their salary toward future benefits, with pensions being figured under a formula that takes into account how long they served, average of their three highest annual salaries and an "accrual rate." But, according to the National Taxpayers Union (NTU), "congressional pensions are typically 2–3 times more generous than those offered to similarly-salaried workers in the private sector, and are even more generous than pensions for most federal workers." Their benefit is also protected with Cost of Living Adjustments, which only one out of ten private plans offer. They can also take part in a Thrift Savings Plan, "a defined contribution arrangement that works like a 401 (k) retirement system."[7]

According to the AARP, "on grounds that working in Congress means uncertain job security, elected members and their staffs receive a larger retirement benefit from FERS for each year of service than other federal employees. They also become eligible for a retirement annuity at a younger age and with fewer years of service."[8]

But congressional incumbents have something like a 95 percent reelection rate—mainly because (in the House) their parties get to create their own safe districts—which the two gangs do together in collusion to make sure they are all safe. Not too much job insecurity there. I'd say few things in life could be more predictable than having the same old gang member back-in-bowl.

In November 2004, 401 of the 435 sitting members of the House of Representatives decided to seek reelection. Of those 401, all but five kept their seats. In other words, incumbents seeking reelection to the House had a better than 99 percent success rate. In the Senate, only one incumbent seeking reelection was defeated. Twenty-five of twenty-six (96 percent) were reelected.[9]

Now the 2010 midterm election was a different kettle of fish. There was a big turnover, with 120 members of the House moving on to something new in life . . . well, sort of. The majority of the departed simply passed through "a revolving door that shuffles former federal employees into jobs as lobbyists, consultants, and strategists just as the door pulls former hired guns into government careers. While officials in the executive branch, Congress and senior congressional staffers spin in and out of the private and public sectors, so too does privilege, power, access and, of course, money." A private study found that almost 33 percent went to work for a lobbying firm, while another 20.3 percent became lobbying clients.[10]

Okay, so what about pensions for our chief executives? Since the 1950s, they've been covered under the Former Presidents Act. NTU's Vice President for Policy and Communications, Pete Sepp, says, "What started as a modest system to help Harry Truman answer his mail has become a millionaires' club for ex-Presidents, and taxpayers are the ones covering the dues." NTU calculated that Bill Clinton's lifetime pension payout is $6.97 million, while George W. Bush's will add up to a likely $5.56 million if he lives to be 83.5. Dick Cheney comes out pretty well, too, even though he was only VP, at around $3.24 million. And this is not to mention the staff, travel, mail, and office expense reimbursements which, for Clinton in fiscal year 2006, equaled $1.16 million.[11] Plus, ongoing Secret Service protection for the an ex-president and his wife.

Speaking of office expenses, the last analysis made by the NTU showed that members of the House in 2005 spent $525 million on their offices, which was 20 percent higher than in 2001. (I'm sure a lot of that was to make the offices more secure after 9/11.) They get what are called "Members' Representational Allowances" to do this, which are based on things like the population of their district and the current rents there. A lot of them go beyond their allowance and are allowed to make "adjustments."[12]

One of the top "perks" of House members and Senators is the ability to send postage-free informational letters or announcements to their constituents on a regular basis. In 2005, the House spent $22.3 million on what's called "franked mail postage"—85 percent of this being mass mailings of 500 or more identical pieces.[13] I wouldn't call that "franked," I'd frankly call it "junk."

The office budget allotments also provide enough money to hire sizeable staffs, both in the nation's capitol and back home, wherever they hail from. Of course, a lot of that staff work (and all those free mailings) mainly goes toward making sure the member of Congress get reelected: helping to ensure the boss is well liked by the constituents.

Congress members also get travel allowances for trips between D.C. and their home districts, as well as for inside their states. And if you've got a yen for foreign journeys, run for office. As for CODELs, which stands for Congressional Delegation foreign trips:

> Travel abroad has tripled over the past ten years, but between $30 and $40 million in travel costs have gone unreported. . . . Members are technically responsible for returning excess per diem, but this rule is not enforced. Furthermore, members are supposed to complete a detailed disclosure of expended funds when they return from a CODEL, but the Congressional Research Service has said these disclosures are of 'limited utility' since they are often filed late and filled with inaccuracies.

In response, the STAY PUT Act was filed in 2010 by Rep. Tim Johnson, a Rebloodlican from Illinois, but you can bet your latest travel voucher that this never got out of committee.[14]

During his first two years in office, Barack Obama became the most widely traveled president in our history. He made fifteen trips to thirty-four countries, traveling abroad for a total of fifty-five days. George W. Bush is in second place with eleven trips, twenty-eight visits, and forty-seven days. Overall, Bill Clinton is still in the lead for a two-termer, with fifty-five total trips and 233 days out of the country. We'll see if Obama ends up topping that one.[15]

And while we're on the subject of travel: In November 2010, Rep Ron Paul introduced HR 6416, a bill "to ensure that certain Federal employees cannot hide behind immunity." Specifically, the legislation was aimed at protecting Americans from physical and emotional abuse by federal Transportation Security Administration (TSA) personnel who conduct the security screenings at our airports. That's what my lawsuit was about, too, but more on that later.

Here's an excerpt from what Paul said in introducing his American Traveler Dignity Act.

> It removes the immunity from anybody in the federal government that does anything that you or I can't do. If you can't grope another person and if you can't X-ray people and endanger them with possible X-rays, you can't take nude photographs of individuals, why do we allow the government to do it? We would go to jail. He'd be immediately arrested if an individual citizen went out and did these things, and yet we just sit there calmly and say, "Oh, they're making us safe."

"Let's make sure that every member of Congress goes through this," Paul said. "Get the X-ray and make them look at the pictures, and then go through one of those groping pat downs. And then I think there will be a difference. Have everybody in the executive branch, anybody who is a cabinet member, make them go through it and look at it. Maybe they would pay more attention."[16]

❖ ❖ ❖

It's a no-brainer: Our elected officials manage to leave D.C. (if they ever do) with more bucks in the bank than when they arrived. One way to do that is by insider trading on the stock market. You've heard about financial bigwigs getting busted for doing the same thing—Raj Rajaratnam of hedge fund fame recently got sentenced to eleven years in prison and socked with a record $92.8 million fine. The SEC, looking to bolster its image after being asleep at the wheel for Bernie Madoff, filed fifty-seven actions against alleged inside traders in 2011.

But if you happen to be a member of Congress, it's long been legal to use such confidential information for personal gain. A paper published by the *Journal of Financial and Quantitative Analysis* in 2004 looked at how the majority of U.S. senators were trading stocks during the "boom years" of the mid-'90s. On average, they were beating the market by 12 percent a year.[17] (There was no difference between Democrips and Rebloodlicans in terms of who made out better.) Compare that to 5 percent beating-the-market by corporate insiders and to underperformance by typical households at 1.4 percent. As one analyst put it, "12 percent is a statistically shocking number, way beyond luck or just being smart. Nobody does that well. Not George Soros. Not Warren Buffett."[18]

In 2004, the STOCK Act was introduced by a former Congressman from Washington state, Brian Baird, trying to establish some rules on conflict-of-interest and a ban on insider trading. It went nowhere until this year—after a hard-hitting report by CBS' *60 Minutes* and a new book called *Throw Them All Out*—when suddenly Congress got antsy about the practice. Lo and behold, the STOCK Act had overwhelming bipartisan support and passed both houses. Now lawmakers and other senior officials, including the president and vice president, will be required to report their investment transactions every month or forty-five days instead of yearly.[19]

We'll see if that makes a difference. In the meantime, here's some of what the *60 Minutes* report revealed:

- Alabama Representative Spencer Bachus, a Rebloodlican who chairs the House Financial Services Committee, attended closed-door meetings in mid-September 2008 with Bush's Fed chairman and Treasury Secretary Hank Paulson, who were warning about a coming global financial meltdown—"and literally the next day Congressman Bachus would engage in buying stock options based on [these] apocalyptic briefings. . . ." He bet against the market in what they call a "short option," and he sold his shares in General Electric at a profit before GE's stock price plummeted. Early in 2012, Bachus came under investigation by the Office of Congressional Ethics. Crips under the microscope for other possible insider trades during the financial crisis are Senators John Kerry and Dick Durbin and Rep. Jim Moran.
- In March 2008, then-House Speaker Democrip Nancy Pelosi and her husband accepted a quite lucrative IPO (initial public stock offering), whereby they bought 5,000 shares of Visa for $44. Two days later, the stock was trading at $64. The timing was interesting, because a piece of legislation that would've been "hurtful" to credit card companies was just starting to work its way through the House and—guess what?—it never got to the floor. (The Pelosis benefited from at least eight IPOs.)
- In 2009, members—including today's Rebloodlican Majority Leader John Boehner—were working overtime to kill the government-funded "public option" on health care that would have competed with the big insurance companies. A few days before Boehner and his buddies succeeded, his financial adviser was buying health insurance stocks—all of which went up once the "public option" was dead.

"In the past few years," the *60 Minutes* report said, "a whole new totally unregulated, $100 million industry has grown up in Washington called political intelligence. It employs former congressmen and former staffers to scour the halls of the Capitol gathering valuable non-public information, then selling it to hedge funds and traders on Wall Street who can trade on it."[20] You scratch my back, I'll get you some more pork. There are massive amounts of money involved here, but the Rebloodlicans managed to get rid of language in the STOCK bill that would have made these outfits register the same as lobbyists do.

To me, this is a level of corruption that defies rational discourse. I mean, corporate insiders are required to disclose their transactions within forty-eight hours. . . . Why shouldn't Congress be held to the same standard? But both Harry Reid, the Senate Majority leader, and his Blood "brother," Mitch McConnell, the Minority leader, were said to be busy doing all they could to weaken the final version of the STOCK Act. The gangs want their equal opportunity rewards.

Here's one you've probably forgotten. Back in 2003, U.S. Rep. Bill Janklow, former governor of South Dakota, had been drinking and was speeding when his car struck and killed a guy on a motorcycle. At his trial, it came out that he'd been stopped for speeding on many occasions but almost never got ticketed because of his office. Janklow got convicted of vehicular manslaughter and was sentenced to a hundred days in jail, but he was released after only thirty days to do community service. Well, Janklow did end up resigning from Congress, so I guess we can count our blessings. He received four more speeding citations after his probation ended in 2007, but by then the South Dakota Supreme Court had granted his petition for early reinstatement of his license to practice law. [21]

If we lie to a judge or falsify documents submitted to a court, it's considered perjury or fraud, and we go to jail. Politicians and their minions do the same things, and nothing happens to them; except on rare occasions, often when it's somebody's payback time (think Illinois' former governor, Rod Blagojevich, sentenced to fourteen years for trying to sell a Senate seat). I suppose lying has always been a "political art," but what does it take to be over-the-top?

Tricky Dick "I am not a crook" Nixon got pardoned for his assorted crimes by his successor, Gerald Ford, whose own malfeasance, I might add, dated back to knowingly falsifying the "single bullet" theory for the Warren Commission looking into JFK's assassination.

In the '90s, we had the Iran/Contra caper under Reagan and Oliver North, his National Security aide for covert ops. North's notebooks, released through the Freedom of Information Act in 1989, show beyond a shadow of a doubt that he was informed many times about the Nicaraguan Contra's ties to drug dealers. Even before that, the Kerry Subcommittee on Narcotics, Terrorism, and International Operations had concluded that "senior U.S. policy makers were not immune to the idea that drug money was a perfect solution to the Contras' funding problems." Behind closed doors, the Congressmen holding the Iran/Contra hearings knew all about this but looked the other way and let North, among others in the Reagan Administration, lie through their teeth.[22]

Meantime, Nancy Reagan's "Just Say No" campaign was in full swing. Consider the results, in terms of the American people, of the "War on Drugs" that began under Nixon. As of 2004, more than half a million people were behind bars for drug offenses in our country. The Justice Department's own statistics showed that 55 percent of all federal prisoners and 21 percent of state prisoners were doing time for drugs.[23]

I find this hypocrisy staggering. Of course, Oliver North ended up running for U.S. Senator in Virginia, and a heckuva lot of people voted for the man. By the way, did you know that his code name was "Hammer"? That was also what people called Tom ("The Hammer") DeLay, who had to resign his leadership spot in Congress in 2006 after being indicted for conspiring to launder corporate money through the Republican National Committee for campaign donations, which was illegal in Texas. DeLay ended up being sentenced to three years in prison but was released the same day on a $10,000 appeal bond. He told the judge, "I can't be remorseful for something I think I didn't do." DeLay said he'd already raised and spent $10 million on legal fees but "I've got some friends who help me pay bills." You may have last seen him as a contestant on "Dancing with the Stars." And I'm not making that up.[24]

Among the Democrips, consider New York Rep. Charles Rangel. He started being investigated a few years ago "after news reports that he had accepted four rent-stabilized apartments at prices hundreds of dollars per month below their market value." In the next months, "he was accused of failing to declare hundreds of thousands of dollars of personal assets on his financial disclosure forms, failing to pay state and federal taxes on rental income on his villa in the Dominican Republic, and helping to preserve a tax loophole worth hundreds of millions of dollars for an oil company at the same time that he was seeking a $1 million contribution to the Rangel Center from a company executive."[25]

In November 2010, a House panel found Rangel guilty of eleven counts of ethics violations, and less than a month later, the full House censured him. What that means is that he had to stand in front of all the other members and listen to the censure resolution against him. Oh, and he also had to resign from the Ways and Means Committee. Less than a year later, a lot of those same members held a big fundraiser for Rangel at a posh D.C. restaurant. And of course he's still sitting in Congress.

Contrast this look-the-other-way treatment with what's happening to U.S. Army Private Bradley Manning, the soldier who's facing possible life in prison for revealing the truth. He's been charged with passing on hundreds of thousands of documents that expose government secrets to the whistleblower website WikiLeaks. These documents are chock-full with revelations about lying, corruption, and other crimes committed by the United States and other nations. Except, like Manning's lawyers have been asserting, a lot of what WikiLeaks published wasn't really secret, or shouldn't have been classified as such.

That hasn't stopped Manning from being held for months, twenty-three hours a day, in illegal solitary confinement at the Quantico Marine Base. According to the medical experts, after sixty days in solitary, a person's mental condition starts to deteriorate severely. In Manning's case, it's been designed to break him down enough to implicate Julian Assange, WikiLeaks' founder, as his co-conspirator. . . . But Manning never has. He may be barely able to stand, but he's still a stand-up guy.

Something you may not know: Congressional staffers and other federal employees must undergo scrupulous background checks and extensive interviews before they can have access to sensitive information. You're considered a risk if you even associate with people who have a history of alcoholism or financial problems or a criminal background, let alone have such things in your own past. Security clearance denied.

But, if you're a member of Congress, you're not subjected to any such background check. You're granted a security clearance just because you've gotten elected. All you're asked is to promise that you won't reveal any of our country's secrets. Well, like Keith Ashdown of Taxpayers for Common Sense puts it, "there are more alcoholics [in Congress] than anywhere in the country. . . . Lawmakers should absolutely have to go through the same security clearance process as employees do."

One example that Winslow Wheeler, author of *Wastrels of Defense: How Congress Sabotages U.S. Security*, has given is Randy "Duke" Cunningham, the California congressman mentioned earlier, who eventually pled guilty to accepting $2.4 million in bribes from defense contractor MZM, Inc. But during the five months Cunningham was under federal investigation, he still retained access to our country's most sensitive information.[26]

Of course, he was still getting his government pension too—"eligible for an initial annual payout of as much as $64,000," according to the National Taxpayers Union. At that time, in 2006, "no member of Congress is required to forfeit a pension unless convicted of crimes related to treason and espionage. As a result, over the past 25 years, at least 20 lawmakers guilty of other serious offenses have enjoyed Congressional retirement payments."[27]

What do former congressmen Dan Rostenkowski [D-IL], James Traficant [D-OH] and Bob Ney [R-OH] have in common with Duke Cunningham? Yup, all are convicted felons still reaping generous pensions—all told, more than $250,000 a year—for the rest of their lives from us, the taxpayers.

In 2007, Congress did finally pass a law that stops cronies who've gotten convicted of particular crimes from raking in the pension profits, but that only applies to eleven different kinds of felonies and not crimes like evading taxes. The law doesn't apply retroactively either, to the Dukes of this realm.[28]

I'll close this chapter with one thought. You probably read about SOPA, the Stop Online Piracy Act that was introduced in the House and looked for a good while like it would become law. I delve into the ramifications in a later chapter on civil liberties, but for now consider what one watchdog group learned: "We wondered how many of the employees there have engaged in unauthorized copying. The answer is . . . they pirate a lot. In total we found more than 800 IP-addresses assigned to the U.S. House of Representatives from where content has been shared on BitTorrent sites. . . . It quickly became clear the House isn't just using it for legitimate downloads." Nope, while tens of thousands of Americans have been sued for file-sharing by the Recording Industry Association of America, I guess they haven't fully cleaned House.[29]

NOTES

1. "No pay raise for Congress in 2011." May 14, 2010, http://thehill. com.
2. The section on congressional benefits is taken from "'Defunding' the Affordable Care Act: Guilty of a Double Standard," found online at www.Familisesusa.org.
3. Ibid.
4. Ibid.
5. Taxpayer-subsidized care: Fritze, John. "Lawmakers get 'generous' health plans." *USA Today*, June 24, 2009.

6. Blue Cross: Ibid.

7. Sepp, Pete. "Congressional Pensions—Ripe for Reform." March 10, 2011, www.ntu.org.

8. "What Kind of Benefits Does Congress Really Get?" December 15, 2010, www.arp.org.

9. www.opensecrets.org/bigpicture/reelect.php.

10. www.opensecrets.org/revolving/index.php.

11. Sepp, Pete. "Golden Years to Bring Golden Pension Payout of $5.6 Million to Bush, $3.2 Million to Cheney, Taxpayer Group Finds." January, 16, 2009, www.ntu.org.

12. Sepp, Pete. "No Belt-Tightening Here: House Members' Office Spending Breaks Half Billion-Dollar Mark; 20% Jump in 4 Years." May 21, 2007, www.ntu.org.

13. Postage: Ibid.

14. "Cosponsor Efforts to Reform Congressional Foreign Travel: An Open Letter to the U.S. House of Representatives," September 15, 2010, www.ntu.org.

15. Brady, Dernian. "Incredible Journey: How Barack Obama Became the Most-Traveled President His First Two Years in Office." November 23, 2010, www.ntu.org.

16. "Ron Paul to TSA: Stop Irradiating Our Bodies and Fondling Our Children!" November 17, 2010, www.RonPaul.com.

17. Senators beating the market: Zingales, Luigi. "Why Congress can freely trade on insider information." November 29, 2011, www.cnn.com.

18. Parramore, Lynn. "Can Rep. Bachus and His Money-Crazed Congressional Colleagues Be Stopped from Insider Trading?" February 18, 2012, www.alternet.org.

19. STOCK Act: "New insider trading law to open window into Congress members' financial transations." *Associated Press*, February 28, 2012.

20. "Congress: Trading stock on inside information?" November 13, 2011, www.cbsnews.com.

21. Bill Janklow: "Politicians in Prison." January 31, 2001, www.socialistunity.com.

22. "The Contras, Cocaine, and Covert Operations": www.gwu.edu/~nsarchiv/NSAEBB/NSAEBB2/nsaebb2.htm.

23. "Drug War Prisoner Count over Half a Million, U.S. Prison Population at All-Time High." http://stopthedrugwar.org.

24. "DeLay sentenced to 3 years in prison, freed on appeal bond." January 10, 2011, www.statesman.com.

25. Kocieniewski, David. "House Panel Finds Rangel Guilty." November 16, 2010, www.nytimes.com.

26. Bennett, William Finn. "Watchdog: Double Standard on Security Clearance Must End." December 11, 2005, www.nctimes.com.

27. "Nearly Two Dozen Citizen Groups Tell Pelosi and Reid: No Tax-Funded Pensions for Congressional Criminals": November 30, 2006, www.ntu.org.

28. http://mediamatters.org/mobile/research/200808010001.

29. December 26, 2011, http://torrentfreak.com.

CHAPTER NINE

THE OBAMA ADMINISTRATION: SPARE CHANGE YOU CAN BELIEVE IN?

Part of the flaw of the two-party system is that it's induced a sense of denial about the extent of our nation's problems. In other words, both sides employ "spin" so effectively that American voters are reduced to mere spectators in a vast political drama that includes partisan bickering and political impasse on the floors of Congress, while the gridlock and cost of fighting two wars has sent the economy toward the brink of disaster.

In 2008, Barack Obama ran on a popular theme to "transcend partisan politics," which appealed to a wide bloc of Independent voters. Unfortunately for us and Obama, it hasn't quite worked out that way. A lot of reasons have been put forward for Obama's drop in popularity, including the mess he inherited from the Bush administration and the ongoing sabotage of anything positive he tries to do by the Rebloodlicans.

But has anything really changed? I honestly don't think so. What I'm going to get into in this chapter is something that deeply disturbs me—all the power Bush gave the presidency, Obama is using as well, and not for good ends. I'll lead off with this example: Where in the Constitution and Bill of Rights does it say "national security" trumps them both?

Back in 2005, then-Senator Obama strongly condemned aspects of the Patriot Act. Among other things, he said: "If someone wants to know why their own government has decided to go on a fishing expedition through every personal record or private document—through library books they've read and phone calls they've made—this legislation gives people no rights to appeal the need for such a search in a court of law. No judge will hear their plea, no jury will hear their case. This is just plain wrong."[1]

But in May 2011, Obama approved a congressional four-year extension of parts of the Patriot Act that would have otherwise expired. These included letting the government "seize records without the owner's knowledge, conduct secret surveillance of suspicious people who have no known ties to terrorist groups, and to obtain secret roving wiretaps on people."[2]

During the presidential campaign, Obama promised to close the Guantánamo Bay detention camp. He didn't. He announced in his first year that no CIA agent would be prosecuted for torturing, and later his administration refused to go after any of the Bush officials who'd been responsible for ordering or justifying the goings-on at Abu Ghraib, Guantánamo, and elsewhere. The surveillance without warrants and the military tribunals denying defendants their basic rights, begun under Bush, have continued. At the same time, Obama's administration "has fought to block dozens of public-interest lawsuits challenging privacy violations and presidential abuses." The new president "not only retained the controversial Bush policies, he expanded on them."[3]

In September 2011 in Yemen, a country we are not at war with, our military murdered Anwar al-Awlaki, an American citizen and supposed traitor/terrorist. He never took up arms but was said to have provided "material support to terrorism." And then two weeks later our drones also killed his 16-year-old U.S.-born son. Supposedly, the Fourth Amendment guarantees that nobody can be seized unreasonably by our government; the Fifth Amendment states that the government can't deprive someone of life "without due process of law," and the Sixth Amendment gives any of our accused citizens "the right to a speedy and public trial" and habeas corpus. We simply blew this guy and his son away from a "safe" distance. Is it now the right of the executive branch to order the execution of an American citizen on the whim of the president? And Obama was a professor of constitutional law!? Even though we have a federal law against murder and an executive order banning assassinations, a secret memo written over a year earlier determined that killing al-Awlaki was lawful in the event it was not feasible to take him alive.[4] Obama and his advisers were judge, jury, and executioners of an American citizen.

Couple this with the vast increase in our capacity for surveillance and remote control killing, and we've entered a very dangerous realm where constitutional rights become essentially meaningless. I'm well aware that our government has carried out murders in the past of U.S. and foreign nationals, but now it's being done in the open and with the full blessing of government, press, and public opinion? We're not just on a slippery slope, we're already well on our way downhill and picking up speed fast. It came out last December in the *Washington Post* that the United States under Obama has carried out top-secret drone attacks in at least six Muslim countries. Who are they killing, and why doesn't this have to be divulged?! The only member of the "team" who objected, Dennis Blair, got fired as director of national intelligence.[5]

In February 2012, the head of our military's Joint Special Operations Command (JSOC), Admiral William McRaven, is said to have asked for "more autonomy" to send elite killer squads to every corner of the globe. This includes the Navy SEALS and the Green Berets, which have gone from only 1,800 troops in 1980 to more than 25,000 today. The SEALS were created by President Kennedy, and I'm proud to say that I served as one of them, with the Underwater Demolition Teams. But I never anticipated seeing special ops forces deployed in more than seventy-five countries in our ever-expanding role as "policeman" to the world.

In both Iraq and Afghanistan, JSOC units have been involved in some of the worst atrocities. They carried out wholesale assassinations of opponents of the Iraqi occupation during the 2007 "surge" ordered by the Bush administration and were implicated in systematic torture of detainees. In Afghanistan, these units were responsible for the infamous 2002 wedding massacre, where they called in an AC-130 gunship to rake a wedding party and other civilian targets, leaving hundreds dead and wounded. Unlike the CIA, the JSOC is not required to secure a "presidential finding" authorizing lethal covert operations, or submit to congressional oversight.[6]

It pains me that the SEALS are today forced to be part of illegal gangland operations.

In early March 2012, Attorney General Eric Holder gave a speech at Northwestern University law school. During that speech, he basically laid out in detail the legal theory behind being able to kill American citizens who are suspected of terrorism without any charges or trial. "Due process and judicial process are not one and the same, particularly when it comes to national security," Holder told the students. "The Constitution does not require the president to delay action until some theoretical end stage of planning when the precise time, place, and manner of attack become clear. . . . We are at war with a stateless enemy, prone to shifting operations from country to country. . . . This is an indicator of our times, not a departure from our laws and our values."[7]

Along these lines, it seems to me that everything Bush implemented, Obama has backed up if not taken farther. So in a way, the Democrips are even more deceitful than the Rebloodlicans. One of Obama's longtime colleagues, and an informal adviser to his 2008 campaign, came out with strong criticism about how the president has done so little to change Bush's policies on government secrecy. Geoffrey R. Stone, a law professor at the University of Chicago and board chair of the American Constitution Society, wrote in June 2011 that Obama has "followed Mr. Bush in zealously applying the state secrets doctrine . . . [which] had been invoked in an unprecedented manner by the Bush administration to block judicial review of a broad range of questionable practices." (Think torture, surveilling people's private communications, and restricting habeas corpus.) After first saying this doctrine should be rarely invoked, since then "the Obama administration has aggressively asserted the privilege in litigation involving such issues as the CIA's use of extraordinary rendition and the National Security Agency's practice of wiretapping American citizens." Senator Obama, Stone added, was a sponsor of the Free Flow of Information Act so journalists could protect confidentiality of sources, but President Obama didn't support it, "in what seems to be a recurring theme." The administration's attitude "is a lesson in 'trust us'. . . . The problem is, 'trust us' is no way to run a self-governing society."[8] During the first year of Obama's administration, the number of new national security secrets increased by 22.6 percent.[9]

Back in 2009, Obama said that "a democracy requires accountability, and accountability requires transparency" and that the Freedom of Information Act (FOIA) encouraged both. The FOIA came into existence after Watergate in 1974 as a landmark law that's made it possible for citizens to learn more about the hidden workings of our government than ever before. It's pretty much forgotten today that President Gerald Ford actually vetoed the legislation— on the advice of his chief of staff (Donald Rumsfeld) and Rummy's Deputy (Dick Cheney). But Congress did the unthinkable—at least it would be unthinkable today—they voted to override the veto.

But, as of October 30, 2011, the Obama administration proposed making rule changes to the FOIA. If a document might be seen to interfere with an enforcement proceeding, the agency could not only deny the request for it but can also pretend the document didn't even exist! Disguised as a minor bureaucratic adjustment, that's legalizing lying! It's a crime for a citizen to lie to the government but fine and dandy for the government to lie to its citizens? And this is the same president who'd just talked about an Open Government Partnership?[10]

It's ironic that as a senator, Obama was a champion of the Federal Funding, Transparency, and Accountability Act that passed in 2006. This was responsible, among other things, for the website USASpending.gov that enabled researchers like Allison Stanger to find out about all that money going to private contractors in Iraq and Afghanistan, which I wrote about in chapter five. Now, Congress has proposed cutting the funding for these open government initiatives from $35 million to $8 million, which Stanger believes would shut that website down and keep still more important information from the American people.[11]

The Obama gang has also charged six whistleblowers under the pre–World War I Espionage Act—and that's more than all the previous administrations in American history put together. One of them was an advisor to the National Security Agency, charged with ten felonies for informing the media "that government eavesdroppers were wasting hundreds of millions of dollars on misguided and failed projects." A federal judge thought the case against Thomas Drake was outrageous and let the fellow plead to a misdemeanor (misuse of a government computer) and walk.[12] But this was after Drake's house was raided at gunpoint and the National Security Agency had dumped him from his job. The most recent case, in January, was going after ex-CIA officer John Kiriakou for telling journalists some classified scoop on our waterboarding of al-Qaeda suspects (the *real* "don't ask, don't tell").

Short of prosecution, there are subtler methods employed to break dissenters. Peter van Buren was a twenty-three-year career Foreign Service officer who wrote a critical book while still employed by the State Department (*We Meant Well: How I Helped Lose the Battle for the Hearts and Minds of the Iraqi People*). It "exposed what State did not want people to know," he says, "that they had wasted enormous amounts of money in Iraq, mostly due to ignorance and a desire for short-term successes that could be trumpeted back home." Not exactly earth-shaking news, but State retaliated by suspending his security clearance, banning him from entering the building where he worked, and threatened felony charges. Not to mention examining all his travel vouchers, his Internet activity, and his credit reports. Oh, and impounding his diplomatic passport.[13]

Speaking of what van Buren revealed about Iraq, we were told that the last American troops were supposedly withdrawn just before 2012 dawned. But the Defense Department is requesting about $2.9 billion to cover the cost of "Post-Operation NEW DAWN (OND)/Iraq Activities." This is for a war, mind you, that we're no longer engaged in.[14]

As for that other war, the one in Afghanistan where American troops have been burning Qur'ans and even gunning down innocent civilians, Lt. Colonel Daniel Davis, a seventeen-year Army vet just back from his second tour there, wrote an eighty-four-page unclassified report of which *Rolling Stone* got a copy. It opened with this: "Senior ranking U.S. military leaders have so distorted the truth when communicating with the U.S. Congress and American people in regards to conditions on the ground in Afghanistan that the truth has become unrecognizable. This deception has damaged America's credibility among both our allies and enemies, severely limiting our ability to reach a political solution to the war in Afghanistan." He's called for holding congressional hearings. Unnamed Pentagon officials are threatening to investigate Davis for "possible security violations."[15]

"During a point in history when our government has been accused of sending prisoners to secret locations where they were said to have been tortured and the CIA is conducting remote-controlled wars in far-flung places, it's not a good time to treat the people who aid in the publication of critical information as spies," David Carr wrote in an op-ed recently for the *New York Times*. "And it's worth pointing out that the administration's emphasis on secrecy comes and goes depending on the news. Reporters were immediately and endlessly briefed on the 'secret' operation that successfully found and killed Osama bin Laden. And the drone program in Pakistan and Afghanistan comes to light in a very organized and systematic way every time there is a successful mission."[16]

On our domestic front, Obama did get the health care reform law passed (if it survives the Supreme Court), watered down though it may be. He did pull America back from the brink of another Great Depression, flawed though the means were to the end. He did to a limited degree expand financial regulation and opened a national education reform initiative. And he took a major stand early in this election year by appointing a tough dude named Richard Cordray to run the new consumer protection agency—while the Rebloodlicans were away on recess. Cordray, blocked earlier by a filibuster, supposedly can now move forward on regulating a wide array of debt collectors, credit bureaus, and other scurrilous scumbags of low finance.[17]

But when dialing for dollars is pretty much the only choice you've got—and that's what our two-party (gang) system has come down to—idealistic promises may never have a prayer of being fulfilled. That is, if they were real in the first place. "The real conundrum," as psychologist Drew Westen has written:

> Is why the president seems so compelled to take both sides of every issue, encouraging voters to project whatever they want on him, and hoping they won't realize which hand is holding the rabbit. That a large section of the country views him as a socialist while many in his own party are concluding that he does not share their values speaks volumes.[18]

Westen pointed out that Obama presents inconsistent positions without apparently recognizing their incoherence:

> He announces in a speech on energy and climate change that we need to expand offshore oil drilling and coal production—two methods of obtaining fuels that contribute to the extreme weather Americans are now seeing. He supports a health care law that will use Medicaid to insure about 15 million more Americans and then endorses a budget plan that, through cuts to state budgets, will

most likely decimate Medicaid and other essential programs for children, senior citizens, and people who are vulnerable by virtue of disabilities or an economy that is getting weaker by the day. He gives a major speech on immigration reform after deporting more than 700,000 immigrants in two years, a pace faster than nearly any other period in American history.[19]

In another example of Obama "double-talk," at his big populist speech in Kansas in December 2011, the president said, "Too often, we've seen Wall Street firms violating major anti-fraud laws because the penalties are too weak and there's no price for being a repeat offender." Five days after that, appearing on *60 Minutes*, Obama said, "Some of the least ethical behavior on Wall Street wasn't illegal." Whaaat? There's been a veritable crime wave of, by, and for the Street![20]

Five big banks recently settled with the Obama administration for about $20 billion for their shady mortgage lending practices. A drop in the bucket, basically, when you consider their size, no criminal charges filed, and the fines being paid by their shareholders—"not by their executives or board members (all of whom carry insurance). . . . As if all of this weren't bad enough, the banks reportedly will be able to use government money to write down the value of mortgages, which amounts to subsidizing them to pay their own meaningless fines." That's Simon Johnson, the co-author of *13 Bankers*, talking. Johnson, again:

> The Obama administration's settlement with the mortgage lenders is consistent with its track record on all of its policies related to the financial sector, which has been abysmal . . . at stake in the mortgage settlement are fundamental and systemic breaches of the rule of law—perjury and fraud on an economy-wide scale. The Justice Department has, without question, all of the power that it needs to prosecute these alleged crimes fully. And yet America's top law enforcement officials have consistently—and now completely—backed off.[21]

Truth be told, the lunatics are pretty much running the government asylum. Government Sachs is still atop the heap, and it plays both sides of the gang world. Clinton's Treasury Secretary was former Goldman CEO Robert Rubin. Another ex-Goldman CEO, Hank Paulson, ran Treasury under Bush, when "coincidentally" (wink) Goldman received $23 billion during the TARP bailout. Not to mention the corporation getting a sizeable chunk of the $180 billion that AIG, the insurance Godzilla, was "awarded" from the Federal Reserve Bank of New York when it was presided over by Timothy Geithner, who is now Secretary of the Treasury.

Here's Bill Black, the savings and loan regulator during the Reagan years and now a professor at the University of Missouri, speaking to Bill Moyers: "The Bush Administration and now the Obama Administration kept secret from us what was being done with AIG. AIG was being used secretly to bail out favored banks like UBS and like Goldman Sachs." In the months leading up to the 2008 meltdown, "he [Geithner] took absolutely no effective action. He gave no warning. He did nothing in response to the FBI warning that there was an epidemic of fraud. All this pig in the poke stuff happened under him."[22]

Geithner helped Goldman Sachs instantly convert from an investment house to a commercial bank, making the company eligible for those ballooning government handouts. He then gave Goldman a $30 billion taxpayer-funded loan at .01 percent interest. Not a bad deal, especially at a time "when ordinary folks who missed a few credit card payments in order to finance their mortgages were being slapped with interest rates of more than 25 percent."[23]

Well, after all, Goldman Sachs gave nearly $1 million to the Obama campaign in 2008. Entering the Obama administration from Goldman were Gary Gensler, to chair the Commodity Futures Trading Commission; Robert Hormats, undersecretary of state for economic, energy and agricultural affairs; and Mark Patterson, an ex-Goldman lobbyist named Geithner's chief of staff. In the meantime, White House counsel Gregory Craig positioned himself to become one of Goldman's legal eagles. Lloyd Blankfein, current Goldman CEO, hired another new lawyer specifically to help with the Department of Justice's investigation into whether he might've done something illegal. The new lawyer, Reid Weingarten, used to work at Justice with Eric Holder. And now that Holder is the U.S. Attorney General, Weingarten is still among his "closest friends."[24]

Lawrence Summers, Obama's other prime economic adviser, got paid $135,000 by Goldman back in '08—for a *one-day* visit to the company. Altogether, his speaking fees in 2008—the year of the financial meltdown—were over $2.7 million from the likes of Citigroup, JP Morgan Chase, Lehman Brothers, and Merrill Lynch. Summers also collected about $5.2 million in compensation from D. E. Shaw, a hedge fund bigwig, for some part-time work that year. And you think those companies weren't thinking ahead about which of them were gonna benefit from how the government responded to the crisis? Summers, back in 1999, along with Robert Rubin and Alan Greenspan, was also the main man in blocking Congress from voting in legislation designed to regulate the derivatives market.

"Just think about how this works," *Salon* columnist Glenn Greenwald has written.

> People like Rubin, Summers and Gensler shuffle back and forth from the public to the private sector and back again. . . . When in government, they ensure that the laws and regulations are written to redound directly to the benefit of a handful of Wall St. firms, literally abolishing all safeguards and allowing them to pillage and steal. Then, when out of government, they return to those very firms and collect millions upon millions of dollars, profits made possible by the laws and regulations they implemented when in government. Then, when their party returns to power, they return back to government, where they continue to use their influence to ensure that the oligarchical circle that rewards them so massively is protected and advanced. This corruption is so tawdry and transparent—and it has fueled and continues to fuel a fraud so enormous and destructive as to be unprecedented in both size and audacity—that it is mystifying that it is not provoking more mass public rage.[25]

Rahm Emanuel, named as Obama's Chief of Staff and now the Mayor of Chicago, used to be a director at the mortgage giant Freddie Mac, a recipient of $150 billion in bailout bucks. In the summer of 2010, an oil well in the Gulf of Mexico exploded, jetting tons and tons of crude oil into the water. This oil well was owned by BP. At the time of the explosion, Rahm Emanuel was living rent free in a Washington D.C. apartment owned by Stanley Greenberg, one of the top advisors to BP—which gave rise to some speculation. Might Emanuel have compromised government efforts to regulate the oil industry? Perish the thought.[26]

Elizabeth Warren, who set up the new Consumer Financial Protection Bureau and is now running for the U.S. Senate in Massachusetts, said of Obama:

> He's got to know that his angry words at Wall Street, at their recklessness and dangerous incentives in compensation, about how they do their business in ways utterly divorced from what's actually good for the economy—that he can't just say that sort of thing, and then dump money in their laps and be credible.[27]

One of Obama's main pledges during the '08 campaign was that he'd get rid of the Bush Administration's tax cuts for the rich that helped create the huge deficit. Instead, when they were set to expire in December 2010, he extended them for another two years. That was a folded hand that a lot of his former supporters found simply baffling. More recently, the Obama administration has proposed to lower corporate taxes from 35 percent down to 28 percent for most companies and 25 percent for manufacturers. This is called being "revenue neutral," because another proposal is closing loopholes like letting corporations send their earnings overseas in order to pay lower taxes. Supposedly, this makes up for the lost revenue. But do these guys really need lower taxes? Back in 1953, under Eisenhower, "corporate taxes accounted for 32 percent of total federal tax revenues. Now they're only 10 percent."[28]

Then came the debt ceiling debacle, where the extortion by the Rebloodlicans seemed to bring the Democrips to their knees once again. "How can American democracy work," asked columnist Paul Krugman, "if whichever party is most prepared to be ruthless, to threaten the nation's economic security, gets to dictate policy? And the answer is, maybe it can't."[29] (And that's a level-headed Nobel Prize-winning economist talking!)

Here's one I really don't get. After the most fraud-riddled financial crisis in our history and not a single bankster being prosecuted, at the same time the Obama Justice Department has decided to *reverse* a campaign promise to leave the medical marijuana dispensaries alone provided they abided by state law. They're shutting down these places like crazy, especially in California where medical pot has been legal for approved patients for fifteen years! And while the mega-corporations manage to avoid taxes altogether, the IRS has told the pot clinics they can't deduct salaries or other operating expenses—meaning their tax bill generally ends up exceeding their profits. The Harborside Health Center in Oakland—biggest dispensary in the country—got sent a $2.4 million tax bill from the IRS in the fall of 2011.

As a longtime advocate for legalization, which would stop the drug cartels in their tracks, I'd really like to know what's going on here. Medical marijuana is legal in sixteen states and the District of Columbia. When he ran for president, Obama said he was "not going to be using Justice Department resources to try to circumvent state laws on this issue" like his predecessor had.

Here's what the Justice Department said during Obama's first year:

> Prosecution of individuals with cancer or other serious illnesses who use marijuana as part of a recommended treatment regimen consistent with applicable state law, or those caregivers in clear and unambiguous compliance with existing state law who provide such individuals with marijuana, is unlikely to be an efficient use of limited federal resources.

Now that was all well and good . . . until there came another memo in early 2011 that redefined what a "caregiver" was and threatened action in states that had made medical marijuana legal. During the first three years of Obama, the feds made more than a hundred raids on pot dispensaries—on track to break Bush's record.[30]

This is outrageous! In July 2010, the Department of Veterans Affairs gave its blessing to medical marijuana for returning soldiers. Then Michele Leonhart, who headed the Drug Enforcement Administration (DEA) under Bush, got renominated by Obama to head the agency. She'd once been told by then-House Judiciary Committee chairman John Conyers that she was going after medical pot dispensaries in a way "typically reserved for the worst drug traffickers and kingpins." But this was the same woman who'd called the murders of almost a thousand Mexican kids by the cartels a "sign of success in the fight against drugs." So her DEA followed up with a report that included headings like "Smoked Marijuana Is Not Medicine." That was when the crackdown really took off.

Federal prosecutors in D.C. have gone so far as to threaten state employees with potential felony charges under the Controlled Substances Act if they didn't take a hard line on new regs for the dispensaries. In response, two governors—Washington State's Christine Gregoire and Rhode Island's Lincoln Chafee—petitioned the DEA to reclassify marijuana as a drug with recognized medicinal value. "It's time to show compassion, and it's time to show common sense," said Gregoire. "We call on the federal government to end the confusion and the unsafe burden on patients." For its part, the White House keeps saying its position is "clear and consistent."

Uh huh, just like the financial institutions. According to an article in *Rolling Stone*, "the federal war on medical marijuana has locked pot dispensaries out of the banking system—especially in Colorado, home to the nation's second-largest market for medicinal cannabis. Top banks—including Chase, Wells Fargo, and Bank of America—are refusing to do business with state-licensed dispensaries, for fear of federal prosecution for money-laundering and other federal drug crimes." Don't you just love how law-abiding the big banks have become lately? Just one problem—if pot dispensaries are forced to work outside the usual system, as Rep. Jared Polis warned Attorney General Holder, "it makes the industry harder for the state to track, to tax, to regulate them, and in fact makes it prone to robberies, because it becomes a cash business."[31]

Look, the number of people put in prison for nonviolent drug offenses has risen more than twelve times since 1980! At the same time, global consumption of opiates has gone up 34.5 percent, cocaine 27 percent, and cannabis 8.5 percent from 1998 to 2008. And this is a successful "war on drugs?" After forty years, our government has spent a *trillion* dollars on this, and for what? How much of that has been spent to arrest over thirty-seven million nonviolent drug offenders, including some ten million for marijuana possession? $121 billion, plus another $450 billion to lock the convicted up in federal prisons.[32] This is what's criminal! And a fiasco! So much so that a Global Commission on Drug Policy recommends "to substitute treatment for imprisonment for people who use drugs but do no harm to others."[33] But try telling that to whichever gang is in control of the White House.

Obama's administration has put in place *some* good new rules—like raising fuel efficiency standards for new cars and trucks. So you'd think he might say something about the anti-regulatory sentiment that's so rampant in Congress. Instead, the president sounded more like the Chamber of Commerce in promising "to root out regulations that conflict, that are not worth the cost, or that are just plain dumb." Obama's White House "has watered down or quashed a series of public health, consumer and other regulatory protections ready for implementation."[34]

In August 2011, Bill Daley, the new White House chief of staff, held same-day meetings with various stakeholders to talk about a proposed EPA rule to tighten air pollution standards. Industry groups, according to the *Wall Street Journal*, handed the White House "a map showing counties that would be out of compliance with the Clean Air Act if the stricter standards were put in place. The map showed that the rule would affect areas in the politically important 2012 election states of Florida, Pennsylvania, Virginia, and Ohio." The Chamber of Commerce, National Association of Manufacturers, American Petroleum Institute, and others told Daley that going ahead with tougher restrictions would hurt Obama's reelection chances. So Obama caved on the tougher ozone regulations, sticking with the exposure level that Bush had set.[35] In October, five environmental and health groups including the American Lung Association sued the administration for what it called an "illegal" action driven by politics.[36] Not long after that, Obama's administration approved a plan by none other than BP to drill four new exploratory wells off the Louisiana coast.[37] "Drill, baby, drill" was back!

Then there's Monsanto, the chemical and biotech behemoth. Back in January 2011, a White House policy analyst got an email from a lobbyist with the Biotechnology Industry Organization (BIO) that represents genetically engineered (GE) seed companies like Monsanto and Syngenta. This apparently was related to a successful lawsuit by the PEER nonprofit to stop the planting of GE crops in northeastern wildlife refuges. The United States wants to step up exports of these, and it looks like there was collusion here. But the White House won't release a portion of the email, supposedly because "it accidentally contained information on BIO's lobbying strategy that, if released, would cause competitive harm to the gr up and the companies it represents."[38]

As a patriotic American, I wish I could give this president the benefit of the doubt. I'd like to think that the speech he gave out in Osawatomie, Kansas, was the start of something different—where he talked about the "breathtaking greed" behind our economic disaster and how what's "at stake is whether this will be a country where working people can earn enough to raise a family, build a modest savings, own a home, and secure their retirement." Maybe the Occupy Wall Street message was breaking through?

But I'm afraid I'm like more and more of my countrymen: I see what our two-gang system has degenerated into as a quagmire that it's well-nigh impossible to extricate from, without an "occupation" of our electoral politics.

NOTES

1. Obama in 2005: Quoted in "Obama Learns Newspeak: The Administration's Perversion of the Freedom of Information Act (FOIA)" by Harvey Silverglate, *Boston Phoenix*, November 9, 2011.

2. Obama Patriot Act extension: Quigley, Bill. "Twenty Examples of the Obama Administration Assault on Domestic Civil Liberties!" December 2, 2011, http://truthaholics.wordpress.com.

3. Turley, Jonathan. "Obama: A disaster for civil liberties." September 29, 2011, www.latimes.com.

4. Savage, Charlie. "Secret U.S. Memo Made Legal Case to Kill a Citizen." *New York Times*, October 9, 2011.

5. Secret drone attacks: Greenwald, Glenn. "Snapshots of Washington's essence." December 28, 2011, citing the *Washington Post*.

6. Van Auken, Bill. "U.S. Special Operations Command fighting global warfare." *Moral Outrage*, February 25, 2012.

7. Serwer, Adam. "When the U.S. Government Can Kill You, Explained." March 5, 2012, http://motherjones.com.

8. Obama and state secrecy: Stone, Geoggrey R. "Our Untransparent President." *New York Times*, June 27, 2011.

9. National security secrets increasing: *Secrecy News*, September 19, 2011.

10. "Obama Learns Newspeak: The Administration's Perversion of the Freedom of Information Act (FOIA)" by Harvey Silverglate, *Boston Phoenix*, November 9, 2011

11. Horton, Scott. "One Nation Under Contract—Six Questions for Allison Stanger." www.harpers.org.

12. Punishing whistleblowers: Quigley, Bill. "Twenty Examples of the Obama Administration Assault on Domestic Civil Liberties!" December 2, 2011, http://truthaholics.wordpress.com.

13. Van Buren, Peter. "Obama's Unprecedented War on Whistleblowers." February 9, 2012, www.alternet.org.

14. "Pentagon wants $3 billion for the War in Iraq that we thought was over." February 14, 2012, http://rt.com/usa/news/billion-war-iraq-us.

15. Hastings, Michael. "The Afghanistan Report the Pentagon Doesn't Want You to Read" *Rolling Stone*, February 13, 2012.

16. Carr, David. "Blurred Line Between Espionage and Truth." *New York Times*, February 29, 2012.

17. Cooper, Helene and Jennifer Steinhauer. "Bucking Senate, Obama Appoints Consumer Chief." *The New York Times*, January 5, 2012.

18. Westen, Drew. "What Happened to Obama?" *New York Times*, August 6, 2011.

19. Ibid.

20. Obama "double-talk": Taibbi, Matt. "Obama and Geithner: Government, Enron-Style." *Rolling Stone*, December 21, 2011.

21. Johnson, Simon. "Why the Banks Are Too Big to Jail." Project Syndicate, February 24, 2012.

22. Bill Black: On Bill Moyers' Journal, April 3, 2009, quoted in "Larry Summers, Tim Geithner and Wall Street's Ownership of Government" by Glenn Greenwald, April 4, 2009, www.salon.com.

23. "Geithner and Goldman, Thick as Thieves," by Robert Scheer, www.truthdig.com, May 31, 2011.

24. Goldman Sachs: Vissa, Preeti. "How Goldman Sachs' Bet on Obama Paid Off." August 31, 2011, www.huffingtonpost.com; Appelbaum, Binyamin. "Report Says New York Fed Didn't Cut Deals on A.I.G." *New York Times*, November 1, 2011.

25. "Larry Summers, Tim Geithner and Wall Street's Ownership of Government": cited above.

26. Rahm Emannuel: Corsi, Jerome. "White House chief tied to BP adviser." *World Net Daily* (WND.com), June 14, 2010.

27. Elizabeth Warren: Nocera, Joe. "Team of Rivals." Review of *Confidence Men* by Ron Suskind in *New York Times Book Review*, October 2, 2011.

28. www.nationofchange.org/corporations-don-t-need-tax-cut-so-why-obama-proposing-one-1330013423.

29. Krugman, Paul. "The President Surrenders." *New York Times*, August 1, 2011.

30. "Obama's War on Weed: White House Launches Crackdown on Medical Marijuana." October 11, 2011, www.huffingtonpost.com

31. New DEA policy . . . banks and pot: Dickinson, Tim. "Obama's War on Pot." *Rolling Stone*, February 18, 2012.

32. Cost figures: "After 40 years, $1 trillion, U.S. War on Drugs has failed to meet any of its goals." *Associated Press*, May 13, 2010.

33. Global Commission on Drug Policy: Carter, Jimmy. "Call Off the Global Drug War." June 17, 2011, www.nytimes.com; 100 busts: Dickinson, Tim. "Obama's War on Pot." *Rolling Stone*, February 18, 2012.

34. Weissman, Robert. "The GOP's Deregulation Obsession." *The Nation*, October 31, 2011.

35. Roberts, David. "The stupid politics behind Obama's ozone cave." September 12, 2011, www.grist.org; Broder, John M. "Obama Abandons a Stricter Limit on Air Pollution." *New York Times*, September 3, 2011.

36. Broder, John M. "Groups Sue After E.P.A. Fails to Shift Ozone Rules." October 12, 2011. WHERE DID THIS APPEAR?

37. Krauss, Clifford. "BP's Plan for Drilling in the Gulf Is Approved." *New York Times*, October 22, 2011.

38. Ludwig, Mike. "White House Refuses to Release Email from Monsanto-Linked Lobbyist." February 21, 2012, www.truth-out.org.

CHAPTER TEN

THE REBLOODLICAN RACE
TO THE BOTTOM

I've got to start this section with an admission. Like more and more guys, I experience electile dysfunction. That's defined as "the inability to become aroused over any of the choices for president put forth by either party in the 2012 election year."[1]

Here's a telling statement that conservative honcho Grover Norquist made at a gathering early this year:

> All we have to do is replace Obama. . . . We are not auditioning for fearless leader. We don't need a president to tell us in what direction to go. We know what direction to go. . . . We just need a president to sign this stuff. We don't need someone to think it up or design it. . . . Pick a Republican with enough working digits to handle a pen to become president of the United States. This is a change for Republicans: The House and Senate doing the work with the president signing bills.[2]

As this book goes to press, it looks like Twit Romney is going to be the man the Rebloodlicans end up nominating when their dele-gangs come together in Tampa Bay for the convention this summer. (Maybe we should resurrect the Know Nothing party as the slogan for the day?) Anyway, Romney is definitely the leader of the PAC— and thus the perfect representative of the top 1 percent.

Every politician probably flips as much as they flop, depending on which group they're trying to gather votes from; but in my opinion, Romney leaves you wondering whether a belly flop is as good as the others' flipped-lids. Joe Klein in *Time Magazine* put it like this: "Sifting through the Romney policy record, in an attempt to find patterns and answers, is an act of geology. There are sedimentary layers on issues like abortion, climate change, health care, gun control—almost any issue you can imagine."[3] For example, Romney used to be pro-choice. Today, he believes life starts at conception, and he has become "firmly pro-life." Firmly, eh? About the only thing that's stayed firm about Romney is his full head of hair, however he pulls that one off.

I mean, most of the candidates made a bid for the role of "Not Mitt Romney"—including Mitt Romney. Bill Clinton might have been a "pander bear," as one of his opponents said in '92, but here's how Jay Leno summed up Romney: "In an effort to clear up his reputation as a flip-flopper, Mitt Romney will give a speech on health care. And then, right afterward, he'll give a five-minute rebuttal." (Would he vote for himself? Dubious.) Not surprisingly, the Democrip National Committee has a four-minute video on this theme at MittyMitt.com.[4] I'm waiting for "A Flip We Can Believe In."

With a net worth of about $250 million, Romney made his fortune as a Wall Street superstar, "a chief architect of the modern executive-compensation-driven corporation." That's a nice way of saying what Newt Gingrich put a little more bluntly when Romney told him he should return that $1.6 million he earned from Freddie Mac: "If Governor Romney would like to give back all the money he's earned from bankrupting companies and laying off employees over his years at Bain [Capital], I would be glad to then listen to him."[5] From 1984 to 1999, Romney and his cronies invested in, acquired, and then sold about 150 companies and made a fortune, while hundreds of workers lost their jobs.[6] Vulture capitalism, as Gingrich called it . . . and for once, he was right!

The "Bain" of Romney's existence has been mighty kind to him. The last deal he made with his old partners was for a retirement package that's given him a share of the company's lucrative profits since 1999, while adding millions to his annual income. So Romney could have his political cake and eat quite well too, all without having to seek further gainful employment.[7]

Next to Bain Capital, no corporation has been kinder to Romney than Goldman Sachs. That's who Romney went to when Bain was looking to raise dough in 1989 for the Staples office supply company they'd acquired. After he became Massachusetts' Governor, Romney's blind trust handed Goldman most of his wealth to manage, and it still has "at least $10.2 million in Goldman funds—possibly much more—earning as much as $6.2 million." And now, Goldman employees are among the largest sources of his campaign money, having contributed upwards of $367,000 as of the end of September 2011.[8]

One thing I'll say for him though: These days, Romney's doing all he can to look like a man of the people. He ditched the jacket and tie in favor of blue jeans and plaid shirts. He told a group of people without jobs that he's "also unemployed." Yuck yuck. At the same time, he called for cutting 10 percent of the federal work force if he gets elected. "You do that through attrition," Romney told some steel workers. The fact is, upwards of 600,000 government workers have already lost their jobs since the recession started and, contrary to what Romney claims, they're underpaid compared to counterparts in the private sector.[9] (Remember when Romney said he also made "not very much" money from speaking—almost $350,000 in a year.)

Romney's duplicity goes that extra mile with his calling the federal government's bailout of the auto industry in '09 "nothing more than crony capitalism, Obama style . . . a reward for the big donors to his campaign." Well, as it happens, two "vulture investors" (otherwise known as hedge fund operators)—John Paulson of Paulson & Co. and Paul Singer of Elliott International—made out like bandits by buying up stock in an auto parts operation called Delphi and then forcing GM to use a heap of its bailout money to shore up the company. They made "a windfall of more than two billion dollars care of U.S. taxpayers"—and now they've "each written checks for one million dollars to Restore Our Future, the Super PAC supporting Romney's candidacy."[10]

I can't think of a better example of hypocrisy than this one. Something new came out in March about Romney's old firm Bain Capital, from which he admitted earning at least $5.6 million from assets to his blind trusts and retirement accounts in 2010, and whose execs and employees are among his biggest campaign contributors. The *New York Times* reported:

> In December a Bain-run fund in which a Romney family blind trust has holdings purchased the video surveillance division of a Chinese company that claims to be the largest supplier to the government's Safe Cities program, a highly advanced monitoring system that allows the authorities to watch over university campuses, hospitals, mosques and movie theaters from centralized command posts.[11]

In the meantime, on Romney's web site, the flip side is offered up: "Any serious U.S. policy toward China must confront the fact that China's regime continues to deny its people basic political freedoms and human rights." Feel like divesting in Bain yet, Mitt?

The big whopper (with extra cheese) in Romney's announced fiscal plan is his announcement that "we will level with the American people about what it will take to truly cut spending and balance our budget." As Matt Taibbi of *Rolling Stone* wrote, Romney's call for government entitlement reform actually amounts to this: "If we don't cut health care and retirement benefits for old people, how can we pay for the carried-interest tax break that allows private equity guys like, well, Mitt Romney to keep paying 15 percent tax rates?"[12] Romney's proposal would "cut food stamps by $127 billion, which would remove millions of people from the rolls during a downturn and cut the benefits of those who remain. . . . Of course, he wants to repeal health care reform, which he claims would save $95 billion but would actually raise the deficit by $124 billion in just the first decade."[13]

As for his tax "reform" plan, Romney says he'd make the top 1 percent pay more of their fair share, but analysts find his reasoning absurd; the overwhelming majority of his $6.6 trillion in tax cuts would go to the rich. The Romney tax cuts, in truth, would be "clocking in at a cost of more than $10.7 trillion over the next decade and reducing revenue to a paltry 15 percent of GDP," according to Michael Linden of the Center for American Tax Progress. "Balancing the budget on those terms, as Romney claims he will do, would be next to impossible."[14]

I guess to his credit, and unlike a lot of his Rebloodlican brethren, Romney doesn't want to shut down the Departments of Education or Energy. He does want to dump Amtrak, along with the Corporation for Public Broadcasting, the National Endowment for the Arts, and the National Endowment for the Humanities. "More Drivers, Less Culture" could be one of his bumper stickers.

And who are the "main men" in Romney's campaign? His national finance co-chairman is Frank VanderSloot of Idaho, a billionaire who's also given a million bucks to Romney's Restore Our Future super PAC, "somehow avoiding the legal barriers that are intended to keep super PACs separate from candidates' campaigns." He made his fortune with Melaleuca, Inc., a "wellness" company that peddles diet supplements and cleaning products, and "has been targeted by Michigan regulators, the Idaho attorney general's office, and the Food and Drug Administration for various marketing violations." VanderSloot has been funding various right-wing causes for years.[15]

Another one of Romney's campaign "stooges" is Larry McCarthy, who helps direct Restore Our Future, and his company (McCarthy Hennings Media) has spent $15 million producing and airing attack ads. It's something that comes naturally to McCarthy. He did the famed Willie Horton TV ad on behalf of George H. W. Bush in 1988, which made his rival Michael Dukakis look like he was soft on crime for letting a murderer loose on a weekend pass from a Massachusetts furlough program. Even though the ad definitely went beyond the pale as far as civility, a lot of people believed it. . . . So much for Dukakis' campaign. McCarthy, who calls himself a "compassionate conservative," came up with the ads in this year's Florida primary that squelched Newt Gingrich's frontrunner status.[16]

Romney's leading foreign policy adviser is Elliott Cohen, a neocon professor of strategic studies at Johns Hopkins University's School of Advanced and International Studies. He is a protégé of Paul Wolfowitz, having helped him form the Project for a New American Century in 1997. Pre-9/11, its blueprint laid out in *Rebuilding America's Defenses* had this clairvoyant line: "The process of transformation, even if it brings revolutionary change, is likely to be a long one, absent some catastrophic and catalyzing event— like a new Pearl Harbor."[17] Right after 9/11, Cohen had a large role in pumping up war under Bush for "the big prize," meaning Iraq. Dick Cheney recommended Cohen for a post as counselor to Condoleeza Rice in 2007. The white paper he wrote for Romney "urges a policy of regime change in Iran including possible coordination with Israel on military strikes to prevent the Iranian regime from developing a nuclear weapon."[18] For Romney and the other Bloods, war isn't hell, it's good for the economy, stupid! Plus, don't we have to still get back at Iran for seizing our embassy in 1979?

In case you could imagine openness in government might perk up under a Romney presidency, here's how columnist Frank Rich summed the man up:

> We don't know who Romney is for the single reason that he never reveals who he is. Even when he is not lying about his history— whether purporting to have been "a hunter pretty much all my life" (in 2007) or to being a denizen of "the real streets of America"

(in 2012)—he is incredibly secretive about almost everything that makes him tick. He has been in hiding through his stints in both the private and public sectors. While his career-long refusal to release his tax returns was damaging in itself, it resonated even more so as a proxy for all the other secrets he has kept and still keeps.[19]

Then there's Rick Santorum, the former Pennsylvania Senator who's a poster boy for the Christianists. He scored big in the Iowa caucuses with their crowd and came out of almost nowhere to finish first. (I guess Iowa was Sanctum Santorum.) Then, just when Romney looked like he had the nomination iced, Santorum started taking many of the primaries. Now it looks like the nominee may not become clear until the convention.

Santorum is a "home-schooling culture-warrior who likes to brag about fathering seven kids, as though morality can be measured in offspring." Before he got clobbered in a Senate race in '06, he was the congressional poster boy for raking in contributions from lobbyists and their family members. He took in around $500,000, almost 40 percent more than his closest rival. As Melanie Sloan, executive director of Citizens for Responsibility and Ethics in Washington, says, "Santorum is portraying himself as this outsider, when he was really the ultimate insider." He worked hard in the Senate to amend a Medicare bill to benefit Universal Health Services, a Pennsylvania-based hospital management company. Months after departing the Senate, he joined their board and garnered $385,000 in director's fees and stock options. He made sure that millions in earmarks went to companies represented by the American Continental lobbying firm, which was one of his contributors—and later on he provided "legislative policy consulting services" and earned $65,000 from the company. And Consol Energy, a big gas and coal producer that he'd advocated for, hired him on as a consultant.[20] In recent years, (as a "senior fellow" at the Ethics and Public Policy Center) Santorum has lived off the far-right gravy train funded by the Koch brothers, Richard Mellon Scaife, and others. Some have called this lifestyle "wingnut welfare."

Santorum does get down to nuts-and-bolts sometimes; before the campaign, he was well known for ranting in '03 to a reporter about "man on dog" sex.[21] Woof! However, Santorum says that to put somebody who's a victim of incest or rape "through another trauma of an abortion, I think is too much to ask."[22] The man is a believer in "the dangers of contraception in this country." He told an editor with CaffeinatedThoughts.com that "it's not okay. It's a license to do things in a sexual realm that is counter to how things are supposed to be."[23] I imagine he had a few extra cups that morning.

Recently, on *Meet the Press*, Santorum said that, as soon as he got elected, he'd bomb Iran's nuclear facilities if they refused to open the sites for international arms inspectors. Well, Rick, so far the International Atomic Energy Agency has conducted quite a number of such inspections but never found a shred of evidence that Tehran's nuclear program has been shifted over into weapons production. Anybody else hear echoes of "Weapons of Mass Destruction" before we invaded Iraq based on a lie?

Of course, Santorum isn't alone in beating the drum for another war. A district judge in New York issued a "finding of fact" that Iran assisted al-Qaeda in planning the 9/11 attacks, based on some testimony by former members of the 9/11 Commission and three defectors from Iran. What the *Associated Press* article didn't say was that at least two of those defectors were long ago described as "fabricators" by American intelligence, and the two "expert witnesses" verifying the "fabricators" are ex-Commission lawyers who think we're at war with Islam.[24] I seem to hear echoes of another lie that led to our invasion of Iraq, don't you?

We'll get into Santorum's fervent Christianism in a later chapter, but for the moment, here are some more policy nuggets:

- He'd keep defense spending where it is but slash $5 trillion out of the federal budget from the EPA, Medicaid, subsidies for job training, energy, education, food stamps, and housing.

- He'd eliminate most of our finance and regulatory laws.
- He'd "continue to stabilize Iraq," probably by reinvading.

In Santorum's words, climate change is "an absolute travesty of scientific research that was motivated by those who, in my opinion, saw this as an opportunity to create a panic and a crisis for government to be able to step in and even more greatly control your life . . . I for one never bought the hoax."[25] Wonder if he saw the recent report that about 3.7 million Americans are at risk of catastrophic coastal flooding from sea-level rise?[26] But after all, "We were put on this earth as creatures of God to have dominion over the Earth, to use it wisely and steward it wisely, but for our benefit not the Earth's benefit."[27] The more energy we consume, the higher our standard of living will be, he believes.

I can't resist going on to do a little dissection of Newt. Oh, let me debate him just once, I'd love it! Here's the poster boy for the Occupy Wall Street protesters. Since he left Congress, the Gang-Rich Group (excuse me, of course I should have said Gingrich Group) consulting firm has reined in over $100 million in contracts since 2000. That includes $1.6 million from none other than Freddie Mac, the belly-up government-backed housing behemoth. At first, Gingrich said the money derived from his analysis as a "historian." I guess that makes some sense, because what does he know about real estate? Then again, what does Freddie Mac need to learn about history? (About the Robber Barons, maybe?) Gingrich was selling influence. Totally. So he profited personally from the bailout, and people want him as their president?

Lest we forget, Gingrich left Capitol Hill in disgrace in 1998. He had to resign from the House after he got whacked for ethics violations with a $300,000 fine. Since entering "private life," Newt has gone to great lengths to say that he's not a registered lobbyist. Except, through his for-profit Center for Health Transformation, clients in the health-care biz have paid him as much as $200,000 a year to be members. Two dozen of those have been promoted in his

Center's booklet, and execs have made their pitches from panels on his podium.[28]

Gingrich got a rise in the polls after Herman Cain imploded due to ongoing allegations about "Yes We Cain" in the latest Zippergate scandal. The irony of it all! Newt was now the most palatable remaining choice for family values conservatives—having successfully pushed as House Speaker for Bill Clinton's impeachment over the Monica matter, while at the same time having a six-year affair with a young intern (who later became his third wife) while he was still married to his second wife, who had been diagnosed with multiple sclerosis. Of course, Gingrich had an affair with the second wife while he was still with the first, after she had been diagnosed with cancer.[29] Turn the other cheek, Newtie? Turnabout's fair play? Or, as he told the Christian Broadcasting Network, "There's no question that at times in my life, partially driven by how passionately I felt about this country, that I worked far too hard and that things happened in my life that were not appropriate." Read that again: Here's a man driven to serial adultery by patriotism and hard work.[30]

The fact is that Gingrich has stepped on it so many times that it won't be surprising if he's toast before this book comes out. He told a crowd in South Carolina, where $42,600 is the median household income, that the reason he didn't need to work as a lobbyist was because he made $60,000 for every single speech like this one.[31] Not much of an applause line there. He also came out in favor of getting rid of child labor laws. My copy of *The Quotable Gingrich* has him telling an audience at Harvard's Kennedy School of Government (where, incidentally, I used to teach the most popular class):

It is tragic what we do in the poorest neighborhoods, entrapping children in, first of all, child [labor] laws, which are truly stupid. Most of these schools ought to get rid of the unionized janitors, have one master janitor, and pay local students to take care of the school.

On *Face the Nation* last December, Gingrich said that "activist judges" need to be held accountable by being subpoenaed before Congress "to explain their constitutional reasoning," and he'd send the Capitol Police or even a U.S. Marshal to arrest them if need be. Separation of powers—out the window! A President Gingrich could decide that where the federal courts wrongly applied the Constitution, "legislation would remove the power of the courts." Or you could just impeach the judges or abolish their seats.[32]

As for those pesky illegal immigrants, Gingrich told an audience that we ought to use UPS and FedEx and "send a package to everyone who's here illegally and when it's delivered, we pull it up in a computer, so we know where they are." Hmmm, wouldn't you already need to know that in order to send them the package?[33]

This is the same man who said that unemployed workers shouldn't keep collecting benefits and just "sit at home for 99 weeks. It's fundamentally wrong, and a violation of the Declaration of Independence commitment that we have the right to pursue happiness."[34] He's also the same man who told the *National Review* a while back that Barack Obama was actually an undercover Kenyan (like his father), intent on dismantling American democracy. "What if [Obama] is so outside our comprehension, that only if you understand Kenyan, anticolonial behavior, can you begin to piece together [his actions]?" Newt was quoted as saying. [35]

In March 2011, "Big Thoughts" Gingrich gave a speech where he expressed grave concern about what the future might hold for his grandchildren. "I am convinced that if we do not decisively win the struggle over the nature of America," he said, "by the time they're my age, they will be in a secular atheist country, potentially one dominated by radical Islamists and with no understanding of what it once meant to be an American." Wow, you could be a secular atheist and a radical Muslim all at once? Who knew you could mix state and church like *that*?! But, damned if he didn't announce a plan to establish "on Day One" of his presidency a commission "to examine and document threats or impediments to religious freedom in the United States."[36]

But here's my favorite. When somebody at a town hall meeting in South Carolina asked what his position was on torture, Gingrich responded, "Waterboarding is by every technical rule not torture. Waterboarding is actually something we've done with our own pilots in order to get them used to the idea of what interrogation is like." Yeah, Newt, the Navy SEALS did it too, and having undergone waterboarding when I was one of them, let me report to you that it *is* torture. Gingrich went on to add that a prisoner should be waterboarded at the direction of the President only "in a circumstance which the information was of such great importance that we thought it was worth the risk of doing it, and I do that frankly only out of concern for world opinion."

So, in the eyes of the world, waterboarding's a no-no, but not *really*?![37] Does anybody remember that the United States tried and executed Japanese "interrogators" for the crime of waterboarding American servicemen during World War II? If Gingrich actually knew anything about interrogation, though, he would realize that it mainly yields false information. But it does make us *feel* better to torture them, doesn't it.

Now, for those of you looking for a solution in the Middle East, here's what Gingrich came up with in an interview with the U.S. Jewish Channel. First, he said that Obama's approach to diplomacy over there is "so out of touch with reality that it would be like taking your child to the zoo and explaining that a lion was a bunny rabbit." That's because, in Newt's view, treating the Palestinians on equal footing with the Israelis is "favoring the terrorists." Palestinians, you see, are an "invented" people "who are in fact Arabs. . . . And they had a chance to go many places, and for a variety of political reasons we have sustained this war against Israel now since the 1940s, and it's tragic."[38] Duh, was there an Israeli state before 1948, and wasn't Palestine there first?

When it comes to the Gingrich tax plan, according to the Independent Tax Policy Center, the middle class would be paying higher rates than millionaires. But the nonmagnitude of the tax

cuts that he's proposing for the top 1 percent and the corporations would also send the national debt booming still higher, even
if federal spending wound up being cut drastically. The analysis
says that, under the Gingrich plan, the debt would hit $25 trillion
(over 100 percent of our GDP) by the end of his possible second
term. That's an additional roughly $12.5 trillion over where we are
now.[39] ("There's no ceiling on a stairway to heaven" might be a
good motto.)

Then there are the candidates who fell out of the race early, and
good riddance. Maybe it's a sign that there are moderate conservatives who just refuse to drink the Kool-Aid, I don't know. But for
dead sure, this was one miserable crew of possible choices.

Rick Perry, the governor of Texas who starred for a short time
as "Front Runner for a Day," wrote a book in 2010 called *Fed Up!*
Therein, he said, "The American people mistakenly empowered
the federal government during a fit of populist rage in the early
twentieth century . . . by changing the way senators are elected (the
Seventeenth Amendment)." According to Perry, "the states were
historically more in control when they decided who those senators
were going to be. . . . The 17th Amendment is when the states started getting out of balance with the federal government, is my belief." He'd like to turn the clock back to a time when the rich could
easily bribe their way into the Senate by paying off insiders. That's
where Perry's "fit of populist rage" came from, an attempt to bring
more democracy into a corrupt system that once let governors and
legislators choose our senators (1789 until 1913).[40] This is also the
guy who thought secession was a good idea because of Obama's
Socialist policies . . . excuse me, but didn't we try that once?

Rick Perry raised more money than any governor in Texas
history, and the cookies from his generous friends cut both ways.
"Nearly half of the Texas governor's 150 most generous political
donors have received business contracts, tax breaks, or appointments from him or his administration." These once included the
late Kenneth Lay of Enron fame, who ponied up $87,000 to a Perry

campaign and, the day after, saw one of his ex-execs named chairman of the Texas Public Utility Commission.

During his eleven years as Texas' governor, Perry has taken free trips— 200 flights worth $1.3 mil—from corporate execs and other big-money donors.[41] "Texas does have this amazing pay-to-play culture," as one political consultant put it.[42] Are we surprised at Perry's "flat-tax" plan calling for a 20 percent across-the-board rate, which would give high-income folks a big break and everybody else modest tax savings or none.[43]

Perry was scary; there's just no other way to put it. He used to hunt and take guests to a West Texas camp that his family leased. The name for part of the property, on a rock at the entrance as late as the '80s and '90s, was "Niggerhead."[44] He's pooh-poohed evolution as "just a theory" that's "got some gaps in it" and accused scientists of making up man-made climate change "so that they will have dollars rolling in their pockets."[45] If truth be told, the pseudo-scientists who've made out like bandits are the ones being bank-rolled by the oil and coal companies to say that the jury's still out on global warming.

Rep. Michelle Bachman, who I'm not proud to say hails from my home state, thinks the founding fathers "worked tirelessly to end slavery." In fact, many of them *owned* slaves and enshrined slavery in the Constitution. We've come a long way, baby: On national TV, Bachmann accused President Obama of planning a trip to India at a cost to taxpayers of $200 million a day." Of course, she also thinks the prez "has virtually no one in his cabinet with private-sector experience." Only about two-thirds of them.[46]

She also believes global warming science is a hoax ("CO2 is a natural byproduct of nature") and that the EPA ought to be rechristened the "job-killing organization of America." Don't lose sight of Bachmann having introduced the Lightbulb Freedom of Choice Act of 2011 after those anti-free-marketeers like George W. Bush's administration set out to ban incandescent bulbs as harmful to our environment.[47] On abortion, she's said: "The Republican Party cannot get the issue of life wrong. It's a seminal issue."[48] I think she might have misstepped on that one—did she mean to say "semen-all?" After all, she's got 23 foster kids. (Speaking of seamy situations, we should recall that Romney once took a family vacation to Canada with his Irish setter Seamus strapped to the roof of the car.)

Herman Cain at least let it be known what his campaign was really all about, calling his book *This Is Herman Cain!* "Shoot-from-the-lip" Cain, as he said of himself at one press conference, comin' at ya. While in charge of construction of the Pillsbury skyscraper in downtown Minneapolis, he was the self-described "CEO of Self." He said he'd left the "Democratic plantation a long time ago," going on to run Godfather's Pizza and the National Restaurant Association (where he apparently encountered a bevy of beauties). His "nein-nein-nein" tax plan would have raised taxes on about 84 percent of American households, and the lower your income, the more you'd have paid. But if you earned more than a million bucks a year, your tax bill would have been cut in half. No more capital gains taxes whatsoever. Oh, and like Gingrich and Bachmann, Cain didn't think waterboarding was torture either.[49]

I watched quite a few of the Rebloodlican debates and have gotta say they could be the pilot for a new reality show called *Gang Survivor*. Or maybe reruns of *The Gong Show* or *Beat-the-Clock*? Obama has naturally been the prime target. Romney purported that Obama "is going to put free enterprise on trial." (Please! Obama goes out of his way to *praise* it!)[50] Gingrich said Obama favors "higher taxes, more regulation, no American energy." Perry accused Obama of waging a "war against religion." Rick Santorum said Obama plans to take wealth and "redistribute it to others." Jon Huntsman Jr. said Obama's time in office has been full of "crony politics." Michele Bachmann was determined that he be a "one-term president."

But their true ways with words come in the pointing of fingers (no middle ones allowed) at each other. Romney outspent Gingrich five-to-one in Florida on negative ads, which basically poisoned the atmosphere to the extent people hardly give a damn. If all the political bullshit encourages you not to vote, you've then given your rights away. . . . Except, they like it if people don't vote! They want you to feel that you don't make a difference, because then you're easier to control.

Who amongst them would snatch defeat from the jaws of victory in 2012? That was a question raised by Paul Krugman in a column headlined "Send in the Clueless." He pointed out just what level of absurdity these politicians have achieved. I mean, Obama's health reform package—designed by the Rebloodlicans, for the most part—gets denounced as another "Big Government" maneuver. And the president who apparently took out Bin Laden is "a radical socialist who is undermining American security."[51]

Taking the oath of office is one thing, but what's amazing is that only one of the Rebloodlican candidates, Jon Huntsman, Jr., refused to sign any of the pledges that various interest groups are asking for. And look what happened to him—early dropout. Rick Santorum and Michelle Bachmann even signed onto the Marriage Vow pledge (I doubt Newt was asked) where candidates agree they're opposed to same-sex marriage and reject Shariah law but will ever remain true to their spouse. This pledging business began with Grover Norquist, who over time has gotten 95 percent of all the Rebloodlicans in the Congress to say unequivocally that they will never *ever* raise taxes!

Can loyalty oaths be far behind?[52] Can you see why a man could experience electile dysfunction?

NOTES

1. Electile dysfunction: www.urbandictionary.com.
2. Frum, David. "Norquist: Romney Will Do As Told." *The Daily Beast*, February 14, 2012.
3. Joe Klein on Romney: "Where Is the Love?" *Time Magazine*, December 12, 2011.

4. "Pander bear"; Leno; MittyMitt.com: Kristof, Nicholas D. "Waiting for Mitt the Moderate." *New York Times*, January 5, 2012.

5. Gingrich on Romney and Bain Capital: "Mitt and Newt Latent Progressives?" *Robert Reich's Blog*, December 13, 2011, www.readersupportednews.org.

6. Barbaro, Michael. "After a Romney Deal, Profits and Then Layoffs" *New York Times*, November 13, 2011.

7. Romney and Bain Capital: Confessore, Nicholas, Christopher Drew, and Julie Creswell. "Buyout Profits Keep Flowing to Romney." *New York Times*, December 19, 2011.

8. Confessore, Nicholas, Peter Lattman, and Kevin Roose. "Close Ties to Goldman Enrich Romney's Public and Private Lives." *New York Times*, January 27, 2012.

9. Romney as man of the people: "Romney, Whose Net Worth is $250 Million, Whines That He Makes Less Than Federal Employees." November 9, 2011, http://thinkprogress.org.

10. Palast, Greg. "Romney's Top Funders Made Billions on Auto Bail-Out." February 23, 2012, www.nationofchange.org.

11. Jacobs, Andrew and Penn Bullock. "A U. S. Tie to Push on Surveillance in Chinese Cities." *New York Times*, March 16, 2012.

12. Romney social security/medicare plan: Taibbi, Matt. "Mitt Romney's Entitlement Plan Is Crazy." *Rolling Stone*, November 8, 2011.

13. Food stamps and health care: "Mr. Romney's Missing Details." Editorial in the *New York Times*, December 6, 2011.

14. Waldron, Travis. "Romney Says He'll Make the Top 1 Percent Pay More While Proposing Plan Giving Them a Massive New Tax Break." *ThinkProgress*, February 22, 2012.

15. "Mitt Romney's Money Man: Who Is Frank L. VanderSloot?" February 24, 2012, www.dailyfinance.com.

16. Mayer, Jane. "Attack Dog." February 13, 2012, www.newyorker.com.

17. "The process of transformation . . .": Cited in Jesse Ventura's *American Conspiracies* (New York: Skyhorse Publishing, 2010), p. 160.

18. Blumenthal, Max. "Elect Romney, Get War in Iran?" *Al-akhbar*, February 5, 2012.

19. Rich, Frank. "Who in God's Name Is Mitt Romney?" February 14, 2012, http://nymag.com.

20. McIntire, Mike and Michael Luo. "When Santorum Left the Senate, Familiar Hands Reached Out." *New York Times*, January 6, 2012.

21. Walsh, Joan. "Why Rick Santorum's Entirely Predictable Brief Success in Iowa Still Means He'll Be Back to Wingnut Welfare Soon." Alternet. com, January 2, 2012 .

22. Santorum on abortion: "Where the Republican Candidates Stand on Key Issues." *New York Times*, December 31, 2011.

23. Krugman, Paul. "Sex and Santorum." *New York Times*, January 4, 2012.

24. Porter, Gareth. "Are Crackpot Liars Being Used to Tie Iran to 9/11?" December 29, 2011, www.alternet.org.

25. Hymas, Lisa. "Crazy talk: Rick Santorum out-denies the climate deniers and spins eco-conspiracy theories." February 15, 2012, http://grist. org.

26. Gillis, Justin. "Sea Level Rise Seen as Threat to 3.7 Million." *New York Times*, March 14, 2012.

27. Quote about creatures of God: "Crazy Talk . . ." *New York Times*, March 14, 2012.

28. Center for Health Transformation: McIntire, Mike and Jim Rutenberg. "Gingrich Gave Push to Clients, Not Just Ideas." *New York Times*, November 30, 2011.

29. Newt Gingrich—Freddie Mac, leaving Congress, affairs: Murphy, Tim. "13 Reasons Why Newt Gingrich Won't Win the Nomination." *Mother Jones Online*, December 5, 2011 .

30. Gingrich to Christian Broadcasting Network: Collins, Gail. "Eye of the Newt." *New York Times*, March 12, 2011.

31. South Carolina speech: Gabriel, Trip. "When Gingrich's Big Thoughts Backfire." *New York Times*, December 6, 2011.

32. Gingrich on judges: "Mr. Gingrich's Attack on the Courts." Editorial in the *New York Times*, December 11, 2011.

33. Stan, Adele M. "The 5 Stupidest Things GOP Presidential Candidates Said . . . in Just One Day." February 13, 2012, www.alternet.org.

34. Ibid.

35. Costa, Robert. "Gingrich: 'Obama's Kenya, anti-colonial' worldview," www.nationalreview.com, September 11, 2010.

36. "On Day One": Dowd, Maureen. "Separation of Newt and State." *The New York Times*, December 12, 2011.

37. Gingrich on child labor, Obama, secular atheists, and waterboarding: Khalek, Rania. "10 of the Craziest Things Newt Gingrich Has Ever Said." *Alternet*, December 8, 2011.

38. Gingrich on Israel and Palestinians: "Gingrich Calls Palestinians 'Invented' People." *Al Jazeera*, December 10, 2011, www.readersupportednews.org.

39. Hanlon, Seth. "Gingrich's Tax Plan Would Cause Perpetual Trillion Dollar Deficits, Triple the Debt by 2024." Citing analysis by Tax Policy Center, December 14, 2011, www.nationofchange.org.

40. Rick Perry on ending direct election of senators: Nichols, John. "Rick Perry's Attack on Democracy." *The Nation*, October 10, 2011.

41. McIntire, Mike. "For Perry, Use of Private Jets As Part of Job." *New York Times*, November 4, 2011.

42. "pay-to-play": Confessore, Nicholas and Michael Luo. "Perry Mines Texas System to Raise Cash." *New York Times*, August 21, 2011.

43. "Flat Taxes and Angry Voters." Editorial in the *New York Times*, October 31, 2011.

44. Oppel, Jr., Richard A. "Snag for Perry: Offensive Name at Texas Camp." *New York Times*, October 3, 2011.

45. Perry on evolution and climate change: Krugman, Paul. "Republicans Against Science." *New York Times*, August 29, 2011 .

46. Gabriel Trip. "With Stakes for Bachmann Higher Now, Her Words Get in the Way." *New York Times*, September 16, 2011.

47. Bachmann on climate and light bulbs: Roberts, Diane. "The Tea Party's Next Target: The Environment." *Guardian UK*, August 3, 2011.

48. Bachmann on abortion: "Where the Republican Candidates Stand on Key Issues." *New York Times*, December 31, 2011.

49. Herman Cain: Tomasky, Michael. "The 'CEO of Self.'" *New York Review of Books*, November 23, 2011.

50. Romney quote: Krugman, Paul. "The Post-Truth Campaign." *New York Times*, December 23, 2011.

51. Krugman, Paul. "Send In the Clueless." *New York Times*, December 5, 2011.

52. Pledges: "Signing Away the Right to Govern." Editorial in the *New York Times*, July 19, 2011.

CHAPTER ELEVEN

THIS IS YOUR TEA PARTY ON KOCH

When the Tea Party showed up on the scene not too long after Obama won the presidency, they cast themselves in a mold that a lot of Americans could relate to. Starting with the name, of course, calling to mind those patriots in disguise who boarded British ships in Boston harbor and dumped all those barrels of tea into the sea in protest of the colonial tea tax back in 1773. It's interesting that the tea the Brits were trying to force down their throats was from the British East India Company (BEIC) that London had set up as a monopoly when the BEIC was having some hard times. The message was, buy BEIC tea or the King's Army will spread freedom all over ya. They figured they'd blockade Boston Harbor until it was all drunk—and taxed—and paid for. Good to the last drop. So this was really a protest against one of the original corporate bailouts. And it helped jump-start the American Revolution. (Americans have never really gotten along with the billionaires' wet dream of government-enforced monopoly, even from the beginning.)

So here came all these folks at the modern-day Tea Party rallies dressed up as George Washington and marching with flags reading "Don't Tread on Me." The motivation behind the Tea Party seemed at first like a valid one. Its members were against how much power the big corporations have, and how the politicians are so willing to bail them out in exchange for having their own pockets lined. They were determined to downsize the government, a grassroots movement that was ready to "take back the country" at the polls in 2012. They knew how corrupt the two-party system had become.

In the 2010 midterm elections, the Tea Party did surprisingly well. In today's Congress, we have fifteen freshmen House members as part of the Tea Party Caucus, and they've been making out quite well, donation-wise, from some very familiar Washington outfits. Their first nine months in Congress, the fifteen all told received more than $3,450,000 from about 700 different PACs. The biggest contributor (52 donations) was Honeywell International, a Fortune 500 defense contractor. Coming in second was the American Bankers Association, followed by Koch Industries, the National Association of Realtors, and Lockheed Martin.[1]

Now you could argue that nobody in politics today has much choice except to keep an open hand (which goes along with a closed mind). Greasing of palm is, after all, the favorite parlor game in D.C. To compete, any party is going to have to corrupt itself, which is why I don't support any parties, including the Tea-baggers. Also, when people like Glenn Beck end up being the spokespeople, I almost view them as worse than what we've got.

Is the Tea Party concept initially a good idea? Absolutely. Follow the Constitution, follow the Bill of Rights. We've strayed so far from those documents that we do need to come back to them. But maybe, in the name of that, there's something insidious going on here; at least that's where the evidence is pointing. The trouble is, supporters of the Tea Party are—whether they're aware of it or not—snorting Koch.

Don't take it from me but from a memo the Mitt Romney campaign dated October 4, 2011, and first revealed by the *Washington Examiner*, stating unequivocally that the Koch brothers (yes, that's pronounced "coke") are the "financial engine of the Tea Party." The same memo went on to discuss Romney's courting of the billionaire bros, Charles and David; they'd endorsed Romney in 2008, and one of Twit's first big campaign fundraisers for 2012 was hosted at a Koch mansion in the Hamptons.[2]

But the Kochs aren't hedging their bets—they're planning on hosting whoever might emerge "over Tea," and we're not talking herbal! Until August 2010, when a 10,000-word article by Jane Mayer appeared in the *New Yorker*, the Koch family of Wichita, Kansas, and Planet Earth had been operating under the radar forever. Primarily, from the oil business they'd amassed quite a sizeable fortune, to the point that each brother is worth between $21.5 and $25 billion. The brothers own almost all of the $100 billion Koch Industries, a conglomerate of refining, pipeline, chemical, and paper businesses. Along with owning Georgia-Pacific, they bring us Stainmaster carpets, Brawny paper towels, and other consumer products (there's an online boycott if you're interested). Theirs is the second biggest privately run company in America. *Forbes* has listed the Kochs as the nation's fifth richest people.[3]

Their father, Fred Koch, was one of the founders of the John Birch Society, so it's no big surprise that the boys are estimated to have given more than $100 million so far to right-wing causes. They put up the seed money for the Cato Institute and the Mercatus Center and are big donors to the Federalist Society. Not to mention donating "directly to 62 of the 87 members of the House GOP freshman class . . . and to 12 of the new members of the US Senate" in 2011.[4] And fronting groups called Americans for Prosperity, FreedomWorks, and Citizens for a Sound Economy, along with about thirty others including Tea Party affiliates. Things go better with Koch, I guess.

FreedomWorks, led by ex-House Majority Leader Dick Armey (who gets $500,000 a year from the group and its foundation)[5], set up a Tea Party Commission in 2011 to give presentations on how to cut the budget deficit. FreedomWorks also founded Tea Party Patriots, another "grassroots" group to stop any tax hikes on the rich from being part of the deficit deal. Freedom works for who? I don't think they're talking about the working class.

So just what *is* the Tea Party in favor of? Small government, anti-regulation, tax cuts, removal of government programs like Medicare, Social Security, and "Obama-Care." What are the Koch Brothers in favor of? All that and a bit more. To keep their oil-and-gas business booming, they've reportedly given about $55 million since 1997 to scientists and others to say that global warming is a hoax.[6] "Koch Industries and its employees form the largest bloc of oil and gas industry donors to members of the new House Energy and Commerce Committee, topping even ExxonMobil. And what do they get for that largess? As a down payment, the House budget bill not only reduces finances for the Environmental Protection Agency but also prohibits its regulation of greenhouse gases."[7]

As Mary Boyle of Common Cause put it, "What makes them [the Kochs] unique is that they are not just campaign contributors; they are a vast political network in their own right."[8] One group the brothers have been courting with arms outstretched is the Christian Right. Tim Phillips, president of the Koch-funded Americans for Prosperity, showed up not long ago to present at the Awakening conference sponsored by the Freedom Federation. "So conservative Christian voters are being told that a radically limited federal government is God's idea, and that right-wing economic policies are mandated by the Bible. . . . Jesus himself is also opposed to progressive taxation, the capital gains tax, the minimum wage, and even collective bargaining."[9] I guess that old parable about money-changers being tossed out of the temple has been relegated to the biblical bin of dust.

The Kochs are also cozy with two of the Supreme Court justices who pushed for the "corporations are people" resolution in the *Citizens United* case that overturned almost a century of limitation on contributions to political campaigns. In fact, Antonin Scalia and Clarence Thomas took part in strategy sessions at the Kochs' annual "retreats" before ruling on that case.[10]

The Kochs' have also funded a campaign to help Wisconsin Governor Scott Walker with his union-busting. There've been petitions gathered with over a million signatures from Wisconsin citizens calling for a recall election that would get rid of Walker. Meanwhile, Americans for Prosperity, funded by the Kochs, is busy running $700,000 worth of TV ads in Wisconsin, claiming Walker's policies are "working"—even though the state has been losing jobs consistently since the Walker budget came to pass. It's called the "Stand with Walker" campaign. And they don't mean pushing yourself around to keep your balance.

Supposedly, this kind of coordinated effort between candidates and "independent" groups like Americans for Prosperity is a violation of IRS law.

> Under the Internal Revenue Code, all section 501(c)(3) organizations are absolutely prohibited from directly or indirectly participating in, or intervening in, any political campaign on behalf of (or in opposition to) any candidate for elective public office. Contribution to political campaign funds or public statements of position (verbal or written) made on behalf of the organization in favor of or in opposition to any candidate for public office clearly violate the prohibition against political campaign activity. Violating this prohibition may result in denial or revocation of tax-exempt status and the imposition of certain excise taxes.[11]

Is anybody out there willing to mount the Koch Challenge?

You've probably heard about the controversy over the Keystone XL oil pipeline, which drew a slew of protesters to the gates of the White House. At the writing of this book, it's still on hold. In January, Obama rejected rapid approval of the pipeline because the Rebloodlican Congress was holding a short-term extension to the payroll tax cut hostage to it. Obama said the "arbitrary nature of a deadline prevented the State Department from gathering the information necessary to approve the project and protect the American people."[12]

Before this happened, Speaker John Boehner and George W. Bush had called the pipeline a "no brainer" that would create "tens of thousands of jobs" right away (if you believe in the tooth fairy), and Mitch McConnell said it was "shovel-ready" (and he's a champion shoveler of you-know-what).[13] They're talking about a 1,700-mile, $7 billion project that would bring *very* crude oil from the tar sands of Alberta, Canada, down through the Great Plains states to be refined on the Texas Gulf Coast. Besides polluting air and water and destroying wildlife, it's set to cross the Ogallala Aquifer, which provides drinking water for two million people and supports $20 billion in agriculture. Parts of the pipeline will also be built on an active earthquake zone. So what happens if there's a leak? Not to mention this being business-as-usual in terms of fossil fuels, while we ought to be making the shift to a cleaner energy economy. According to James Hansen, a prominent climate expert with NASA, if this development isn't stopped, it's "game over" for the global climate. Removing and burning all that oil would send so much carbon dioxide into the atmosphere that it'd be impossible to stabilize in future years.[14] Plus, most of the Keystone oil is actually for export, not for U.S. "Energy Independence."

But in a classic case of the fox guarding the henhouse, Hillary Clinton's State Department was allowing a Keystone XL contractor in Houston—chosen by the TransCanada company that plans to build the pipeline—to manage the project's environmental review![15] And TransCanada's top lobbyist in Washington is Paul Elliott, who happened to have been a deputy national manager for Hillary's 2008 presidential campaign. As soon as she became Secretary of State, he got hired by TransCanada. It turns out that he's so tight with folks in the State Department that one of them "provided Fourth of July party invitations, subtle coaching and cheerleading, and inside information about Secretary Hillary Rodham Clinton's meetings" to him.[16] What's so different about this from when Dick Cheney held secret meetings with Big Oil during the first months of the Bush Administration, which offered them pretty much anything they wanted?

Like the phrase from Latin class goes, *Cui bono*? Who benefits from all this? None other than the Brothers Koch. They stand to make millions from the pipeline's construction, since they run a subsidiary called Koch Exploration Canada, LP, and are admittedly "among Canada's largest crude oil purchasers, shippers and exporters."[17] They're spreading the word to state legislators about such matters through the American Legislative Exchange Council (ALEC) by sending out "model bills" promoting their agenda. ALEC only makes the details available to its 2,000 legislative and 300 corporate members. One of these tries to refute all the evidence about climate change. Another model would cut various regulations and public services and is called—don't laugh!—the Economy Civil Rights Act.[18]

ALEC bills itself as "the nation's largest, non-partisan, individual public-private membership association of state legislators." That's a mouthful, which ought to raise eyebrows from the get-go. It was founded back in 1973 by conservative activists like Paul Weyrich, and today, ALEC is intent on privatizing education, breaking unions, and passing voter ID laws. Nobody knows just how much money the Kochs have given ALEC, but it's sure to be more than a million bucks. ALEC's current chairman is now the Koch brothers' top lobbyist; and, in return for $25,000 a year, Koch Industries gets to be an "equal" board member among ALEC's state legislators.[19]

A footnote on all this: If you want to talk real jobs—not just more money to the rich—the power plant upgrades that need to happen because of the new rule curbing mercury emissions will create at least 45,000 temporary construction jobs and 8,000 permanent ones. The loan guarantee programs that the Department of Energy has in place for solar and wind, and companies working on more fuel-efficient cars and advanced battery technology, would mean more than 60,000 direct jobs. And that's just for openers.[20]

Once a year, like clockwork, the Kochs bring together some of America's Righteously Richest for a secret strategy seminar. In June

2011, this was held in Bachelor Gulch, outside Vail, Colorado, at a Ritz-Carlton. *Mother Jones Magazine* reported:

> Though the Vail guest list is a jealously guarded secret, the Koch network includes Rich DeVos, cofounder of Amway, owner of the Orlando Magic, and a prolific donor to Focus on the Family and other conservative causes; John Childs, a "notoriously media-shy" Boston private-equity guy who's worth an estimated $1.2 billion and who last year doled out $750,000 to outside expenditure groups like Karl Rove's American Crossroads; Diane Hendricks, a billionaire roofing-supply magnate who joined the Kochs in supporting Wisconsin Gov. Scott Walker's recent attacks on public-sector unions.

They and a few hundred more listened to talks on, among other things, "Winning the Fight between Free Enterprise and Big Government." Charles Koch gave acknowledgment to "32 individuals and families who had given more than a million dollars each in the past year to the 'Kochtopus'—what political insiders call the network of advocacy groups the brothers have employed in their discreet attempt to shape American political life to their whims."[21]

What came out of that gathering at Crony Island? Well, at least in the backroom closets, they surely discussed the Koch brothers' plan to have a national database to connect up millions of their like-minded citizens. Apparently, the Kochs started the voter file with $2.5 million back in 2010. "It has been given the name Themis, after the Greek goddess who imposes divine order on human affairs. . . . Themis will in effect become an electoral roll of right-wing America, allowing the Koch brothers to further enhance their power base in a way that is sympathetic to, but wholly independent of, the Republican party."[22]

Charles, seventy-five, and David, seventy-one, are no spring chickens, but they've obviously got plenty they're planning to squeeze in while they're still kicking. Like Charles told his "masters of the universe" at Bachelor Gulch (you can't make this stuff up),

"This is the mother of all wars we've got over the next 18 months, for the life or death of this country."[23] We'll see what happens in 2012 to top the freedom-loving advice they gave their 50,000 employees just before the midterm elections. They all received an urgent letter instructing them who to vote for "and warning them about the dire consequences to their families, their jobs and their country should they choose to vote otherwise."[24] Let freedom ring!

When the Kochs convened their four-day retreat early in 2012 at a golf resort in Indian Wells, California, "helicopters, private security and police officers from neighboring cities patrolled the area constantly." Every entrance to the Esmerelda Renaissance conference venue was blocked. A number of private planes belonging to wealthy Rebloodlican donors flew into a nearby airport, including one that belonged to billionaire investor Phil Anschutz.[25] Coming for the first time to a Koch event was Sheldon Adelson, the billionaire casino tycoon who's primed to be the most Super PACman of them all.[26] That is, if the Koch brothers don't beat him to the punch.

Yup, the Tea Party bills itself as the protector of our Constitution, which they claim was established to restrain our federal government. It's hard to figure out what document they're reading, since the real text of the Constitution leans heavy on ensuring that the new government had enough power. The framers thought the old Articles of Confederation were way too weak. What the government *can* do—not what it can't—is what the Constitution tries to define. The Tenth Amendment leaves whatever powers aren't enumerated in the Constitution to the states. So maybe the Tea Party is confusing the Constitution with another document— perhaps the Bible? I read one article about a whole bunch of "patriots" coming to a seminar, only to find out that supposedly the Constitution is based on the Law of Moses and "restores the fifth-century kingdom of the Anglo-Saxons." Besides that, they look at Social Security, the EPA, and the 1964 Civil Rights Act as violations of God's law.[27]

The story goes that the Tea Party began when Rick Santelli of CNBC got on the floor of the Chicago Mercantile Exchange and called for the traders to hold a tea party to stop Obama's proposal to "subsidize the losers," meaning folks who couldn't keep up with their mortgage payments. That same day, the Koch Brothers' Americans for Prosperity put a Tea Party page on Facebook and started organizing events, whereby a whole bunch of "angry, God-fearing, government-loathing populist insurgents . . . fired up the town halls."[28] This is actually the biggest Astroturf campaign in history. Passing itself off as a spontaneous uprising of concerned Americans, it's a completely fabricated grassroots movement.[29] In 2009, Tea Party organizers reported back to David Koch at their Defending the Dream summit. "Five years ago," Koch told the gathering, "my brother Charles and I provided the funds to start Americans for Prosperity. It's beyond my wildest dreams how AFP has grown into this enormous organization."[30]

Here's the irony of it all. The Koch brothers wouldn't be bankrolling the Tea Party, except for the money made by the old man in Stalin's Soviet Union. He had just graduated from college with a degree in chemical engineering, and in 1929, with a partner named Winkler, Fred Koch signed a $5 million contract—a ton of money in those days—to become Comrade Stalin's No. 1 builder of oil refineries, five altogether. Four years later, Koch had cleared half a million bucks in the midst of the Great Depression . . . and that was the original source of all the family's assets. The communists loved Koch's refineries and sent a number of engineers to be trained in Wichita, Kansas. Later, in the mid-1950s, after a final trip to the USSR, the old man started talking about a commie conspiracy to take over our country. According to son Charles, all the engineers who'd worked with his dad had ended up imprisoned by Stalin, which turned Fred into an anti-communist who "thought the values of economical freedom and prosperity [were] more important than ever before."[31]

I don't know about you, but I'm feeling a little Koched-up right about now. When the Tea Party was stolen by the same party system that's running the show, the next thing we got was Occupy Wall Street—which hasn't been captured because it refuses to participate in the political process. The great evil, to me, is that the party system can buy out the righteous anger people have for the way the system works.

NOTES

1. Caucus contributions: Mehta, Aaron and Bob Biersack. "15 Tea Party Caucus Freshmen Rake In $3.5 Million in First 9 Months in Washington." November 31, 2011, www.nationofchange.org.

2. Romney memo on Kochs: Fang, Lee. "Romney Campaign Memo: The Koch Brothers Are the 'Financial Engine of the Tea Party.'" November 3, 2011, http://thinkprogress.org.

3. Koch Brothers ownings and wealth: "Koch brothers now at heart of GOP power." *Sacramento Bee*, February 5, 2011.

4. Koch donations to Congress: Stan, Adele M. "You Thought the Koch Brothers Were Bad? Turns Out They're Even Worse Than You Thought." April 5, 2011, www.alternet.org.

5. Armey salary; Tea Party Patriots: Stan, Adele M. "In Bid for Control of GOP, Tea Party Brings U.S. to Brink of Economic Calamity." July 23, 2011, wwwalternet.org.

6. $55 million to climate change deniers: Pilkington, Ed. "Koch brothers: secretive billionaires to launch vast database with 2012 in mind." November 7, 2011, www.guardian.co.uk.

7. Oil and gas contributions: Rich, Frank. "Why Wouldn't the Tea Party Shut It Down?" *New York Times*, February 27, 2011.

8. Mary Boyle quote: Ibid.

9. Kochs and Awakening conference: Montgomery, Peter. "Tea Party Jesus: Americans for Prosperity Sidles Up to Religious Right for 2012 Campaign." April 15, 2011, www.alternet.org.

10. Tencer, Daniel. "Supreme Court justices 'participated in political strategy sessions' before Citizens United." January 20, 2011, www.rawstory.com.

11. Nichols, John. "David Koch Admits Big Spending to Help Scott Walker Bust 'Union Power.'" February 20, 2012, www.nationofchange.org.

12. "Obama rejects Keystone pipeline from Canada to Texas." January 18, 2012, www.usatoday.com.

13. Republican deal, Boehner and McConnell: "Keystone Claptrap." Editorial in the *The New York Times*, December 13, 2011.

14. James Hansen: Broder, John M. and Dan Frosch. "Politics Stamps Out Oil Sand Pipeline, yet It Seems Likely to Endure." *New York Times*, December 24, 2011.

15. "State Department Letting Keystone XL Contractor Mange Its Environmental Review." September 28, 2011, www.thinkprogress.org.

16. Rosenthal, Elisabeth. "Cozy U.S. Tie to Builder Is Seen by Resisters of Pipeline Project." *New York Times*, October 4, 2011; McKibben, Bill. "The Cronyism Behind a Pipeline for Crude." Op-ed in the *New York Times*, October 4, 2011.

17. Koch Brothers and Keystone pipeline: Greenwald, Robert. "The Kochs' Keystone Clique Exposed." *Guardian UK*, September 8, 2011.

18. ALEC: Kilkenny, Allison. "Koch Brothers' ALEC Tentacles Creep into Your State." July 18, 2011, www.truthout.org.

19. ALEC and Koch background: Nichols, John. "ALEC Exposed"; Graves, Lisa. "The Koch Connection." *The Nation*, August 18, 2011.

20. "Where the Real Jobs Are." Editorial in the *New York Times*, January 2, 2012.

21. "Koch Brothers retreat: "Spying on the Koch Brothers." *Mother Jones*, November/December 2011.

22. Themis: Pilkington, Ed. "Koch brothers: secretive billionaires to launch vast database with 2012 in mind." November 7, 2011, www.guardian.co.uk.

23. "Spying on the Koch Brothers," *Mother Jones*, November/December 2011.

24. Letter to employees: Ames, Mark and Mike Elk. "Big Brothers: Thought Control at Koch." *The Nation*, May 9, 2011.

25. Fang, Lee. "Koch Brothers Convene Super-Secret Billionaires' Meeting for 2012 Elections." *Alternet*, February 4, 2012.

26. Stone, Peter H. "Adelsons Attend Koch Brothers Conference for Mega Donors." *iWatch News*, February 3, 2012.

27. Seminar: Epps, Garrett. "Stealing the Constitution." *The Nation*, February 7, 2011.

28. "Angry, God-fearing, government-loathing . . .": Keller, Bill. "Is the Tea Party Over?" Op-ed in the *New York Times*, October 10, 2011.

29. Tea Party beginnings: "The Tea Party movement: deluded and inspired by billionaires," by George Monbiot, October 28, 2010, www.guardian.co.uk.

30. Defending the Dream and Koch quote: Monbiot, George. "Anger, Deceit and a Billionaires' Coup." *Guardian UK*, August 2, 2011.

31. Koch family and Soviet Union: Levine, Yasha. "Tea Party Financiers Owe Their Fortune to Josef Stalin." April 21, 2010, www.alternet.org.

CHAPTER TWELVE

POLL-CATS: THE STEALING OF DEMOCRACY

The dictionary definition of a polecat is either any of various North American skunks or a European weasel-type critter that ejects a fetid fluid when attacked or disturbed. This chapter is about our political equivalent: poll-cats. They come in a number of weaselly shapes and sizes.

First some historical background: More than sixty years after the United States was founded, all men were not equal, no matter what the Declaration of Independence said. Most black people were slaves, counted as three-fifths of a man in the Constitution to boost the populations in southern states and their representation in Congress. In exchange for the representation, southerners also had to pay increased taxes. In order to vote back then, you had to be white (except for brief periods in a few northern states), male (except in New Jersey, where women voted until 1807), and a landowner (nearly everywhere; there were twenty-six states at the time). In some places, that meant that only 15 percent of the population could vote. It's hard to imagine today how small a number of citizens were allowed to the polls: 15 percent?!

In 1841, Thomas Dorr, a congressman from Rhode Island, decided this was unfair to the poor and fought to get the law changed.

He secretly wrote a new constitution (with some supporters) to try to make all white males over the age of twenty-one eligible to vote. Six months later, two separate elections for governor were held, and two men were elected: The landowners choose a man named Samuel Ward King, and the other party—known as the "People's Charter"—chose Thomas Dorr himself. (Despite good intentions, he might have been a little *too* partisan.) When Dorr showed up with 3,000 citizens and two beat-up cannons to take the city arsenal from the "illegal" government, he was arrested and tried for treason. He was pardoned after two years in prison.

Eventually the land owning requirement was dropped in Rhode Island, and the other states followed. So I guess Dorr opened the door, in a way. But even with the enfranchisement of the poor, it took decades to allow everyone else to come to the polls. Women fought for suffrage and finally gained it in 1920 with the passage of the Nineteenth Amendment, but only after staunch resistance.

Some who study our history might remember when the "Dixiecrats" later used literacy tests and poll taxes to keep black Southerners away from the voting booth. In case you think a lot has changed as we've become more "enlightened," think again. There are a whole slew of new measures in various states that will likely keep minorities, immigrants, elderly people, students, and ex-cons from their fundamental right to vote in 2012.

In a behind-the-scenes move pushed by the American Legislative Exchange Council (ALEC)—who, as I mentioned in the Tea Party chapter, are largely funded by the billionaire Koch brothers—no less than thirty-eight states introduced legislation and a dozen approved efforts to keep the "wrong people" at home on Election Day. Before 2006, not a single state forced voters to produce a government-issued photo ID. But here's what an article in *Rolling Stone* revealed in September 2011:

> Kansas and Alabama now require would-be voters to provide proof of citizenship before registering. Florida and Texas made

it harder for groups like the League of Women Voters to register new voters. Maine repealed Election Day voter registration, which had been on the books since 1973. Five states—Florida, Georgia, Ohio, Tennessee and West Virginia—cut short their early voting periods. Florida and Iowa barred all ex-felons from the polls, disenfranchising thousands of previously eligible voters. . . . States controlled by Republican governors and legislatures—Alabama, Kansas, South Carolina, Tennessee, Texas, and Wisconsin—will require voters to produce a government-issued ID before casting ballots. More than 10 percent of U.S. citizens lack such identification, and the numbers are even higher among constituencies that traditionally lean Democratic—including 18 percent of young voters and 25 percent of African-Americans.

Bill Clinton described what's happening like this: "There has never been in my lifetime . . . the determined effort to limit the franchise that we see today." Since that article came out, a total of nine states—including Pennsylvania and Virginia—have passed new voter ID requirements. The measure in Pennsylvania is almost exactly what ALEC drafted up as its "model legislation."[1] "In 2012, states in which voting rights have been restricted will provide 171 electoral votes, 63 percent of what is needed to win the presidency, according to the Brennan Center for Justice at the New York University Law School."[2]

The hypocrisy boggles the brain. After the Supreme Court awarded a false victory to Bush over Al Gore in 2000, W's administration—led by Karl Rove—declared that voter fraud was "an enormous and growing problem." Well, that's certainly true when it comes to computerized elections, which we will get to shortly. But a report examining these claims by the Brennan Center said, "It is more likely that an individual will be struck by lightning than that he will impersonate another voter at the polls."

So 2011 was a record-setting year for new legislation—nineteen laws and two executive actions in fourteen states that are dominated by Republicans—that is obviously intended to keep more

Democrat voters from the polls.[3] Let's take a closer look at some of the shenanigans. Out in Florida, where democracy got creamed in the recount mess of 2000, the Rebloodlican legislature passed a law that makes anybody out there registering voters—such as the League of Women Voters and Rock the Vote— "hand in registration forms to the state board of elections within 48 hours of collecting them, and to comply with a barrage of onerous, bureaucratic requirements. . . . The registration law took effect one day after it passed, under an emergency statute designed for 'an immediate danger to the public health, safety or welfare.'" Emergency? There had been three arrests for suspected voter fraud in Florida over a three-year period.

Early voting, a strategy that Obama used successfully in 2008, is getting cut back in Florida (from fourteen to eight days) and Ohio (from thirty-five to eleven days), and state government-issued photo IDs are being touted since our "impartial" Supreme Court upheld one such law in Indiana in 2008. Used to be you could use your Social Security card or a bank statement or utility bill. Now, in Texas, Governor Rick Perry signed "emergency" legislation that makes a concealed-weapon permit an acceptable ID—but *not* a student ID.

Under a new law in Wisconsin implemented by Koched-up Governor Scott Walker—which a circuit court judge declared was unconstitutional, but his ruling is being appealed—students in Wisconsin wouldn't be able to vote without IDs that show their birthday, current address, signature, and two-year expiration date. Not a single school of higher education in the whole *state* requires that! Until this go-round, Wisconsin made it easy for students and was one of the top states with young voter turnout.[4]

In South Carolina, in order to get a state ID needed to vote, 178,000 people without one would first be required to pay for a passport or a birth certificate. In the name of stopping voter fraud, nothing like prodding a few more folks to get a phony birth document, eh?[5] The Justice Department, after reviewing the legality of the photo ID cards and also the early-voting restrictions, blocked the South Carolina law on photo ID under the Voting Rights Act, because it would have "significant racial disparities."[6]

It's happening in my home state as well. ALEC's state chairman for Minnesota is a State Rep named Mary Kiffmeyer. She's also the legislator who wrote a photo ID bill that passed both chambers of our state house last year, before Governor Mark Dayton vetoed it. A watchdog group called TakeAction Minnesota issued a report early this year that "describes how Minnesota's wealthiest finance institutions and their executives, lobbying groups, PACs and the chamber of commerce have been pooling funds together, sharing resources, and in some cases sharing office suite space in a collective effort that's at least partially responsible for a Republican takeover of the state legislature in 2010." They've set up a mega-lobby called MN Forward, which is backing efforts of the ALEC-linked Rebloodlicans to get a photo ID requirement on a referendum ballot in November.[7]

Prisoners who've done their time are citizens who ought to be allowed to join everyone else at the polls. But four states—Kentucky, Virginia, Florida, and Iowa—have laws that permanently disenfranchise anyone convicted of a felony. Alabama, Arizona, Delaware, Mississippi, Nevada, Tennessee, and Wyoming do the same for at least some offenders. Nineteen other states restore voting rights after somebody completes his or her sentence, including parole and probation. Only two states—Maine and Vermont—have no disenfranchisement for felony offenders.[8] No such thing as a reformed crook, I guess (unless your name is Richard Nixon).

Charlie Crist, Florida's former Republican governor, restored voting rights to 154,000 ex-cons who'd been jailed for nonviolent crimes. The new Florida governor, Rick Scott, in March 2011 overturned that decision, "instantly disenfranchising 97,491 ex-felons and prohibiting another 1.1 million prisoners from being allowed to vote after serving their time." Most of those, as Bill Clinton pointed out, were African Americans or Hispanics who don't customarily go for Rebloodlicans.[9]

This is especially true, of course, in the South. Some call this "the new Jim Crow laws." It's also a means for social control and destroying minority communities. There's been a conscious decision by our government to increase income inequality and deal with the malcontents by putting them in jail. But think about how much more it costs to incarcerate a young man than to educate him. You could pay tuition at Harvard for the price tag of keeping the same guy behind bars.

As far as democracy is concerned, the worst thing in previous elections has been the shift to electronic voting. In Minnesota, we still have the old hand-counted ballots. But paper ballots have become, for the most part, passé now that we're in the digital age. More and more state officials have opted to use computerized technologies to tabulate election results. According to Jonathan D. Simon, Executive Director for the Election Defense Alliance, "as a nation, our votes are counted in virtual secrecy on computer equipment owned, operated, programmed, distributed and maintained by a few corporations situated squarely and unabashedly at one pole of the political spectrum," the right-leaning pole.[10]

Currently, there are three main companies that produce these machines: Premier Election Solutions, Elections Systems and Software (ES&S), and Sequoia Voting Systems. Time and again, the integrity of this computerized equipment has been questioned—and for good reason. The way I see it, they're stealing our democracy—one byte-sized piece at a time.

Premier Election Solutions was founded in January 2002, which was then part of a larger company called Diebold. The CEO of Diebold was a man named Walden O'Dell, who was later revealed to be one of George W. Bush's "most active fund-raisers," and who had previously expressed his "commitment to help deliver the electoral votes of Ohio . . . to President Bush" in 2004.[11]

ES&S was founded in 1979 as American Information Systems, AIS for short. In the 1996 and 2002 elections, AIS was responsible for tabulating 85 percent of the votes in the state of Nebraska. Up until 1995, Chuck Hagel served as chairman of AIS. The very next year, Hagel was elected as a Senate Republican and, in 2002, won reelection. While a Senator, Hagel never properly disclosed his former relationship with AIS.[12]

These are two blatant examples of what at best could be described as a conflict of interest. But generally speaking, there are more subtle and far more nefarious ways to manipulate the outcome of elections tabulated by computerized equipment. Take, for example, the situation in California in 2007. The Secretary of State, Debra Bowen, a Democrat, withdrew approval for Sequoia Voting Systems after it was found that "significant security weaknesses throughout the Sequoia system" raised "serious questions as to whether the Sequoia software can . . . protect the integrity of elections."[13]

To provide more context, consider the following: Under George W. Bush, the Help Americans Vote Act was passed by Congress. HAVA 2002, as it was called, required the replacement of punch-card and lever-based voting systems and mandated all states to "upgrade their voting machines." Many jurisdictions then opted to computerize their elections. Those three major election-tech companies are, for the most part, protected under the notion of "proprietary rights" via "proprietary software." In short, this means that Premier Election Systems, ES&S, and Sequoia are not required to hand over items such as "electoral computer codes" or any other "trade secrets" for independent verification, citing issues of copyright and "material ownership" of technology.

This means that the public can't demand or even request that these companies exhibit the tabulations computed on their software for review and certification. The public *can* demand to see these materials and, in 2008, the state of New Jersey announced plans to send some of the Sequoia voting machines to a pair of Princeton computer science academics. Via email, the powers-that-be at Sequoia claimed that allowing these academics to examine their machines would, among other things, present an "infringement of [their] intellectual property." In fact, the two academics from Princeton, Edward Felten and Andrew Appel, received "threatening" emails from Sequoia stating the company "will also take appropriate steps to protect against any publication of Sequoia . . . behavior."[14]

The state of Georgia has used computerized touch-screen technology for every election since 2002. Back then, Georgia Secretary of State Cathy Cox signed a $54 million contract with Diebold. Ray Cobb, an academic at Kennesaw State University, stated in a deposition given in 2007 that those Diebold machines did not have an independent audit trail—a requirement of Georgia state law at the time. Cathy Cox, no longer in state politics, remains linked to a Diebold Electronic Systems lobbyist, Lewis Massey, who had been Cox's boss when *he* was Secretary of State. Small world, isn't it.[15]

The ES&S voting machines also appear to be prone to many "technical difficulties." In 2006 in Sarasota, Florida, the ES&S systems "inexplicably lost a full 18,000 votes." In the end, a Republican candidate "won" the election by just 369 votes. Despite evidence suggesting that ES&S machines are prone to "vote-flipping," the U.S. Elections Assistance Commission has "failed to take any action to decertify the systems."[16]

When a special Senate election was held in Massachusetts in 2010 as a result of the death of Edward Kennedy, the assumption was that Democratic candidate Martha Coakley would be a shoo-in for his seat. But Scott Brown, a Republican, ended up winning, thus changing the balance of power in the Senate. What wasn't talked about much at the time was that 97 percent of the ballots cast in this special election were counted by optical scan equipment manufactured either by ES&S or Diebold. There was no systematic audit of the vote count, no exit polls were performed, and none of the ballots stored in the equipment were allowed to be examined, let alone verified.

Based on a lengthy, multijurisdictional study conducted by Jonathan D. Simon of the Election Defense Alliance, it seems that in places where the votes were counted by hand, Martha Coakley defeated Scott Brown by a margin of 2.8%. But when the votes were tabulated by computer, unobserved and not subject to outside "human scrutiny," Brown defeated Coakley by a margin of 5.2%. According to Simon, "We cannot say with 100% certainty that the 97% of votes counted [by optical scan equipment] were subject to manipulation. But we can fairly ask: 'What evidence exists that they were not?'"[17]

Also in 2010 came stories about "vote-flipping" in Texas. Citing the YouTube clip of a Texas voter named Don Relyea, the Brad Blog reported that the ES&S touch-screen voting system "flipped votes" for Governor Rick Perry to candidates of other parties—showing that this kind of manipulation is a bipartisan problem.[18]

One of the most damning stories about computers and elections comes from the sworn testimony of Clinton Eugene Curtis. On December 13, 2004, Curtis testified in Ohio regarding the rigging of software during the 2000 elections in Florida. Asked "Are there programs that can be secretly used to fix elections?" Curtis responded, "Yes . . . In October of 2000, I wrote a prototype . . . in Florida . . . that did just that. It would flip the vote 51/49 to whoever you wanted it to go to and whichever race you wanted to win."

When the good lawmakers of Ohio asked Curtis why he would write such a program, he blamed his employers, Yang Enterprises International, and also named a Florida lawmaker: "I was asked by Tom Feeney. He's now a Congressman. At that time, he was speaker of the House in Florida." Before Feeney was an elected official, he'd been a lobbyist. U.S. Representative Gerry Nadler continued the questioning: "And he was your lobbyist, the lobbyist for your company . . . and he asked you to design . . . code to rig an election?"

Curtis: "Yes."

Nadler: "While he was the speaker of the Florida House?"

Curtis: "Yes."[19]

Here's what we know about a guy who might have blown the whistle on an even bigger scale: Michael Connell. He was only forty-five when he died in the crash of his private plane not long after the 2008 election. Before that, Connell was president of GovTech Solutions, a company that designed websites and provided various levels of IT support for government and elected officials, mainly from the Republicans. In 2008, Connell was subpoenaed to testify in an Ohio federal court regarding voter fraud in the 2004 presidential election. He was expected to be the star witness.[20]

Cliff Arnebeck is the chair of the Legal Affairs Committee of Common Cause Ohio and an attorney for the Alliance of Democracy, who subpoenaed Michael Connell. Arnebeck believes that Connell's plane was sabotaged, because he'd been instrumental in rigging the outcome of the Ohio vote for George W. Bush in 2004— and was prepared to talk about it. Ohio was where Bush's "victory" put him over the top in the Electoral College for a second term.

Arnebeck was the lead attorney in a somewhat related case charging Ken Blackwell, the Ohio Secretary of State, with disenfranchising black voters in the '04 election. You want to talk cronyism, just start with Blackwell. In 2000 he'd been Bush's main "electoral system adviser" during the Florida recount. He also happened to co-chair Bush's reelection committee in Ohio. A report by Congressman John Conyers on what happened there in '04 set forth "massive and unprecedented voter irregularities and anomalies in Ohio . . . caused by intentional misconduct and illegal behavior, much of it involving Secretary of State J. Kenneth Blackwell."[21]

Cliff Arnebeck thinks that a cadre of conservative operatives under the guidance of Karl Rove used a network of computers to manipulate the outcome of the race. Connell, the GOP's IT guru, had been working "to build a cyber system that could assure permanent control by Republicans of key offices, state and federal." According to Arnebeck, "Michael Connell's business was involved in every aspect of this complex conspiracy."

Arnebeck harkens back to the spring of 2000, when Bush lost the New Hampshire primary to John McCain, as the main impetus for certain Republicans to use computer technologies for their benefit. That was when Rove went looking for ways to ensure Bush's election to national office . . . and Connell was their go-to guy. When he appeared ready to come out of the high-tech closet, Rove reportedly first threatened Connell's wife and then perhaps took another step.[22]

I detailed in my book *American Conspiracies* how another computer expert and friend of Connell's, Stephen Spoonamore, described a duplicate control center set up by Connell in 2004. The Rebloodlicans used a company in Chattanooga, Tennessee, called SMARTech, Inc., a backup server that received the Ohio results. These could then be observed and changed using remote access through high-speed Internet. Spoonamore said: "There could have been twenty Republican operatives and from that point they could have made a direct hop to the White House. They could have been running this from the War Room."[23]

So what, if anything, has been done to fix the problems presented by computerized elections? Ever since the term "hanging chad" entered the American political lexicon in 2000, and ever since the passing of the HAVA bill in 2002 (which burdens each state with the need to "upgrade" their election-tabulating process), more and more states are going for optical-scan, touch-screen computerized technologies for election vote counting and tabulation. In October 2010, according to *USA Today*, "New York [State] became the latest to make the switch this year when it replaced lever machines. . . . The verdict [is that] elections are more accurate: There is less chance that voters will make mistakes, and there are safeguards in case they do."[24]

Since then, though, "experts at Princeton University, New York University's Brennan Center, Johns Hopkins University, indeed Congress' own Government Accountability Office, have all sounded the alarm that the system is highly vulnerable to outcome-determinative hacking and/or insider manipulation."[25]

It seems pretty obvious to me. To get rid of the likelihood of voter fraud hanging over our elections, we've got to outlaw the electronic voting machines and go back to a system where there's a paper trail. Isn't the conflict of interest obvious, with the computer companies and the vote counters being dominated by the Rebloodlicans? Not to mention all the new voter ID requirements. But give the Democrips enough years in power, and it's a pretty safe bet they'd follow the same pattern. Gotta keep up with the Joneses.

NOTES

1. Berman, Ari. "GOP War on Voting Targets Swing States." *Rolling Stone*, March 10, 2012.

2. DuBose, Lou. "Republicans Block the Vote." *Washington Spectator*, February 26, 2012.

3. New legislation: "The Myth of Voter Fraud." Editorial in the *New York Times*, October 10, 2011.

4. "Keeping Students from the Polls." Editorial in the *New York Times*, December 27, 2011.

5. Justice Department review: Savage, Charlie. "Holder Signals Tough Review of New State Laws on Voting." *New York Times*, December 14, 2011.

6. Savage, Charlie. "U.S. Cites Race in Halting Law Over Voter ID." *The New York Times*, December 24, 2011.

7. Mock, Brentin. "The Wealthy One Percent That's Behind Minnesota's Racist Voter ID Push." *ColorLines*, February 12, 2012.

8. "Felon Voting Rights by State," www.projectvote.org.

9. All the material on state regulations for 2012 comes from: Berman, Ari. "The GOP War on Voting," *Rolling Stone*, September 15, 2011; also at www.readersupportednews.org.

10. Simon, Jonathan D. "Counting Votes in a Tarnished Era." http://electiondefensealliance.org.

11. Diebold: "The Business of Voting." *New York Times*, December 18, 2005; see also: Smyth, Julie Carr. "Voting Machine Controversy." *Cleveland Plain Dealer*, August 28, 2003.

12. Chuck Hagel and AIS: Bolton, Alexander. "Hagel's Ethic Filings Pose Disclosure Issue." *The Hill*, January 29, 2003.

13. "Withdrawal of Approval of Sequoia Voting Systems, Inc." California Secretary of State, August 3, 2007. Also: "Source Code Review of the Sequoia Voting System." California Secretary of State, February 13, 2008.

14. Sequoia and scientists: Masnick, Mike. "E-Voting Firm Threatens Ed Felten If He Reviews It's E-Voting Machine." *TechDirt.com*, March 18, 2008.

15. Favorito, Garland. "The Greatest Scandal in Georgia History." www.voterga.org, October 14, 2010.

16. Friedman, Brad. "Incident Challenged by Election Official, Reported to DA, Highlights Familiar Problem with Unverifiable Machines." *Brad Blog*, October 22, 2010.

17. *Massachusetts Coakley vs. Brown*: Simon, Jonathan D. "Believe It (or Not): The Massachusetts Special Election for U.S. Senate." August 27, 2010, ElectionDefenseAlliance.org.

18. Texas vote-flipping: *Brad Blog*, October 22, 2010.

19. Clint Curtis: 2004 Election Forum held at Columbus, Ohio, City Hall, December 13, 2004. Sworn testimony of Clinton Curtis, available also on video.

20. "Stark Co. Plane Crash: Who Was Michael Connell?" Online version of WKYC.com, December 20, 2008.

21. Conyers and Blackwell: Fitrakis, Bob and Harvey Wasserman. "The Suspicious, Disturbing Death of Election Rigger Michael Connell." December 21, 2008, www.freepress.org.

22. Spinelli, John Michael. "GOP Threatens 'Valerie Plame' Style Strike Against Wife of IT Mastermind if He Doesn't Become Fall Guy for Gaming the 2004 Ohio Election." Ohio News Bureau; Renner, James. "Point of Impact: If There Was a Plot to Steal the 2004 Election, Michael Connell Knew About It. Is That Why He's Dead?" www.clevescene.com.

23. Jesse Ventura, *American Conspiracies*, p. 136.

24. New York making switch: *USA Today* article by Richard Wolf, October 19, 2010.

25. Simon, "Counting Votes in a Tarnished Era, http://electiondefensealliance.org.

CHAPTER THIRTEEN

BIG MEDIA'S COLLUSION WITH THE GANGS

The loss of liberty in general would soon follow the suppression of the liberty of the press; for it is an essential branch of liberty, so perhaps it is the best preservative of the whole. Even a restraint of the press would have a fatal influence. No nation ancient or modern has ever lost the liberty of freely speaking, writing or publishing their sentiments, but forthwith lost their liberty in general and become slaves.
—James Alexander, *New York Weekly Journal*, 1733[1]

L et's start with a look back at what happened to Howard Dean when the Vermont Governor was the front runner for the Democratic nomination in 2004. He was independent, he was tough, and his honest talk was inspiring an army of young people to finally get involved in politics. Besides Dennis Kucinich, Dean was the only candidate that year who opposed the United States invasion of Iraq, thus alienating a vast industry: the military-industrial complex that gorges at the government trough, no matter which gang is in power. Not to mention, of course, the insurance industry—since Dr. Dean was first of all calling for a new approach to health care.

The date that sealed his fate was December 1, 2003, when Dean was twenty points ahead in the polls. At that time he'd raised much more money than any of the other Democrips, although it came primarily from many small donations, outside the control of the rich gangsters. But that was the day Dean went on MSNBC's *Hardball* with Chris Matthews and said, "We're going to break up the giant media enterprises."

Uh oh: A leading candidate for the presidency talking about reregulating the communications industry?—in what "amounted to a declaration of war on the corporations that administer the flow of information in the United States," as blogger David Podvin later put it. This happened to be the same month that my own show on MSNBC got dumped, but more on that in a moment.

Within a couple of weeks after his comment, "the news divisions of the four major television networks were reporting as fact that Dean was unelectable. The print media echoed the theme." Every major paper in the U.S.—*New York Times, Washington Post, Wall Street Journal, Los Angeles Times, Boston Globe, Chicago Tribune,* and more were touting the same "unelectable" theme before the year was out. Then came *Time* and *Newsweek*.[2] All this, despite a *Time* poll indicating that George W. Bush was only ahead of Dean by six points—closer than Al Gore's numbers shortly before the 2000 election, lest we forget he won the popular vote nationwide.

So on January 19, 2004, after all the negative coverage (as well as an alliance among the party line Democrip candidates to get him out of the race with negative ads), Dean finished third in the Iowa caucuses—after which the infamous "Dean scream" was emitted in front of 3,500 staff and supporters. He'd ended a listing of the early-primary states where he could do better, by raising his fist and giving out a gleeful "Yalp," which the cable-canines proceeded to play endlessly at us, that "bizarre" rally incident obviously showing "unpresidential" and "emotionally unstable" behavior. Howard Dean, everybody chorused, had self-destructed. Thus, the big media's unified precaucus clucking was fully justified.

Except here is what CBS News reporter Eric Salzman, who was traveling with the Dean campaign, wrote soon afterward: "What you might not know, because it doesn't play 30 times a day on the cable news channels, is what was happening in the rest of the room. You don't see the visual and you don't hear the audio. The television crews recording the event plug into an audio source picking up Dean's microphone, not the sound of the room. The cameras focus in to a tight shot of the candidate, not the rest of the room.

"What you are not hearing is a room with thousands of people screaming and cheering.

"What you are not seeing are hundreds upon hundreds of American flags waving.

"What you are not hearing are members of the audience shouting out state names urging Dean to list more.

"What you are not seeing is the way Dean's supporters were lifted out of their slump by the speech.

"In a nutshell, you are not seeing that Dean's speech fit the tone of the room."[3]

After that, though, Dean's campaign was history. Maybe it's better that the media assassinated him rather than the powers-that-be sending out someone with a gun to do the same, which I was very afraid would happen as he was tapping into people's desperate desire for an honest and fearless man in the gang-land politics. . . . But to me, this was proof positive: Anything or anyone that the two gangs don't own or can't co-op, they'll sic their media dogs on to destroy.

As I mentioned above, the timing was personally interesting. In February 2003, I signed a three-year contract with MSNBC to host a talk show. Having recently decided not to run again for governor of Minnesota, I was still a pretty hot commodity. The show was originally scheduled for an hour, four nights a week. Soon after the deal was made, I was riding with MSNBC's then-president Erik Sorenson to start doing preliminary setup of the show out in L.A. Later, what he said came to haunt me. Right after I'd gotten hired,

Sorenson told me he'd gotten phone calls from two very high-ranking men in Washington. They wanted to know why MSNBC was giving me a national forum, and they clearly weren't pleased about this. I asked Sorenson to name names, but he said he couldn't.

They'd told me I'd have complete artistic control, but almost from the get-go, I had to tell the cable network that I hadn't been hired to read off a teleprompter. However, they wanted all the subjects and guests to be handed down from upstairs, and I started having to fight the brass on a daily basis. I wanted to do meat-and-potatoes journalism about things that impact people in the big picture—not tabloid stuff like they were feeding me. Before long, they'd scaled everything back; I'd go on once a week at 5:00 p.m. on Saturdays. In the worst possible time-slot, I still had the second-highest rated news-talk show on MSNBC, right after *Hardball*. I'd completed five shows when the network cancelled it and bought out my contract that December. "And so it goes," as Linda Ellerbee used to say (she got canned, too).

You think things have changed since Obama got elected? For starters, how about what's been happening to Rep. Ron Paul's campaign in 2012? (He hasn't screamed yet, but he sure ought to.) When the *Washington Post* saw fit to include Paul in its series of candidate profiles, the opening paragraph described Paul as "not the standard presidential candidate—he lacks the factory-built appearance of Mitt Romney or Rick Perry. He's thin, bony, a bantam rooster." Cock-a-doodle-who? A second *Post* piece went on to say: "Consider if Paul had the heftier, more serious bearing of a Romney or a Gingrich. Would he be so easy to dismiss? In the Darwinian world of public perception, it's easy to discount what you hear from someone who looks a little smaller, and perhaps a little weaker; especially when his voice tends to spiral into the upper registers."[4] Not enough of a manly man, eh? Or maybe stepping on too many big toes? Maybe another honest and fearless man not playing by gang rules. . . .

According to the *National Journal*, as of last December, "Paul is mentioned on air far less frequently than most of his rivals, including Bachmann and Texas Governor Rick Perry, both of whom trail him in national and state-level polls. And when pundits talk about him, they frequently do so in a far more negative tone. It is also true, as his campaign has asserted that Paul gets less time to air his views in debates."[5] Cable news channels, otherwise chomping at the bit, in Jon Stewart's words are "pretending Ron Paul doesn't exist."[6]

Even after his strong performances in Iowa and New Hampshire, the Pew Research Center's Project for Excellence in Journalism noted that mainstream media coverage of Paul went back to nearly zero—with less than 5 percent of all campaign stories focused on him toward the end of January, even as his poll numbers kept rising.[7] It was even worse in Florida, where Paul came in fourth in the primary while up against an almost total blackout of coverage in the state—appearing in less than 1 percent of print-based media, while Romney got 60 percent of the attention, Gingrich and Santorum receiving 20 percent each.[8]

Contrast this to how *Time Magazine* crowed about Rick Perry when he first entered the Rebloodlican race. "When you look at Perry, it's easy to picture him in an old Western. His late arrival in the primary field in August [2011] certainly felt like that moment when the big stranger steps through the swinging saloon doors and all heads pivot and the plinky-plunk piano dies away." The secret of Perry's appeal, *Time* also said, was that "he can cite job-creation statistics in Texas that are the envy of the nation's other 49 governors." The secret? Texas' unemployment rate is higher than that of 26 of the 50 states. And it's based on cheap labor, too. . . . But I guess envy comes cheap these days.[9]

❖ ❖ ❖

Not long ago, an interesting unsigned memo from 1970 surfaced at the Richard Nixon Presidential Library. It was titled "A Plan for Putting the GOP on TV News." "People are lazy," the fifteen-page plan began, which is why they got most of their news from TV where "the thinking is done for you." So how about creating a network "to provide pro-Administration, videotape, hard news actualities to the major cities of the United States." By going more local, you could avoid "the prejudices of network news selectors and disseminators." This was back in the day before cable and satellite channels dominated the news airwaves.

The thought was heartily endorsed as an "excellent idea" by Roger Ailes, then a top Rebloodlican media consultant. He responded to H.R. Haldeman that he'd like to get the gig, which at the time didn't get off the ground. But after he got fired by the White House, Ailes did start Television News Incorporated, with financing from right-wing beer-monger Joseph Coors, which turned out to be a trial run for the "fair and balanced" Fox News Channel that Ailes founded a quarter-century later in 1996.[10]

So I guess we have Nixon to thank for helping launch what we have today. Make no waves and keep the status quo afloat: If you buck that tide, you're in deep shit with the media barons.

Let's make it clear whom we're talking about. The roster isn't all that big; in fact:

> The U.S. media landscape is dominated by massive corporations that, through a history of mergers and acquisitions, have concentrated their control over what we see, hear and read. In many cases, these giant companies are vertically integrated, controlling everything from initial production to final distribution.[11]

The "Big Six" in fact control *90 percent* of what we read, watch, or listen to. In 1983, fifty companies had that kind of control. Today, it's 232 media executives who basically run the programming of 277 million Americans. In 2010, the total revenues for the "Big Six" came to $275.9 billion.[12] (The political data below comes from www.opensecrets.org.)

- General Electric (GE) is at the top of the list, with revenues of $157 billion (2009), including 49 percent ownership in NBC, as well as big shares of Telemundo, Universal Pictures, Focus Features, plus 26 American TV stations and cable networks, including MSNBC, Bravo, and the Syfy Channel (formally the Sci-Fi Channel). Most recent figures show GE spent more than $26 million on lobbying. Back in 2000, they donated $1.1 million to the Bush campaign. Most recently, Romney has received $37,750 and Obama $30,493 from their equal opportunity PAC.

  When it came out last year that GE paid zero taxes in 2010 on its global profits of $14 billion, NBC didn't mention anything until the *Washington Post* started questioning. So *NBC Nightly News* gave GE's CEO, Jeffrey Immelt, a forum. His solution? "Immelt says that everyone should pay their fair share of taxes, including GE, and that the corporate tax code needs to be reformed to make it more competitive and eliminate loopholes."[13]

  Since Immelt happens to head up Obama's Jobs Council, maybe he could ask Barack to raise GE's taxes? That is, unless he's too busy moving the headquarters of GE's 115-year-old x-ray business to China. Since Immelt took over at the helm in 2001, GE has laid off 34,000 workers in the United States and added 25,000 jobs overseas.[14]

- Walt Disney ($36.3 billion revenues) owns ABC TV, ESPN, Disney Channel, A&E, Lifetime, 277 radio stations, music and book publishing companies, and production companies Touchstone, Miramax, Pixar Animation, and Walt Disney Pictures. According to the Center for Political Accountability in Washington, the Disney company is the worst among big U.S. corporations in terms of political transparency. Disney admitted funneling $3.6 million into state and local campaigns in Florida, home of Disney World, but "they aren't really interested in telling you who they're buying off or why."[15]

- News Corp. ($30.4 billion) owns Fox TV, *National Geographic*, *Wall Street Journal*, *New York Post*, *TV Guide*, and book publisher HarperCollins, along with production companies including 20th Century Fox, not to mention most of the British and Australian media. The mogul is Rupert Murdoch—Mr. Tabloid himself and phone-hacker extraordinaire. It might surprise you to know that News Corp. recently become an equal-opportunity giver—more than $50,000 to gang members on both sides of the aisle in June 2011 ($32,500 to Democrips and $20,000 to Rebloodlicans). They're both the same to Murdoch, who managed to avoid $875 million in U.S. taxes in 2010.[16]

- TimeWarner ($25.8 billion) is the biggest media conglomerate on the planet; its holdings including CNN, HBO, Cinemax, Cartoon Network, TBS, TNT, America OnLine, MapQuest, Moviefone, Warner Bros. Pictures, Castle Rock, and New Line Cinema, as well as more than 150 magazines including *Time*, *Sports Illustrated*, *Fortune*, and *People*. TimeWarner ranked eighth among corporations for donating to political gangs in 2008 ($624,618, including $64,312 to Obama).

- Viacom ($13.6 billion) owns MTV, Nickelodeon, VH1, BET, Comedy Central, Paramount Pictures, and more. In the past, 62 percent of its contributions went to Democrips. The 2012 PAC's $165,500 (as of February 2011) had given 43 percent to Democrips and 56 percent to Rebloodlicans.

- CBS ($13 billion) owns CBS TV, Showtime, Simon & Schuster publishers, 30 TV stations, and CBS Radio with its 130 stations. Supposedly, the company has cracked down on its contributions, but the PAC dished out $105,265 for 2012.

- Clear Channel Communications doesn't rank quite as high as those guys, but it owns more radio stations (1,200) than anybody else in the country. That's despite a ruling by the Federal Communications Commission (FCC) back in 1995 forbidding any single outfit to own more than forty, but I guess somebody's been looking the other way. Clear Channel's parent company, CC Media Holdings, boasts nearly $6 billion in annual revenue. Its website also says the overall Media and Entertainment arm reaches 238 million monthly listeners in the United States, while Clear Channel Outdoor "operates close to one million [billboard] displays in 45 countries across 5 continents."[17] Nearly 90 percent of its radio stations feature right-wing content, including syndicating the programs of Rush Limbaugh, Glenn Beck, and Sean Hannity.

After 9/11, the Clear Channel brass issued a list of 165 "lyrically questionable" songs that their stations might not want to play. That included everything recorded by Rage Against the Machine, and "Knockin' on Heaven's Door" by Bob Dylan and Guns N' Roses. Later, they took the Dixie Chicks off their playlists after the ladies said of George W. Bush, "We're ashamed the President of the United States is from Texas."

So who do you figure bought Clear Channel in November 2006, after the company announced its plans to go private: two private-equity firms, Thomas H. Lee Partners and Bain Capital Partners for $18.7 billion.[18] Lest we forget, Bain Capital was the outfit started by Mitt Romney, and from which he continues to profit handsomely as a mega-stock owner. Can we be that surprised at Rush Limbaugh chanting "right on, right on, right on" after "Mitt's Best Speech So Far" on January 12, 2012?[19] Rush still supported Gingrich, but I guess he was hedging his bets.

So there you have it, in case you were still wondering about whether you're getting "independent" unbiased fair and balanced news. But news isn't what makes the execs and the shareholders rich, it's . . . ADVERTISING, dummy! According to the *Fiscal Times*, "television advertising accounts for about 60 percent of all political spending. . . . Between primary races, national and state elections, political advertising is expected to reach $4.9 billion in 2012 . . . a

17 percent increase from then-record spending in 2008." Private TV companies, broadcasting on our so-called public airwaves, are expected to bag about $3 billion of that total from political ads this year. Keep in mind this is all the result of the *Citizens United* decision opening the door to unlimited corporate spending.

Buzzflash editor Mark Karlin says:

> What that means is that there is every reason for the mainstream media—particularly television—to underplay issues such as Citizens United. The increased flow of dollars to candidates means more profit for commercial television in election years. . . . Selling democracy to the highest bidder is a lucrative business for the mainstream media.[20]

So it's no surprise that the National Association of Broadcasters (NAB) is fighting hard against the new rules proposed by the FCC that would force TV and radio stations to post their public inspection files online. These include the "political files," which show how much these outfits are profiting from air time purchases of political ads. To cite just one example, for only the Florida Republican primary in February, Romney spent $15.6 million and Gingrich $3.3 million on advertising.

A group called MapLight has analyzed the campaign contributions made by interest groups representing TV and radio stations that are benefiting financially from these political ads. Members of the Senate, for a six-year period starting in summer 2005, got $2,043,666 from the interest groups, including $383,423 from the NAB and its employees. Members of the U.S. House got $1,495,325 from the same groups, with the NAB throwing in $549,450 of that.[21] Just in case anybody was seriously thinking about changing the rules of the game.

Once upon a time, broadcasting over public airwaves meant that they had to serve the public interest. But since the gangs believe that *they are* the public, all the media really serves is gang interest.

❖ ❖ ❖

I know I've already offered quite a few "history lessons" in this book, but this is one I think is quite important. Back in 1735, on the main floor of New York's City Hall, an indictment was filed against John Peter Zenger, a German-born printer and publisher of the newspaper *New York Weekly Journal*. Zenger stood charged with libelous sedition against New York's colonial governor, William Cosby, after having printed editorials speaking out against the governor's corrupt practices and abuse of power. Zenger had already spent eight months in jail. After a failed attempt at jury tampering by the governor, the trial went forward. Zenger was called "a seditious person and a frequent printer and publisher of false news and seditious libels."

Zenger's lawyer, Andrew Hamilton, didn't have a legal leg to stand on: At that time under British law, *the truth could not be used to defend a charge of libel!* A person could be convicted of slander or libel, even if what he said was the absolute truth! But Hamilton put forth a powerful defense, saying:

> It is natural, it is a privilege, I will go farther, it is a right, which all free men claim, that they are entitled to complain when they are hurt. They have a right publicly to remonstrate against the abuses of power in the strongest terms, to put their neighbors upon their guard against the craft or open violence of men in authority, and to assert with courage the sense they have of the blessings of liberty, the value they put upon it, and their resolution at all hazards to preserve it as one of the greatest blessings heaven can bestow.

The jury returned with a verdict of "not guilty" for Zenger, followed by shouts of joy from the courtroom. It was the birth of freedom of the press.

The press is supposed to critique our political leaders. That's the main reason the founding fathers gave us a free press when the very first Congress of the United States debated the Bill of Rights.

It's the media's *job* to help keep politicians honest and their actions transparent. But our media today are accountable to no one—except the two gangs they promote and whose interests they serve. It seems that the more arrogant they get, the higher their ratings go. They've got no incentive to report reliable, unbiased news. The profits are just too good.

Today's journalists love to portray every story as a battle, because that's what gets the public's attention. Look how often the headlines describe two opposing viewpoints as a "war." They did that with me and Ross Perot: "Venturans vs. Perotbots: Open War in Reform Party!" was one headline. Come on! I wasn't at war with the man. We disagreed on some aspects of the Reform Party platform; but instead of debating the merits of each of our positions, which would have been helpful, this reporter chose to make it sound like Perot and I were dukes-up in some stupid clash of egos.

This is a dangerous game, and the media plays it all the time. In order to create a war, you need two opposing sides, right? So in the name of presenting "both" sides, they go looking for an opponent. It's almost comical to watch a TV debate and see two people who basically agree look blankly into the cameras fumbling for strong words against the other. Or two "angry" pundits who moments earlier were shouting over each other, chatting cozily while the credits are rolling. For the media to present them as mortal enemies spouting no-holds-barred jargon, when they're in the same game, is disingenuous at best; theater of the absurd at worst. It really is just a game.

The two-gang war has become standard practice, but who says there are only two sides to every issue? Who says that every issue even has another side? Not every viewpoint is equal, but when the media go looking to match up every newsworthy figure or issue with an opponent, they can make it seem as though they are. When you pit so-and-so versus such-and-such, as you do in a wrestling ring, it's implied that the two opponents are a fair match; but I'm here to tell you it ain't necessarily so.

The media's turning every story into a fight has got to frustrate the hell out of many of our public officials, because they can't get their information across without it being twisted into a stupid showdown. Due to this nonsense, the media is ultimately dumbing-down the American public, because when we're getting it reinforced to us day in and day out that there are only two sides (the Democrips and Rebloodlicans) to every story, after awhile we start to believe it. We begin to assume that the issues really are as cut-and-dry as the media tell us. You're either with us or against us. When it comes to politics and choosing our leaders, we stop remembering that there can be many points of view, and they aren't necessarily represented by just a two-party system. We get caught up in paying attention only to those who are wearing gang colors (red or blue) and flashing gang signs. Instead of thinking for ourselves, we wait for all those big shiny graphics to tell us immediately whose "side" someone is on.

Did you ever consider that this whole "fight club" which puts us all into a war zone mentality might ultimately be serving the interest of the *real* warmongers? It's a long-established idea that war is good for the economy . . . at least if you come out a winner, like we did in World War II. Not so much when billions get poured into rat hole wars like Iraq. But *somebody* is making a financial killing, right? Not just the weapons contractors but, in recent times, the private mercenary forces like Blackwater (now XE).

And what are we looking at in 2012? The "threat" from Iran is rampant among the same big media who trumpeted about Iraq's weapons of mass destruction (WMDs), except that phrase seems to have gone out of style (maybe due to the fact that it was a blatant lie). Turn back the clock a moment to 2003. That was when the *New York Times* did a series of page-one stories about Iraq's purported arsenal. One source was an unnamed Iraqi scientist who supposedly "led Americans to a supply of material that proved to be the building blocks of illegal weapons, which he claimed to have buried. . . ." The same person allegedly explained Iraq's ties to al-Qaeda and its efforts to ship WMDs to Syria. The only problem was, correspondent Judith Miller, who reported this information, never actually interviewed the scientist, and she cleared her copy with the military before publishing the story! Most of the *Times'* "exclusives" were provided by Ahmed Chalabi, an opponent of Saddam Hussein whose credibility has since turned out to be almost zero.[22]

The "liberal" *Times* was cheerleading for the Bush Administration to invade, and there's no doubt about that. Here is one of their top columnists, Thomas Friedman, saying to Charlie Rose soon after we toppled Saddam that it was "unquestionably worth doing," because we were hitting the "terrorist bubble" and "needed to go over there and take out a very big stick." Friedman went on to say:

> What they needed to see was American boys and girls going house to house, from Basra to Baghdad, and basically saying: "What part of this sentence don't you understand? You don't think, you know we care about our open society, you think this bubble fantasy, we're just gonna let it grow? Well, suck. On. This." That, Charlie, is what this war is about. We could have hit Saudi Arabia; it was part of that bubble. Could have hit Pakistan. We hit Iraq because we could.

Wow, a rare bit of gobbledygook insider candor from the can-do crowd. A house-to-house, suck-on-this democracy crusade! That was May 30, 2003, and you can look that quote up. Brought to you by another of our American Chickenhawks . . . just like Cheney and Bush. Now let's cut to December 21, 2011, and a Friedman column that bites the bullet while rewriting his own sorry history:

> Iraq was always a war of choice. As I never bought the argument that Saddam had nukes that had to be taken out the decision to go to war stemmed, for me, from a different choice: Could we collaborate with the people of Iraq to change the political

trajectory of this pivotal state in the heart of the Arab world and help tilt it and the region onto a democratizing track? But was it a wise choice? My answer is twofold: No and Maybe, sort of, we'll see.[23]

No more sucking up for some suckers, I guess. But now, heeeeere's Iran! In two articles that both ran on January 15, 2012, the *New York Times* misled its readers about what was going on with Iran's nuclear program. On the front page was this statement: "The threats from Iran, aimed both at the West and at Israel, combined with a recent assessment by the International Atomic Energy Agency [IAEA] that Iran's nuclear program has a military objective, is becoming an important issue in the American presidential campaign."

Well, it turns out that the IAEA never did any such assessment. They did raise questions —most of them years old—that outside analysts then challenged. But truth be told, the IAEA report "noted that its inspections of Iran's facilities continue to show no diversion of uranium for military purposes" and came to no conclusions like the *Times* was claiming. End result was, the *Times* changed the Web version of its article and removed that paragraph but never admitted the reporter had been mistaken. Another piece maintained that if the United States and Europe imposed an oil embargo on Iran to head off their development of nukes, Iranian officials had said they'd blockade the Strait of Hormuz. "Again, Iran has said repeatedly and emphatically that they are doing no such thing."[24]

They do have a right—according to the Non-Proliferation Treaty—to process uranium to levels of peaceful use, as long as they allow IAEA inspections. . . . Which is exactly what is happening now. They are enriching uranium to 35 percent—peaceful levels—while 95 percent is necessary for weaponry; so why the rush to war???

The *Times* wasn't alone in wrongly ballyhooing what the IAEA report had concluded. Here is a quote from Diane Sawyer on ABC World News: "And now, a long-dreaded headline about Iran and nuclear weapons. After a decade of debating whether Iran would build one, a UN report says tonight they will, and it has begun."

Here was Scott Pelley on CBS Evening News: "Iran is on the threshold of being able to build a nuclear bomb."

Here was NBC's Today Show: "UN reported for the first time Tuesday that Iran is conducting secret tests with the sole purpose of building nuclear weapons."

A *Washington Post* editorial said the IAEA report "ought to end serious debate about whether Tehran's program is for peaceful purposes."

And on and on: "Red Alert over Iran's Secret Nuke Program," headlined *USA Today*, the hype about "red alert" coming from U.S. Rep. Ed Royce, California Rebloodlican and Chairman of the congressional Subcommittee on Terrorism, Nonproliferation, and Trade.[25]

Excuse my French, but what the fuck!? What's the source behind all the misinformation? It couldn't be the report itself, so could it be somebody pushing for us to do to Iran what we did to Iraq (or worse)? Have we learned *nothing* from that debacle? Does anyone realize that Iran is a much larger and more unified country than Iraq—where our "liberation" was of course so easy and successful.

As Matt Taibbi of *Rolling Stone* pointed out,

> our newspapers and TV stations may blather on a thousand times a day about attacking Iran and bombing its people, but if even one Iranian talks about fighting back, he is being "aggressive" and "threatening;" we can impose sanctions on anyone, but if the sanctioned country embargoes oil shipments to Europe in response, it's being "belligerent" ... now the [American] public openly embraces circular thinking like, "Any country that squawks when we threaten to bomb it is a threat that needs to be wiped out."[26]

Just to make sure the big media are fully prepared for their next "in-bedded" assignment, in February retired four-star General Barry McCaffrey did a PowerPoint seminar for about twenty NBC execs and producers that got leaked to the news website Salon. It was called "Iran, Nukes & Oil: The Gulf Confrontation," where Mc-Caffrey said "they will not under any circumstances actually be deterred from going nuclear" and Israel has a "threat to their survival looming in their very near future." Be prepared, be very prepared, went the message.

McCaffrey is still on board at NBC News as an "objective analyst." He's also one of the retired generals who've been part of a Pentagon propaganda program for some time, though viewers are never informed about that little nugget. Back in 2009, a *New York Times* reporter, David Barstow, won a Pulitzer for a two-part series on how the networks utilize these guys. McCaffrey seems to have had his own military-industrial media complex and "consistently advocated wartime policies and spending priorities that are in line with his corporate interests. . . . He is held out as a dispassionate expert, not someone who helps companies win contracts related to the wars he discusses on television."

Of course, NBC News never mentioned this story, even though anchor Brian Williams reported on other Pulitzers that year. But just in case anybody at the network had second thoughts, McCaffrey pointed out on the last page of his recent presentation, "The accompanying chart showed that 78 percent of Americans have faith in the military—by far the most admired institution in America—but near the bottom was 'television news,'" at 28 percent. Subliminal message: Push the Pentagon line, and your faith ratings will go up.[27]

❖ ❖ ❖

So how is coverage of the big political year coming along? Foxily fair and balanced? Here's one that takes the cake. The *New York Times* fessed up in December 2011 concerning a story it ran about Newt Gingrich. The piece had quoted an anonymous "senior aide in the Gingrich campaign," who elaborately refuted criticisms of Gingrich as "untrustworthy and unprincipled" made by Romney supporter John Sununu. The envelope, please. The source was . . . "actually Mr. Gingrich, who did not want to be identified to avoid the impression he was getting into a fight with the Romney camp."[28] Obviously a trustworthy and principled fellow, not to mention the newspaper reporter involved.

Sometimes it gets hard to tell the difference between campaign journalism and campaign advertising. Take the *Washington Post*'s profile of Mitt Romney in its series on the Rebloodlican candidates last December. It was headlined: "The Problem Solver: Mitt Romney doesn't want to talk about feeling voters' pain. He just wants to get to work relieving it." Reporter Ann Gerhart went on to inform readers that "Romney is Dudley Do-Right in a Kim Kardashian world." Here was "a man with a prodigious intellect who has been married to his high school sweetheart for 42 years, donates 10 percent of his money to his church (a considerable sum, as his self-made fortune is upward of $250 million) and, those close to him say, acts generously, earns the loyalty of his staff, and drives himself relentlessly to get the job done, whatever it is." In service of his "overriding philosophy about caring for people" (the quote was from Romney's own brother!), the candidate's "flip-floppery could be interpreted as a flexibility of thinking that might help him burst through warring ideologies in Washington."[29] Funny that they now mentioned flip-flopping as a good thing, while they blasted John Kerry for the very same.

Romney Romney, he's our man, if he can't do it, no one can! Could any propaganda be more blatant? Care we can believe in? In what he's called his "former life" with the Bain Capital private equity outfit, Romney claims to have "helped create over 100,000 new jobs." But when he worked at Bain, as mentioned earlier, he was busy buying up and bankrupting companies, while laying off their workers. "Mr. Romney's claims about being a job creator would be nonsense even if he were being honest about the numbers, which he isn't," as columnist Paul Krugman put it.[30]

But it cuts both ways in terms of the two gangs. Glenn Greenwald summed things up on Salon:

> A presidential term is 48 months; that the political media is transfixed by campaign coverage for 18 months every cycle means that a President can wield power with substantially reduced media attention for more than ⅓ of his term. Thus he [in this case, Obama] can wage a blatantly illegal war in Libya for months on end, work to keep U.S. troops in Iraq past his repeatedly touted deadline, scheme to cut Social Security and Medicare as wealth inequality explodes and thereby please the oligarchical base funding his campaign, use black sites in Somalia to interrogate Terrorist suspects, all while his Party's Chairwoman works literally to destroy Internet privacy—all with virtually no attention paid . . . the media coverage all but ignores even these pretenses of policy positions in lieu of vapid, trite, conventional-wisdom horse-race coverage—who will be the next American Idol?[31]

Or the last Survivor . . . ?

When it comes to pushing something *outside* the mainstream, things get more than a little insidious. Consider media coverage of the Tea Party. Of course, the origins of the Tea Party did represent a real populist movement of folks who were angry that the gangster parties were spending billions of dollars bailing out the banksters who got us into this whole financial mess. We've already looked at how it's being bankrolled by the billionaire Koch brothers and their ilk. Once they were co-opted by the Rebloodlicans, they became media darlings.

We've also seen how the name came straight from a rant by CNBC's Rick Santelli, who was enraged about the home loan modification programs by the Obama White House. ("It's time for another tea party," the commentator said.) Then came the anti-tax protests and the angry citizens denouncing Obama's health care plans at town hall meetings in the summer of 2009. Even though most of the latter gatherings weren't large, the cable news channels religiously covered them. Next up was Scott Brown's surprising victory in the special election for Ted Kennedy's Senate seat, which the *New York Times* called "the coming of age of the Tea Party movement"—despite its supporters having nothing much to do with Brown's ascension.

The corporate media built up this so-called "populist" movement like gang-busters. (Would that they had been, instead of being bamboozled by some of the richest gangsters of all.) Did you see this kind of coverage with the huge anti-war protests before we invaded Iraq? No, those were pretty much greeted with flat-out hostility; but when Sarah Palin came to keynote the Nashville Tea Party convention in February 2010, with about 600 people in attendance, the press turned out in droves. David Broder of the *Washington Post* described Palin's speech as offering "pitch-perfect populism." The *New York Times'* David Carr opined that if her supposedly broad appeal wasn't appreciated enough by the likes of his paper, "maybe we deserve the 'lamestream media' label she likes to give us."

What the media didn't say much about were the racist signs— "Obama's Plan: White Slavery"—and the Confederate flags at a lot of the Tea Party events. At the Nashville convention, anti-immigrant spokesman Tom Tancredo said of the 2008 election: "Something really odd happened, mostly because we do not have a civics literacy test before people can vote in this country. People who could not even spell the word 'vote' or say it in English put a committed socialist ideologue in the White House. His name is Barrack Hussein Obama."

You already know that I'm not a fan of what Obama has done in office, but this is outrageous! The fact is that most people had no idea what the Tea Party really stood for or who was behind it. But the *Washington Post* assigned a reporter to "make sure the movement's covered fully in its pages."[32] Then came the real coup d'tea: In September 2011, CNN teamed up with the Tea Party Express and a hundred local Tea Party groups to stage a "first-of-its-kind debate" among Rebloodlican candidates from the site of its

2012 convention in Tampa Bay. Gee, I don't recall any such "media event" happening with the Occupy Wall Streeters; but the Tea Party movement, according to CNN political director Sam Feist, was "a fascinating, diverse grassroots force." So "topics for the debate will be tailored for the interests of this political insurgent movement."

Nobody saw fit to mention that the former Tea Party Express chairman, Mark Williams, was a "birther" who'd called Obama an "Indonesian Muslim turned welfare thug and a racist-in-chief." After the NAACP complained about Tea Party racism, Williams had posted a "satirical" letter from "We Colored People" to Abraham Lincoln including this sample "joke": "How will we coloreds ever get a wide screen TV in every room if non-coloreds get to keep what they earned?" The Express then got kicked out of the National Tea Party Federation, and Williams got replaced by a female "birther," Amy Kremer—who'd leapt to the defense of "a fellow Tea Partier after he sent out racist emails depicting President Obama as a witch doctor." She was still running the Express when CNN partnered up.[33]

Coverage of Occupy Wall Street (OWS) is a whole other story. Case in point: Erin Burnett last fall moved over from CNBC to CNN with a new show called *OutFront*. She'd gone down there "to see those protests for myself. I saw dancing, bongo drums, even a clown . . . I asked several protesters what it was that they wanted. Now, they did not know. . . . They did know what they don't want. . . . It seems like people want a messiah leader, just like they did when they anointed Barack Obama."

So Miz Burnett tried pointing out to the protesters that "taxpayers actually made money on the Wall Street bailout," which is more than a stretch. Duh, the Wall Street giants made out like bandits, the unemployment and foreclosure crises continued, and AIG never paid us back their many billions. This is why OWS is happening, among many other reasons. But Erin Burnett, in fact, "used to work for the same financial companies that profited from the bailouts— Goldman Sachs, Citigroup—and she is engaged to be married to a

Citigroup executive."[34] That's why she's the perfect commentator to be interviewing the OWS folks, of course.

National Public Radio at first declined to cover the story at all, with then-executive editor Dick Meyer explaining, "The recent protests on Wall Street did not involve large numbers of people, prominent people, a great disruption or an especially clear objective." When the worldwide demonstrations happened on October 15, the *Washington Post* directed readers to page A20 for news about protests in "more than 900 cities in Europe, Africa and Asia." One of the paper's columnists, Charles Krauthammer, called our American variety "Starbucks-sipping, Levi's-clad, iPhone-clutching protesters [who] denounce corporate America even as they weep for Steve Jobs." Another one, Richard Cohen, called OWS "above all, a conspiracy to have left-leaning writers make jackasses of themselves by imparting grave and grand meaning to what is little more than a vast sleepover." And this is the same paper that brought us Woodward and Bernstein to uncover Watergate? (Of course, both of those guys have since become war-loving neo-cons.)

Not to be out-foxed, the *New York Times'* Ginia Bellafante told readers she'd discovered "a default ambassador in a half-naked woman . . . with a marked likeness to Joni Mitchell and a seemingly even stronger wish to burrow through the space-time continuum and hunker down in 1968." The movement's cause, she went on, "was virtually impossible to decipher . . . [with] lack of cohesion and its apparent wish to pantomime progressivism rather than practice it knowledgeably." And who knows more about grassroots "progressive" activism than the *Times*, after all?[35]

If my jaw dropped when *Time Magazine* named "The Protester" its Person of the Year for 2011, I regained composure when I saw who their runner-up was: Rebloodlican "seer" and deficit slasher Paul Ryan from Wisconsin. His "tough budget" had "brought President Obama down from his cloud of happy talk about windmills and high-speed trains to acknowledge that America has a plateful of peas to choke down after its binge at the dessert bar." Yup,

$4.3 trillion in budget cuts on social programs, offset by $4.2 trillion in tax cuts mainly for the top 1 percent. Let's see, that amounts to maybe a point-one reduction in the deficit over the coming years?[36] And the rich get richer . . .

Getting back to where this chapter opened, I've gotta hand it to MSNBC though. They did finally see fit to get rid of Pat Buchanan as a commentator. Here was a man who called for getting control of our borders before "Americans of European descent will be a minority in the nation their ancestors created and built"; who blamed the "Penn State thing" on the states that have sanctioned gay marriage; who said Poland and the United Kingdom had it coming in World War II for not negotiating with Nazi Germany, where Hitler was an individual of "great courage." Where is Glenn Beck now that we really need him?[37]

❖ ❖ ❖

The media's job is to report facts and events. I think they should leave opinions to the op-ed section. It's a principle of journalistic ethics to present a balanced perspective on the stories of the day. Journalists are supposed to go looking for more than one opinion on a given topic. But today's journalists have gotten hung up on the idea that stories are supposed to be "balanced" like a seesaw, not "balanced" like a nutritious diet.

Imagine the difference in news coverage if reporters followed the "nutritious diet" idea of a balanced news instead. You'd get a broad spectrum of views, from many angles and many voices. If they simply presented a range of views, instead of diametrically opposing the two most strident (within gangster limits) among them, they would leave us free to decide for ourselves the validity of each perspective.

The news media have no business trying to entertain us. What happened to the sober journalist, whose words had gravitas? We're distracted by scandal. It was one thing when it was a truly political scandal: Watergate spanned many breathtaking months with so many players it took a who's-who score card to keep up. But it seems that when the Monica Lewinsky mess sucked our hard-earned taxpayer money out of our pockets, it sucked our ability to distinguish between what's important and relevant and what's a distraction on the political landscape right out of our heads. All you have to do is type "hand signal" and "men's room" in Google, and up pops Larry Craig. Similarly, Anthony Wiener. Perhaps more seriously, John Edwards. We're too busy listening to moot debates about the President's birth certificate to pay attention to what's really going on. How many people really know what your senator or representative or governor is really up to if it's not a juicy scandal?

We can blame the media for many things, but in the end, we have only ourselves to blame for allowing our media to be dumbed down. We don't live in North Korea, where we would be required to have our televisions modified to receive only state-owned stations. We have a choice. The only reason the media can make a profit off the scandals they generate is that we provide them with an audience! What is the matter with us? Are we so desperate for entertainment that we have to go looking to the evening news for it? We need to take responsibilities for our choices. When we become passive consumers and allow them to do our thinking for us, we've agreed to let them lead us into any opinion they like. If we don't speak up and tell them to knock it off, what's their incentive to stop?

NOTES

1. James Alexander quote: www.law.umkc.edu/faculty/projects/ftrials/zenger/zengeraccount.html. ("The Trial of John Peter Zenger: An Account" by Bruce Linder, 2001.)

2. Podvin, David. "The Scream." http://rabbit-hole-journey.blogspot.com/2007/11/truth-about-howard-dean-scream-and.html.

3. Salzman, Eric. "Dean's Scream: Not What It Seemed." www.cbsnews.com.

4. Hart, Peter. "Why WaPo Won't Cover Ron Paul: He Looks Funny, Sounds Funny." December 15, 2011, www.fair.org.

5. Naureckas, Jim. "Ron Paul Has NOT Been Ignored by Media—Except, Well, Yes He Has." December 22, 2011, www.fair.org.

6. Jon Stewart: Sanneh, Kelefa. "Party Crasher." *New Yorker*, February 27, 2012.

7. "The Ron Paul Media Blackout Is Back On." www.theatlanticwire.com/politics/2012/01.

8. "Study reveals almost complete Ron Paul media blackout in Florida." Melina Mara/*Associated Press*.

9. *Time Magazine* on Rick Perry: "2011 P.U.-litzers: Journalism That Doesn't Pass the Smell Test." December 22, 2011, www.fair.org.

10. Cook, John. "Roger Ailes' Secret Nixon-Era Blueprint for Fox News." June 30, 2011, http://gawker.com/5814150.

11. "Ownership Chart: The Big Six." www.freepress.net/ownership/chart/main.

12. "Big Six": "Illusion of Choice." *NationofChange/Infographic*, February 21, 2012.

13. GE and taxes on NBC: "2011 P.U.-litzers," www.fair.org, December 22, 2011.

14. GE and jobs: http://theeconomiccollapseblog.com.

15. Disney lack of transparency: Minsky, David. "Walt Disney Doesn't Want You to Know Which Political Campaigns It's Paying For." October 28, 2011, http://blogs.miaminew.toimes.com/riptide/2011/10.

16. Murdoch and taxes: *NationofChange/Infographic*, February 21, 2012.

17. www.clearchannel.com.

18. Ibid.

19. www.rushlimbaugh.com.

20. *Fiscal Times* quote/Buzzflash: http://blogbuzzflash.com/node/13357.

21. Costa, Jay. "Not News: National Broadcasters Want to Hide Their Political Ad Profits." February 3, 2012, http://maplight.org.

22. "Troubles at the Times." June 10, 2003, www.fair.org/index.php?page=1856.

23. Thomas Friedman: Hart, Peter. "Tom Friedman Not Sucking It on Iraq War." December 21, 2011, www.fair.org.

24. "NYT Misleads Readers on Iran Crisis: Paper Disappears Some Inaccurate Reporting." January 6, 2012, www.fair.org.

25. "Iran, Nukes and the Failure of Skepticism." November 16, 2011, www.fair.org.

26. Taibbi, Matt. "Another March to War?" *Rolling Stone*, February 18, 2012.

27. Greenwald, Glenn. "Gen. McCaffrey privately briefs NBC execs on war with Iran." February 28, 2012, www.salon.com.

28. Hart, Peter. "Great Moments in Campaign Journalism." December 12, 2011, www.fair.org.

29. Hart, Peter. "Washington Post: Campaign Journalism or Campaign Advertising?" December 13, 2011, www.fair.org

30. Krugman, Paul. "Bain, Barack and Jobs." *New York Times*, January 6, 2012.

31. Greenwald, Glenn. "2012 Election? Or American Idol Reality TV Soap Opera?" Quoted on www.policymic.com.

32. Tea Party: Hart, Peter and Steve Renday. "At last a citizen movement corporate media can love." *Extra!*, May 2010, www.fair.org.

33. "CNN Throws a Tea Party." September 12, 2011, www.fair.org.

34. Erin Burnett's ties to finance: *Business Insider*, September 30, 2011; show quotes in "CNN's Factcheck Failure on Occupy Wall Street," October 4, 2011, www.fair.org.

35. NPR, *Washington Post*, and *New York Times*: "Occupy the P.U.-litzers!." December 27, 2011, www.fair.org.

36. Hart, Peter. "Time Paints Paul Ryan as Deficit-Slashing Superhero." December 15, 2011, www.fair.org.

37. Peck, Adam. "Why MSNBC Dumped Pat Buchanan: His 10 Most Outrageous Statements." *ThinkProgress*, February 18, 2012, at www.alternet .org.

CHAPTER FOURTEEN

THE DEVILISH MARRIAGE
OF CHURCH AND STATE

I contemplate with sovereign reverence that act of the whole American people which declared that their "legislature" should "make no law respecting an establishment of religion, or prohibiting the free exercise thereof," thus building a wall of separation between church and state.

—Thomas Jefferson, 1802 letter to the Danbury Baptists

Not long after I became governor of Minnesota in 1999, I got in a whole lot of hot water with certain politicians and media types for saying in an interview with *Playboy*: "Organized religion is a sham and a crutch for weak-minded people who need strength in numbers. It tells people to go out and stick their noses in other people's business. . . . The religious right wants to tell people how to live."

Later I clarified my comments. I said that I don't have any problem with the vast majority of religious folks, though I now consider myself an agnostic. I don't believe in a "Supreme Being" that overlooks everything and that we must pay homage to. There are lots of people out there who think they know the truth about God and religion, but does anybody really know for sure? I'm still proud of

209

the fact that I was the only governor who wouldn't declare National Prayer Day. Why do you need government to tell you to pray? That's not the government's job. It's called separation of church and state! That's why the founding fathers built freedom of religious belief into the structure of this nation, so that people could make up their minds for themselves. Of course, both the political gangs are always wearing their religious beliefs on their sleeves and throwing them down like a gauntlet. I have a big problem with the people who think they have some right to try to impose their beliefs on others.

I hate what the fundamentalist fanatics are doing to our country. It seems as though if everybody doesn't accept their version of reality, their beliefs are somehow invalidated. Everybody must believe the same things they do. That's what I find weak and destructive. They seem to me to be a lot like the Muslim fundamentalists they hate so much. They are always trying to tell other people what they should be doing and not doing—especially women. They're Christianists instead of Islamists, with their own petty jihads and enforced morality.

Since I first talked publicly about this more than a decade ago, we've seen Christianism become part of our "body politic" in ways even I hadn't imagined possible. This caused me to say flat-out on CNN in October 2010, "Religion is the root of all evil." This has become pretty damned clear since 9/11, with fanatics on both sides envisioning a "holy war" between Christians and Muslims. Does anybody remember John Adams signing the Treaty with Tripoli in 1797 and assuring the Muslim nation that "the Government of the United States of America is not, in any sense, founded on the Christian religion"?

Students of our colonial history might recall the name of Roger Williams, a Puritan preacher from Massachusetts. When he heard about the British General Court's plan to force everybody in the colony to take a loyalty pledge to the governor ending with "So help me, God," Williams hit the roof, publicly declaring how dangerous it was to force people to swear a religious oath. Williams was found guilty of "disseminating new and dangerous opinions" and ordered to head back to England. Instead, he went into the wilderness, bought land from some Native peoples, and set up a new settlement he called Providence. Today, it's the capital of Rhode Island. "Forced religion stinks in the nostrils of God," Williams said—and penned a warning about opening up "a gap in the hedge, or wall of separation, between the garden of the church and the wilderness of the world."[1] This prefigured Jefferson's words by 150 years!

No, the precise phrase "separation of church and state" doesn't appear in the Constitution, but that doesn't mean the idea isn't there loud and clear. Article VI specifically states that "no religious test shall ever be required as a qualification to any office or public trust under the United States." The Establishment Clause of the First Amendment asserts that "Congress shall make no law respecting an establishment of religion," which means no church *and* no religion could ever be construed as America's "official faith." And the Free Exercise Clause states that Congress can't make any laws "prohibiting the free exercise" of religion.

By design of the founders, there is not a single reference to God in the entire Constitution. They didn't want government interfering with the choices people made about who, what, how, and where they worshipped. Thomas Jefferson once even "took a pair of scissors to the Christian New Testament and cut out every passage that suggested a divine origin and mission for Jesus."[2] That'd be blasphemy (if not cause for stoning) to a lot of today's bible-toting Crusader Rabbits.

Here's what James Madison wrote in 1785, in his *Memorial and Remonstrance Against Religious Assessments*: "Who does not see that the same authority which can establish Christianity, in exclusion of all other Religions, may establish with the same ease any particular sect of Christians, in exclusion of all other sects?" Government involvement with the church, Madison also wrote, "implies either that the civil magistrate is a competent judge of religious truth; or that he may employ religion as an engine of civil policy. The first is an arrogant pretension falsified by the contradictory opinions of rulers in all ages, and throughout the world: the second an unhallowed perversion of the means of salvation."[3]

John Leland, a Baptist minister, worked alongside Jefferson and Madison to put an end to the state church in Virginia, and he did the same thing in Massachusetts and Connecticut. "Government has no more to do with the religious opinions of men than it has with the principles of mathematics," Leland sermonized in 1791. "Let every man speak freely without fear, maintain the principles that he believes, worship according to his own faith; either one God, three Gods, no God, or twenty Gods, and let government protect him in so doing." He was a big admirer of Jefferson's unwillingness to mix religion with government. "Guard against those men who make a great noise about religion in choosing representatives," he told his parishioners. "It is electioneering intrigue."[4]

So I feel like I'm in good company and on pretty solid ground with what I've had to say about the situation. In this chapter, I want to delve into how close we are today to becoming a theocracy—defined as "a government ruled by or subject to religious authority," which several of the Rebloodlican presidential candidates would be only too happy to see happen.

❖ ❖ ❖

Among the theo-candidates, first there was Newt Gingrich, who wrote a book called *Rediscovering God in America*, where he posits that our nation's greatness is directly related to a divinely-sanctioned American exceptionalism. The Newt has said that, when it comes to judicial rulings, he'd ignore the ones he doesn't agree with and get rid of courts altogether in some instances, especially when it comes to church-and-state problems.

According to Mitt Romney, since he became a front runner for the nomination, life begins "at conception," and he'd like to see that enshrined in the Constitution. Consider that his new debate coach is the same dude who taught the Jerry Falwell-funded law students at Liberty University about following God's law instead of man's. Maybe that's why, at the GOP debate in Florida, Romney called the Declaration of Independence a theological document that creates a covenant "between God and man." After all, Romney—"a seventh-generation direct descendant of one of the [Mormon] faith's 12 apostles"—was singled out as a Michigan teenager (and son of the then-governor) as having great expectations from the Lord.

A bit more history, if you'll allow me: The founder of the Church of Jesus Christ of Latter-day Saints, Joseph Smith Jr., ran for president back in 1844 "as an independent commander in chief of an 'army of God' advocating the overthrow of the U.S. government in favor of a Mormon-ruled theocracy. . . . He had predicted the emergence of 'the one Mighty and Strong'—a leader who would 'set in order the house of God.'" Smith didn't get too far, being murdered by anti-Mormon vigilantes, but what his church called the "White Horse Prophecy" got passed down through the generations—"that the day would come when the U.S. Constitution would 'hang like a thread as fine as a silk fiber' and the Mormon priesthood would save it."[5] That's the culture Romney came out of, and his fellow students at Brigham Young University are said to have only half jokingly called him the "One Mighty and Strong."

Today, the Mormon Church is one of the fastest-growing in the world, a multibillion-dollar business empire in which Romney is one of the richest members. He's been a missionary, a bishop, and a stake president—which is equivalent to being a Cardinal of the Roman Catholic Church. Investigative journalist Sally Denton writes:

> The seeds of Romney's unique brand of conservatism, often regarded with intense suspicion by most non-Mormon conservatives, were sown in the secretive, acquisitive, patriarchal, authoritarian religious empire run by "quorums" of men under

an umbrella consortium called the General Authorities. A creed unlike any other in the United States, from its inception Mormonism encouraged material prosperity and abundance as a measure of holy worth, and its strict system of tithing 10 percent of individual wealth has made the church one of the world's richest institutions.[6]

Then there's Rick Santorum. He comes from a Catholic background, and for at least a decade, his family has been part of a church called St. Catherine of Siena, which strangely he didn't choose to mention when he published his book in 2005, *It Takes a Family*, which is essentially his manifesto on personal faith and politics. "The church claims 3,400 parishioners. Supreme Court Justice Antonin Scalia and his wife attend Mass there; so have . . . the head of the National Rifle Association and former FBI Director Louis Freeh." The church sprung up in 1981 in Great Falls, Virginia, and the Santorums have been sometimes daily attendees. They were allowed to join, even though they lived outside of the district.

So who do you think St. Catherine's has connections to? No less than the Catholic conservative secret order known as Opus Dei. I know this may sound conspiratorial—and who knows, I might yet look into it for my TV show—but a lot of Opus Dei priests are said to hear confession at St. Catherine's. Unlike many of the churchgoers, Santorum has said he's not a member but only an "admirer" of Opus Dei, but he did journey to Rome in 2002 for the 100th birthday of the group's founder. That's where he first tossed out criticism of John F. Kennedy's "separation of church and state" speech in 1960.[7] More on that in a moment.

First, let's flash back to a speech Santorum made in 2008 to Catholic students at Ave Maria University in Florida. He began by saying that we're not in a political or cultural war, but in a:

Spiritual war. And the Father of Lies has his sights on . . . a good, decent, powerful, influential country—the United States of America. If you were Satan, who would you attack in this day and age.

There is no one else to go after other than the United States and that has been the case now for almost two hundred years, once America's preeminence was sown by our founding fathers.

I don't think Santorum has read Jefferson or Madison's views on religion anytime lately.

Eventually, he continued, "that great, acidic quality of time corrodes even the strongest foundations." And Satan had used "those great vices of pride, vanity, and sensuality" to attack America's great institutions. Academia had fallen a long time ago, followed by "mainline Protestantism [which] is in shambles, it is gone from the world of Christianity." (Not Catholicism, of course, that particular exclusive sect of the kind Madison referred to.) Next came "the corruption of culture" and "manners" and "decency." And now came politics and government.[8] Save us from our sins, Saint Sanctorum!

By the way, shortly before that speech, in a column Santorum wrote, "Would the potential attraction to Mormonism by simply having a Mormon in the White House threaten traditional Christianity by leading more Americans to a church that some Christians believe misleadingly calls itself Christian, is an active missionary church, and a dangerous cult?"[9] Hmmm, wonder which candidate he was talking about and who felt threatened?

Here are a few of the more recent Santorum statements, in case anybody thinks he's mellowed over the past four years.

- "The idea that the Crusades and the fight of Christendom against Islam is somehow an aggression on our part is absolutely anti-historical. . . . What I'm talking about is onward American soldiers. What we're talking about are core American values."[10]
- "The question is—and this is what Barack Obama doesn't want to answer—is that human life a person under the Constitution? And Barack Obama says no. Well if that person—human life is not a person, then—I find it almost remarkable

215

for a black man to say, 'We're going to decide who are people and who are not people.'"[11] (That was a bit garbled, Rick, but are black people persons?)

- "You know that statistic that at least I was familiar with from a few years ago—I don't know if it still holds true but I suspect it may even be worse—that 62 percent of kids who enter college with some sort of faith commitment leave without it. This is not a neutral setting."[12] (Down with higher ed!)

- Contraception is "not okay. It's a license to do things in a sexual realm that is counter to how things are supposed to be."[13] (Like Monty Python once said, "Every sperm is sacred.")

- "When you marginalize faith in America, when you remove the pillar of God-given rights, then what's left is the French Revolution. What's left is a government that will tell you who you are, what you'll do, and when you'll do it. What's left in France became the guillotine."[14]

Just which mushroom cloud Rick was on when he said that is unclear, but on his show, Stephen Colbert responded by holding up a banana with a condom wrapped around it . . . and guillotining it.

So how do Santorum's views translate into what the man would try to make happen if elected to the highest office in the country? He wants "a blanket ban on abortion," turning back the clock before 1973. He wants not only a ban on gay marriages but also a return to the anti-sodomy laws, equating consensual gay sex in one's home to bigamy, polygamy, incest, and adultery. As for Islam, it's a religion "stuck in the seventh century." In short, Santorum would like to see the U.S. become a "faith-based" Christian nation by imposing all the "family values" that he's decided come straight from God. (Sounds like his own seventh century religion.) He even quotes the Declaration of Independence for backup, that people "are endowed by their Creator with certain inalienable rights." So the role of government is just to make sure those divine rights are put in place and protected. I hardly think that's what Thomas Jefferson intended, who wasn't even a Christian but a Deist who emphasized morality and didn't see God being directly involved with humankind.[15] But Santorum pulls the Constitution out of his hat, too: "This is about a country that believes in God-given rights, and a Constitution that is limited to protect those rights."

❖ ❖ ❖

The founders are likely turning over in their graves at some of the shenanigans over "God-given rights" this year. First there was the big cancer charity, Susan G. Komen for the Cure, pulling its funding of cancer screenings from Planned Parenthood because the women's health group was being investigated by Rebloodlican Congress members for supposedly using federal money toward providing abortions. Planned Parenthood, which gets about $300 million a year from the feds to provide health services and family planning to the poor, has been in the crosshairs of Religious Right politicos for a long time. Led by Congressman Mike Pence, there's been a drive to de-fund the organization as part of "addressing" the budget deficit.[16]

Anyway, three days after the Komen Foundation outraged women across America by its move, the organization changed its tune and reinstated the funding.[17] Turned out that a leading Foundation strategist on Planned Parenthood was Ari Fleischer, who used to be George W. Bush's press secretary and is close friends with Komen's CEO Nancy Brinker. Fleischer has been an outspoken critic of Planned Parenthood for years, and he ended up getting paid to interview Komen's candidates for Senior Vice President for Communications. [18]

Komen's reversal didn't stop Romney from coming out and saying that not only the Foundation but also the government should stop giving Planned Parenthood money. "Look, the idea that we're subsidizing an institution which is providing abortion, in my view, is wrong." (Evidence, Mitt?) "Planned Parenthood ought to stand on their own two feet and should not get government subsidy. I am a pro-life individual—I was a pro-life governor (served as a pro-life governor)—I'm a pro-life candidate. I simply do not want to participate in anything that takes away the life of an unborn child." This, like an Obama spokeswoman said, was "the ultimate hypocrisy." That's because Romney, who once attended a Planned Parenthood fundraiser, supported the same birth control policy that the Obama Administration does, when he was Massachusetts' governor. Abortion rights are one of his bigger flip-flops.[19]

Komen's change of mind didn't stop the House from passing a bill to strip all federal funding from Planned Parenthood on February 17, and we'll see where it goes from there in the future. That same month, things went from bad to worse when the House Oversight Committee's Chairman, Rep. Darrell Issa, prevented a female witness from giving testimony at a hearing that was "examining the Obama administration's new regulation requiring employers and insurers to provide contraception coverage to their employees." Issa said that the hearing was actually about infringement on "religious liberty," with the first panel of witnesses consisting only of male religious leaders who opposed the rule. Two Democratic female reps walked out of the room in protest.

Joe Lieberman, who ought to be nominated for the Self-Righteous Hypocrite Award, came down with the Rebloodlicans, tweeting that "Government should not compel religious organizations to provide services to their beliefs." Sometimes, you have to wonder if the man who Al Gore would have had as his vice president fell victim to the CIA's MKULTRA mind control program or its latest iteration. John Hagee, the Texas pastor who heads up Global Evangelism Television, has been a major supporter of hard-line Zionists and once opined that Hitler had been sent by God to get "the Jewish people" to "come back to the land of Israel." When some of those "Jewish people" took offense, Lieberman said Hagee's remarks were taken "out of context." After all, Jumpin' Jehosophat Joe had spoken at the pastor's Washington-Israel Summit and compared Hagee to Moses.

But I digress.

Santorum was in a snit on the campaign trail and called Obama "hostile to people of faith, particularly Christians, and specifically Catholics." He didn't happen to mention that a lot of Catholic hospitals and universities already offer contraceptive coverage as part of their health insurance. Romney, whose Mormon church explicitly says birth control is okay, got his digs in also, saying Obama is looking to "impose a secular vision on Americans who believe that they should not have their religious freedom taken away."[20] Puh-leeze, but here came Foster Friess—the billionaire mega-donor to Santorum's Super PAC—with an answer on MSNBC. "Back in my day, they used Bayer Aspirin for contraceptives. The gals put it between their knees and it wasn't that costly," Friess told Andrea Mitchell.[21]

Then along came Rebloodlican Senator Roy Blunt from Missouri, who proposed that any employer could object on moral grounds to deny any employee insurance coverage. In other words, if a boss believed that AIDS is the Good Lord's punishment for immoral behavior, he could cut off to AIDS victims those very expensive insured benefits. The argument goes that any government "interference" along these lines goes against the First Amendment, right in line with Issa and Lieberman. The Senate rejected Blunt's plan by only three votes.[22]

What in God's name are they trying to do to the women of this country? House Rebloodlicans passed one bill that would let hospitals receiving federal funds deny their patients access to abortion procedures, even if these were needed to save a woman's life! In another bill trying to end taxpayer funding for abortions, they're looking to redefine rape as "forcible rape" only—excluding statutory rape, or women who've been drugged or threatened verbally, from being allowed abortions.

The Virginia legislature passed a bill that would force women to undergo an invasive ultrasound before they could have an abortion, until a citizen outcry forced the governor to think twice about signing it. Altogether, sixty-nine anti-choice measures were voted into law in twenty-five states in 2011, some of these aimed at forcing abortion clinics to close.[23] A state legislator in North Carolina thinks that doctors who do abortions ought to be publicly hanged, along with rapists and kidnappers. And "fundamentalists in state legislators are trying to get legal personhood status to the unborn 'from the moment of conception,' however that would be determined. This would enable birth control, abortion and even in vitro fertilization to be criminalized."[24]

The president of the Family Research Council, Tony Perkins, claims that Obama has "created an atmosphere that is hostile toward Christianity." That one is hard to swallow—unless you're part of the crowd that sees Obama as a Muslim or a non-American citizen—especially considering that, rightly or wrongly, $140 million just from his stimulus bill went to fund faith-based organizations.

The government's authorizing of federally-funded partnerships with these groups started under George W. Bush a decade ago. For the first time, our taxpayer dollars were going to local churches and other religious organizations to help them expand their social services in local communities. The most recent data published shows that over $2.1 billion in these federal grants were awarded in 2005.[25] At the time, this caused the watchdog organization TheocracyWatch to say that, under Bush's administration, "our country is experiencing a major transformation from a secular to a religious government. The President's faith-based initiative is central to this transformation and raises serious questions about church-state separation."

Obama, when a candidate for president, first indicated he was going to get rid of Bush's program. Instead, he left it in place, saying that "as someone who used to teach constitutional law, I believe deeply in the separation of church and state, but I don't believe this partnership will endanger that idea." Why? Because the grant money couldn't be used "to proselytize to the people you help and you can't discriminate against them—or against the people you hire—on the basis of their religion." Also, the federal bucks could only be used on secular programs, not "directly to churches, temples, and mosques." (Pity the Prez if any of that dough went to the last one, there'd be wailing at the White House wall like you wouldn't believe.)

Reverend Barry Lynn, who is the executive director of Americans United for Separation of Church and State, thought the Bush program "ought to be shut down, not continued."[26] He's "particularly frustrated that President Obama still has done nothing to ban hiring bias by publicly funded religious charities. . . . No American should be denied a government-funded job because he or she holds the 'wrong' views about religion." This was after, in 2010, Obama issued an executive order adding some supposed safeguards to "strengthen the constitutional and legal footing" of the policy.[27]

So what's going on? Are the Crips on a policy of "appeasement" toward the Blood(y) zealots? Seems to me that this is all political posturing using the guise of morality. By stark contrast, Ron Paul says: "We're not supposed to nationalize these problems. The founders were very clear that problems like this, if there needs to be legislation of sorts, the state has the right to write the legislation that they so choose. And that solves a lot of our problems."[28]

❖ ❖ ❖

Birth control as the new battlefield? Battle terms are what House Speaker John Boehner used when he addressed the National Religious Broadcasters in February 2011, not long after the Rebloodlicans took back the Congress. He was talking with a reporter for Pat Robertson's "700 Club" program, about the House having just voted to cut off tax funding of family planning and health programs for women. "I met with a lot of religious leaders earlier today to talk about the strategy," Boehner said, "and I think it's important that we understand that what we want to do here is win the war, not just win a battle. And there will be an opportunity some time in order to win the big war, and we're looking for that opportunity."[29]

Seems like 2012 is what the culture warriors have set their "victory" sights on, and there's a lot of dough involved. The big groups are lavishly funded, collectively raising more than three-quarters of a billion dollars every year—most of it being *tax-exempt*. Here's a list of the most powerful entities on the Christianist Right:[30]

- Pat Robertson's Christian Broadcasting Network has an annual budget of almost $300 million. He's also got Regent University ($80 million), the Christian Advocates Serving Evangelism ($43.8 million), and the American Center for Law and Justice ($13.3 million). It's basically a media-education-legal empire that includes a daily TV show.
- The empire built by Jerry Falwell includes Liberty University ($395 million), the Jerry Falwell Ministries ($4.2 million), and the Liberty Counsel ($1.3 million). He died in 2007 but left it all to his two sons. They pushed for Mike Huckabee in '08 and last year hosted "The Awakening" conference featuring Gingrich and Bachmann.
- Focus on the Family ($130 million) was founded by a child psychologist named James Dobson to push "biblical" solutions for various family problems. They're all over the world, and in the U.S. have a network of thirty-five "family policy councils" that lobby in state capitals.
- Alliance Defense Fund ($30 million) got set up by a coalition of TV and radio preachers in 1993. ADF president Allan Sears believes the bricks in the old church-state wall are being taken down "one by one." They do a lot of funding for legal groups working toward that end.
- American Family Association ($21 million) was founded by Reverend Donald Wildmon to push for censoring sexy TV shows, and now his son Tim runs the day-to-day affairs. One staffer, Bryan Fischer, calls church-state separation a "myth" invented by Adolf Hitler and has said the First Amendment only protects Christians. They hold regular "pastor policy briefings."

- Coral Ridge Ministries ($17.2 million), whose late founder D. James Kennedy liked to attack evolution and tout America as a "Christian nation," is today run by his daughter Jennifer.
- Family Research Council/FRC Action/FRC Action PAC ($14.5 million) is the biggest group based in Washington D.C. Their goal is to merge fundamentalist Christianity with government, and they are active in Tea Party circles. Top honcho Tony Perkins is an ex-state rep from Louisiana with ties to white supremacists. They sponsor a yearly "Values Voter Summit" that brings in congressional and presidential candidates.
- Concerned Women for America ($11.7 million) was formed over thirty years back to counteract the women's rights movement. It was founded by Tim LaHaye of *Rapture*-fiction fame and his wife Beverly. They mainly focus on stopping abortion, gay rights, and public "sex-ed" education. Also, they demand less government support for Public Broadcasting, the National Endowment for the Arts, and Planned Parenthood. They've got a PAC that spent almost $300,000 endorsing right-wing candidates in 2010.
- Traditional Values Coalition ($9 million), best known for gay-bashing and for bad-mouthing Islam, claims to work closely with 43,000 churches around the country. Reverend Louis P. Sheldon, the founder, was called "Lucky Louie" by lobbyist Jack Abramoff, who had some gambling buddies contribute to the TVC in exchange for "Lucky Louie" pushing for more Internet gaming.
- Faith & Freedom Coalition is a new group started up by Ralph Reed, who used to head the Christian Coalition and then became a political consultant. His ties to Jack Abramoff thwarted a possible political career in Georgia. "We have not only the right, but the moral obligation to overthrow the government by force if necessary," he tells crowds.

You think these guys don't lobby the gangs in D.C.? A study came out in November 2011, conducted by the Pew Research Center, which found that religion-related advocacy has increased roughly fivefold in only four decades. There were less than forty such lobbying groups in 1970, but there are more than 200 today. They employ upwards of a thousand people in the nation's capital and spend at least $300 million a year "on efforts to influence national public policy." The biggest is the American Israel Public Affairs Committee (AIPAC), which in 2008 spent almost $88 million. Next is the U.S. Conference of Catholic Bishops, followed by the Family Research Council mentioned above. The outfit with "the most dramatic increase in spending" is the National Organization for Marriage, formed in 2007 to combat those sinister same-sexers.[31]

Under George W. Bush, such:

> Political support was rewarded with weakened legal protections against tax dollars being used to fund religious discrimination and proselytizing, changes that have yet to be fully reversed by the Obama administration. A phalanx of conservative Christian legal organizations fights daily to weaken the legal separation of church and state, and to reverse restrictions on overt electoral activity by tax-exempt churches.[32]

❖ ❖ ❖

Do you ever think that all these "issues"—like banning abortion, denying gay Americans their civil rights, forcing more religion into public schools—are a distraction from the *real* problems that the gangs won't address about our faltering economy and our honest-to-God warmongering overseas? "It could also be simple ignorance," as columnist William Rivers Pitt has written. "After all, a fair portion of these knuckleheads don't believe in dinosaurs because they aren't mentioned in the Bible, don't believe in science generally, and have come to believe that the best thing for America is to revert to some 'Leave It To Beaver' fantasy about gender roles in society."[33]

Either way, the end result is glossing over the truth about the sorry state we're in. I'll say this, I'm glad Rick Perry and Michele Bachmann are no longer in contention for the Rebloodlican nomination. They both have strong ties to what's called Dominionism. This "strain"—and it really is *that*—is convinced that Christians have a divine right to rule over all earthly institutions. It "derives from a small fringe sect called Christian Reconstructionism, founded by a Calvinist theologian named R. J. Rushdoony in the 1960s. Christian Reconstructionism openly advocates replacing American law with the strictures of the Old Testament, replete with the death penalty for homosexuality, abortion, and even apostasy." (There are seventeen different offenses in all, including blasphemy, witchcraft, worshipping false gods, putting out false doctrine, juvenile delinquency, and adultery.) Rushdoony (rhymes with Rush-Loony) "pioneered the Christian homeschooling movement" and came up with the "revisionist history . . . that paints the U.S. as a Christian nation founded on biblical principles. He consistently defended Southern slavery and contrasted it with the greater evils of socialism." TV preachers like Pat Robertson, Jerry Falwell, and D. James Kennedy were all influenced by Reconstructionist ideas.

Michelle Bachmann appeared in one of the Truth in Action Ministries documentaries where she said that "government has no right to collect taxes in excess of 10 percent, the amount that believers are called to tithe to the church." She got her law degree, by the way, from Anal—whoops, of course I mean Oral—Roberts University, which has since been taken over by Pat Robertson's Regent University. Bachmann often makes reference to Francis Schaeffer, a Dominionist who's considered "the godfather of the anti-abortion movement." Her website when she ran for state senate in Minnesota had recommended the book *Call of Duty: The Sterling Nobility of Robert E. Lee*, which—if you can believe it—portrayed the Civil War as the Christian South versus the Godless North.[34]

These days, Truth In Action Ministries is after "dominion . . . not just equal time. . . . World conquest." This harkens back to God telling Adam and Eve in the garden to "have dominion" over every living thing (Genesis 1:26–28). Santorum goes after Obama's environmental policies for the same reason. He claims Obama's "phony theology" worldview "elevates the Earth above man."[35] (Here we have represented, I'd say, both sides of the Santorum stupidity equation: Santorum's press secretary, Alice Stewart, called MSNBC to say she misspoke in an interview on *Andrea Mitchell Reports* and did not mean to accuse President Obama of "radical Islamic policies." Instead—and the tape shows this—she meant to say, and did repeatedly during the same interview, "radical environmentalist policies.")

Texas Governor Rick Perry has ties to a different branch of Dominionist ideology called the New Apostolic Reformation, which talks about the "Seven Mountains" of society (family, religion, media, government, education, business, arts and entertainment), "the nerve centers of society that God (or his people) must control." Perry was seen by many of these Apostolic folks as their ticket to control. A pastor who's close to him preached about infiltrating "the governmental mountain" and said Perry was their man. "Some have told Perry that Texas is a 'prophet state,' destined, with his leadership, to bring America back to God." When he held a big prayer rally in Houston in July 2011, eight members of his Response "leadership team" were affiliated with the movement.[36]

And who might be described as one of their mentors? None other than Chuck Colson, the Watergate felon who once said he'd walk over his grandmother to get Richard Nixon elected. He told the Baptist Convention Pastors Conference in 2007 that the purpose of Christians was "to take command and dominion over every aspect of life, whether it's music, science, law, politics, communities, families. . . ."[37] No control freak, he. All who think Chuck's seen the light, raise your hands.

There's a new project called Champion the Vote (CTV), with a goal of registering five million "conservative Christians" who'll pull the lever or punch the tab in 2012 according to "the Biblical worldview." It's an initiative of United in Purpose, a nonprofit group that was founded last year by some Silicon Valley venture capitalists. The CEO is a kind of "Colson clone" named Bill Dallas, who did time in San Quentin for embezzlement charges relating to his lucrative real-estate business. After he got out in 1995, Dallas started the Church Communications Network, which today is the biggest satellite-based training ground for churches on the planet. Sounds like he traded one con game for another. . . .

Most of the financial support behind United in Purpose is anonymous, but "one of the main backers is technology entrepreneur Ken Eldred, a generous Republican Donor" and a friend and contributor to Reverend Donald Wildmon's American Family Association. As the *L.A. Times* reported, Eldred "founded companies such as Ariba Technologies and Immac, [and] has donated $1.1 million to Republican candidates since 2005." He told the paper that Champion the Vote "did not have a partisan agenda." The organization's "core mission" was only "to change American culture for the good, with the Bible as our standard of truth. . . . Our goal is to raise up a body of believers and that they elect a Godly leader. We're about the agenda of the lamb, Jesus Christ." The *Times* said the group is using "sophisticated data-mining techniques to compile a database of every unregistered born-again and evangelical Christian and conservative Catholic in the country."[38]

Theocracy, here we come! Sure is curious that this is the same gang that so happily wants to invade Iran because it's a theocratic dictatorship. In fact, that sounds like the kind of government they wish they could set up here. Maybe these Christianists are just jealous that the mullahs succeeded before they did. Keep in mind that they're firmly allied with the ultra-right-wing Orthodox in Israel. We give Israel $3 billion a year, which comes to about $1,000 annually from each one of us, man, woman, and child. The Christianists would be thrilled to follow Israel into a war with Iran, and the only politician who will speak out against all of this is Ron Paul . . . once again.

"The Christian activist right is the largest, best organized and, I believe, the most powerful force in American politics today," according to Democrip strategist Rob Stein. "No other political group comes even close."[39] (Look for Reverend Wright's name to become a subject of attack ads this fall.)

Keeping a low profile at the moment is the C Street house in Washington, which is affiliated with the Fellowship, sponsor of the yearly National Prayer Breakfast. The townhouse is registered as a church, and it's where a lot of our Christian lawmakers not only pray but also live. C Street hit the news back in 2009 after it came out that Senator John Ensign and Representative Chip Pickering had extramarital affairs while residing there, and South Carolina Governor Mark Sanford had confided in his "Christian friends" in-house about the cross-continent liaison that he'd kept secret from his wife ("hiking the Appalachian trail," as he called it).

"A formal foundation does exist—a 501(c)(3) called the International Foundation, which oversees three hundred or so ministries associated with the Fellowship, and has a board of directors that approves a budget for the ministries (in the fifteen-million-dollar range) and the salaries of the parent entities relatively few employees," according to an article in the *New Yorker*.

Jeff Sharlet wrote a book, *The Family: The Secret Fundamentalism at the Heart of American Power*, exposing how C Street's overseer liked to call itself a "Christian Mafia." It dates back more than seventy-five years to when a coalition of businessmen opposed to FDR's New Deal started what became the country's first fundamentalist lobby. They'd been under the radar forever, until Sharlet came along and the sex scandals broke. Some of the Congressmen under counsel in recent years include Rebloodlican Senators Chuck Grassley, Jim DeMint, and Lindsey Graham, along with Democrip Senators Mike McIntyre and Mark Pryor. In case you think the Rebloodlicans have a monopoly on this stuff, McIntyre is big on putting the Ten Commandments in public places, and Pryor once explained his bipartisan nature by saying, "Jesus didn't come to take sides. He came to take over."[40] And Hillary Clinton, in her memoir *Living History*, wrote that the Fellowship's secretive main man for forty-some years, Doug Coe, was "a unique presence in Washington: a genuinely loving spiritual mentor and guide to anyone, regardless of party or faith, who wants to deepen his or her relationship to God."[41]

An inquiry was launched in 2010 by the Office of Congressional Ethics into how the politicos residing at C Street paid below-market-value rents of about $900 a month. It soon came out, too, that some of these members had accepted over $100,000 worth of free international travel from the Fellowship Foundation. I'm sure they had their Bibles in tow on their way to Greece and other Mediterranean climates.

❖ ❖ ❖

Here was John F. Kennedy, in a speech delivered shortly before he got elected our first Catholic president in 1960:

> I believe in an America where the separate of church and state is absolute . . . that is officially neither Catholic, Protestant nor Jewish . . . where no religious body shall seek to impose its will directly or indirectly upon the general populace or the public acts of its officials. . . . Today I may be the victim, but tomorrow it may be you—until the whole fabric of our harmonious society is ripped at a time of great national peril.

That last line sounds a little like prophecy to me. Rick Santorum, when he read the speech, said he "almost threw up."[42]

I wonder if many people remember that, besides his leadership of the civil rights movement, Reverend Martin Luther King, Jr. was a clergyman who pushed for family planning "at a time when it was illegal in many states for even married couples to buy artificial contraceptives" and also endorsed the Supreme Court's striking down of mandatory prayer and Bible reading in public schools. "In a pluralistic society such as ours, who is to determine what prayer shall be spoken, and by whom?" King asked.

He also said this: "The church must be reminded that it is not the master or the servant of the state, but rather the conscience of the state. It must be the guide and the critic of the state, and never its tool."[43]

To that, I can only add: Amen.

NOTES

1. Roger Williams: Boston, Rob. "5 Brave Religious Leaders Who Fought Christian Theocracy in America." February 13, 2012, www.alternet.org.

2. Jefferson "took a pair of scissors . . .": Epps, Garrett. "Constitutional Myth #4: The Constitution Doesn't Separate Church and State." www.theatlantic.com.

3. James Madison: Epps, "Constitutional Myth #4. . . ."

4. John Leland: Boston, "5 Brave Religious Leaders. . . ."

5. Denton, Sally. "Is Mitt Romney's Candidacy Part of 'The Eternal Plan' of the Mormon Church?" January 30, 2012, www.salon.com.

6. Ibid.

7. Redden, Molly. "Rick Santorum's Virginia Church and Opus Dei." *New Republic*, March 6, 2012, www.tnr.com.

8. "Santorum: Satan Is Systematically Destroying America." February 16, 2012, www.rightwingwatch.org.

9. Santorum on Mormonism: *Philadelphia Inquirer*, December 20, 2007.

10. Santorum at South Carolina campaign stop: Barr, Andy, "Santorum: Left Hates 'Christendom,'" www.politico.com, February 23, 2011.

11. Santorum on CBS News interview: January 19, 2011. Quoted in "9 Controversial Rick Santorum Quotes," *The Week*, http://the week.com, January 5, 2012.

12. Parry, Robert. "Santorum 'Throws Up' on JFK and Obama." *Consortium News*, February 28, 2012.

13. Santorum on contraception: October 18, 2011, www.Caffeinated Thoughts.com.

14. "Former Senator Alan Simpson Calls Rick Santorum Homophobic and Disgusting": http://blog.buzzflash.com/node/13340.

15. Davidson, Lawrence. "A Christian Conservative in Every Bedroom? Rick Santorum's Nightmare Vision for America." *Consortium News*, February 14, 2012, www.alternet.org.

16. Planned Parenthood funding and de-funding: Boston, Rob. "The Sneaky Ways the Christian Right Has Re-Entrenched Itself in Our Politics." Americans United for Separation of Church and State, May 2, 2011.

17. Condon, Stephanie. "Susan G. Komen Reverses Course, will keep funding Planned Parenthood." February 3, 2012, www.cbsnews.com.

18. Legum, Judd. "Ari Fleischer Secretly Involved in Komen Strategy on Planned Parenthood." February 4, 2012, www.ThinkProgress.org.

19. Planned Parenthood: Romney on Scott Hennen Show, February 6, 2012; Obama administration quote by Stephanie Cutter in "Romney: No Komen money for Planned Parenthood." http://articles.boston.com/2012-02-07.

20. Santorum and Romney quotes: Jaffe, Sarah. "5 Big Lies About the Phony 'War on Religion.'" February 8, 2012, www.alternet.org.

21. Issa hearing and Friess quoted in "To My Mother" by William Rivers Pitt, February 7, 2012, www.truthout.org.

22. Parry, Robert. "GOP Confusion over the First Amendment." *Consortium News*, March 2, 2012.

23. Anti-choice laws: Montgomery, Peter. "5 Signs the Christian Right Still Wields Too Much Power in America," www.alternet.org, January 31, 2012.

24. North Carolina legislators/fundamentalists: Gibson, Linda. "Rick Santorum's American Jihad." Buzzflash, February 21, 2012.

25. $2.1 billion: Government Accountability Office cited in "President Obama issues executive order on faith-based initiative" on November 28, 2010, www.abcnews.com.

26. Theocracywatch, Obama position, Lynn comment: http://biggovernment.com/wthuston/2010/05/16/obamas-faith-based-programs-pushing-global-warming.

27. Lynn frustration and Obama executive order: www.abcnews.com.

28. "Ron Paul on Social Conservatism: 'I Think It's a Losing Position.'" Feburary 19, 2012, http://csnnnews.com.

29. Boehner quote: Boston, Rob. "The Sneaky Ways the Christian Right Has Re-Entrenched Itself in Our Politics." www.alternet.org, May 2, 2011.

30. Boston, Rob. "The 12 Worst (and Most Powerful) Christian Rights Groups." Americans United for Separation of Church and State, www.alternet.org.

31. "Lobbying for the Faithful." November 21, 2011, www.pewforum.org.

32. Montgomery, Peter. "5 Signs the Christian Right Still Wields Too Much Power in America." January 31, 2012, www.alternet.org.

33. Pitt column cited above.

34. Perry, Bachmann, and Christian religion: Goldberg, Michelle. "A Christian Plot for Domination?" August 14, 2011, www.thedailybeast.com.

35. Santorum on Obama and environment: www.buyttown.com/cc-common/news/sections/newsarticle.html?feed=104707&article=9784537#ixzz1nKxUhXGf.

36. Dominionism, Bachmann and Perry: Goldberg, Michelle. "A Christian Plot for Domination?" August 14, 2011, www.thedailybest.com.

37. Chuck Colson: Conn, Joseph L. "Dominionism and Democracy." October 2011, www.au.org.

38. United in Purpose/Champion the Vote: "Silicon Valley Gives Conservative Christians a Boost." *Los Angeles Times*, September 15, 2011.

39. Rob Stein: Conn, "Dominionism and Democracy."

40. Sharlet, Jeff. "Sex and power inside 'the C Street House.'" July 21, 2009, www.salon.com. See also: "Inside C Street, Washington's frat house for Jesus." September 13, 2010, www.newyorker.com.

41. "Inside C Street. . . ."

42. JFK speech quoted; Santorum reaction: Parry, Robert. "Santorum 'Throws Up' on JFK and Obama." http://consortiumnews.com, February 27, 2012.

43. Martin Luther King: Boston, Rob. "5 Brave Religious Leaders Who Fought Christian Theocracy in America. . . ." www.alternet.org, February 13, 2012.

CHAPTER FIFTEEN

IS THE BILL OF RIGHTS IN THE SHREDDER?

In January 2011, I sued the federal government, specifically the Transportation Security Administration (TSA) that's assigned to do all the screening at airports. My reasoning was simple: I had a hip replacement a few years ago, and the titanium the surgeon implanted sets off the metal detectors. They'd previously used hand-held wands to scan my body . . . , but after I was subjected to a frontal pat-down, I sued on grounds that these things amounted to unreasonable search and seizure and violated my Fourth Amendment rights.

It's unbelievable, but a district judge threw my case out of court last November, ruling that my lawyer should have filed it in a Circuit Court of Appeals. That's how they get rid of cases these days; by claiming they don't have jurisdiction. How can a federal judge do that when it's a constitutional question? If she doesn't have jurisdiction, then no one does. How do you go to the Court of Appeals if you don't have a case to appeal? The Court of Appeals doesn't give you a jury or the right of discovery.

This goes back to that scoundrel Woodrow Wilson and how he created the Federal Reserve. It's called administrative law. What happens is this: The President signs an executive order, Congress then approves that order and tells a department to carry it out.

When that happens, it's above the Bill of Rights and the Constitution. So it basically turns Congress and the President into dictators. With the Federal Reserve, the Constitution states there shall be no central bank. But this is how Wilson and the big shots loop-holed it and avoided the Constitution.

Here was an interesting component to my case. The judge turned to me at a hearing in July and said, "Governor, could you cite the time that you were abused at an airport?" My attorney stepped in and said: "No, because of national security the TSA rules are not made known to the governor or anyone else. So how can you possibly cite an abuse when you don't know what the rules are?" And the judge acknowledged that! If they do something wrong, you can't call them on it—because you, the public, are not made privy to the rules. That's absurd.

I found it interesting that, about a week after my case got dismissed, the European Union prohibited using x-ray body scanners in airports because their ionizing radiation has been shown to damage DNA and cause cancer. The TSA had no comment, except to say that it "deploys the most advanced technology available to provide the best opportunity to detect dangerous items, such as explosives." I'd call that avoiding the question, wouldn't you?[1] It's like with steroids; nobody knew back in the '70s or '80s what the two-year outlook on steroids would be. Now you're seeing all these guys dying prematurely in their fifties, and clearly anabolic steroids played a big role in this. So what is it about airport security that they don't want us to know in terms of future health effects?

Well, once again, follow the money. Michael Chertoff, who ran Homeland Security for a while under George W. Bush, today has a private security firm (the Chertoff Group), and included among its clients is Rapiscan. This is the leading company manufacturing the full-body scanning systems, which Chertoff was promoting at DHS back in 2005 when the government placed its first order. After the underwear bomber got arrested on Christmas 2009, the TSA ordered 300 machines from Rapiscan—even though, according to the Government Accountability Office, "it remains unclear whether [the scanners] would have been able to detect the weapon." No matter, since then $118 million in stimulus funds went to purchase Rapiscan technology. The only other company making these scanners, L-3 Systems, has as its chief lobbyist Linda Daschle, wife of the former Senate Majority Leader. Oh, by the way, an inter-agency report about radiation exposure from these machines concluded that pregnant women and children should not be scanned, even though the radiation levels are "extremely small."[2]

What I want people to realize is, when you go to any airport in America, you are not protected by the Bill of Rights. It does not apply. They can do what they want, and it's already starting to spread further. You're going to see Homeland Security in bus terminals and other public transportation, even down to the highways, which is happening already in Tennessee where they're doing random checks of vehicles all across the state. The logic of Bill Gibbons, Tennessee's Department of Safety & Homeland Security Commissioner, is: "Where is a terrorist more apt to be found? Not these days on an airplane, more likely on the interstate."[3] Not only can they scan and probe our body cavities at airports, now they can invade the contents of our cars! They're turning our country into East Berlin!

It makes you wonder what's next for our right to freedom of movement. Never thought I'd even imagine that about my own country. John Pistole, an appropriate name for an ex-FBI agent who now runs the TSA, has said he wants to expand what's called the Visible Intermodal Prevention Response (VIPR) task forces. There are currently twenty-five of these teams, which include TSA agents, federal air marshals, behavior detection (!), and canine officers, and over a year's time they made more than 9,300 searches of our railway and bus stations, ports and ferries, subways, bridges, private cars, and trucks. In fiscal 2011, some $110 million got spent on "surface transportation security," including the VIPR program (compared to over $5 billion for airport security).

Over at Homeland Security, they're testing a new technology called FAST. Don't you love these acronyms? This one stands for Future Attribute Screening Technology, which involves sensors that can check out how quickly your eyes are blinking or how high your blood pressure is. There's also the Insider Threat Detection Project, looking for "observable indicators of potential insider threats before the insider commits a hostile act," and the Violent Intent Modeling and Simulation Project, analyzing to determine "whether radical groups are likely to engage in political violence." You can't make this stuff up. We're all potential suspects now.[4]

In 2010, the Office of Management and Budget reckoned that 31 separate federal agencies were involved in homeland security-related funding that year to the tune of more than $65 billion. The Census Bureau, which has itself been compromised by War on Terror activities—mapping Middle Eastern and Muslim communities for counter-terrorism officials—estimated that federal homeland security funding topped $70 billion in 2010. But government officials acknowledge that much funding is not included in that compilation.[5]

Have you heard about the National Defense Authorization Act (NDAA), with its "Homeland Battlefield" provision? That they're planning on giving the military free rein to operate inside our own borders? Technically, it's a $660-billion military funding bill that authorizes things like pay raises and contracts, along with funding for weapons systems and the war in Afghanistan; but a provision in the bill means that, for the first time in our history, the government will be able to decide who goes to trial and who can get detained without due process, *by the military*. In fact, military custody would be mandatory for most terrorist suspects.

Early in December 2011, the Senate voted 86-to-13 and the House 283-to-136 to pass a bill that's been called "an historic threat to American citizens" by the ACLU—and was also opposed by Defense Secretary Leon Panetta, FBI Director Robert Mueller, and

Director of National Intelligence James Clapper. They all say we're doing just fine in combating terrorism and in fact, "the military does not want new powers to interrogate and investigate terrorist suspects, especially those arrested in the United States."[6] No matter. The final passage occurred on December 15, which just happened to be the 220th anniversary of the ratification of the Bill of Rights. Ironic, isn't it? The only candidate in the presidential campaign fighting to stop the bill was Ron Paul.

After first threatening to veto the legislation as "inconsistent with the fundamental American principle that our military does not patrol our streets," President Obama changed his mind after a caveat was added saying that none of this could be construed as altering legal rights for Americans. He rang in the New Year by signing the NDAA into law, saying he was only doing this to keep on funding our troops! By denying the very principles for which they're supposedly fighting and giving a president authoritarian powers? Give me a fucking break! Supposedly, the bill would only impact "a person who was a part of or substantially supported al-Qaeda, the Taliban, or associated forces that are engaged in hostilities against the United States or its coalition partners." Check the language again, folks. What does "substantially supported" mean? Is it that much of a stretch to call those people occupying Wall Street and the ports "associated forces that are engaged in hostilities"?

Lindsey Graham of South Carolina, one of the Senate bill's prime supporters, is very pleased that the law "basically says . . . for the first time that the homeland is part of the battlefield. . . . If you're an American citizen and you betray your country, you're not going to be given a lawyer . . . I believe our military should be deeply involved in fighting these guys at home or abroad."[7]

Excuse me, Senator Graham? Have you read recently Article III, Section III of the Constitution? It says, flat-out, "No Person shall be convicted of Treason unless on the Testimony of two Witnesses to the same overt Act, or on Confession in open Court." This bill in effect revokes the Posse Comitatus Act of 1878, which outlawed any law enforcement by the military within our borders.

Coleen Rowley was a Special Agent with the FBI, turned whistleblower in questioning whether we've been told the whole truth about 9/11. Here's what she had to say recently:

> Does anyone remember that none of the first thousand people the FBI rounded up after 9/11, and who were imprisoned for several months (some brutalized) were ever charged with terrorism? Does anyone remember that hundreds of the Gitmo detainees who were handed over to their American military captors in exchange for monetary bounties were found, after years of imprisonment, to have no connection to terrorism?[8]

Hey, no-questions-asked is a lot simpler solution than going through cross-examination before a jury of your peers, right? Already under the revised Patriot Act, "material support for terrorism" can include humanitarian aid or even advocating for some suspicious group. Coleen Rowley also writes:

> Corrupted, compliant politicians have already allowed their fears to get the better of them by going along with pre-emptive war in violation of the Nuremberg Principles and international law and torturing in violation of the Geneva Conventions and the Convention against Torture. So why should they also not go for detaining American citizens without constitutional rights or trial?[9]

Here's an excerpt from the original version of the NDAA that the House passed:

> "Congress affirms that the Department of Defense has the capability, and upon direction by the President may conduct offensive operations in cyberspace to defend our Nation, Allies and interests. . . ."[10]

The Pentagon already has on the boards a "domain of war" plan for the Internet, claiming hostile groups are out to infiltrate its information infrastructure.

Here's what Ron Paul had to say about the NDAA.

The founders wanted to set a high bar for the government to over-come in order to deprive an individual of life or liberty. To lower that bar is to endanger everyone. When the bar is low enough to include political enemies, our descent into totalitarianism is virtu-ally assured. The Patriot Act, as bad as its violations against the Fourth Amendment were, was just one step down the slippery slope. . . . The president's widely expanded view of his own au-thority to detain Americans indefinitely on American soil is for the first time in this legislation codified into law. That should chill all of us to our core.[11]

Ray McGovern, a retired CIA officer turned political activist, has written that the NDAA reminds him of the "extraordinary meas-ures" introduced by the Nazis after they took power in 1933. The writer/activist Naomi Wolf points out a lesson of history, drawing on what happened in Nazi Germany, Fascist Italy, and the Soviet Union—suggesting that Congress has probably signed its own ar-rest warrant. "Congress will no longer be directing and in charge of the military: Rather, the military will be directing and in charge of individual Congressional leaders, as well as in charge of everyone else." I hate to say it, but there would be something fitting about some of these same gang members getting incarcerated.[12]

This ties in to my TV show, *Conspiracy Theory*, where we ex-posed that Homeland Security had FEMA build six internment camps. So when the military goes out and takes people or puts 'em under arrest, they've got a place to put 'em. This is outrageous. They're heading us right into martial law. Things are already well in motion, and I'm sure we don't know the half of it. Senator Ron Wyden, a member of the Joint Intelligence Committee, told the Sen-ate in May 2011, "When the American people find out how their government has secretly interpreted the Patriot Act, they will be stunned and they will be angry." Wyden added that he couldn't talk about it without disclosing classified information.[13]

It just got worse. A few months back, the Federal Restrict-ed Buildings and Grounds Improvement Act of 2011 passed by unanimous consent in the Senate and 388-to-3 in the House, where only Ron Paul and two of his Blood brothers voted against it. A title like that sounds innocuous enough, doesn't it? Who wouldn't want to improve the grounds of our grand old institutions? But it's also known as the "Trespassing Bill," and one of the main sections states that anyone who knowingly "enters or remains in any restricted building or grounds without lawful authority to do so," with the "intent to impede or disrupt the orderly conduct of Government business or official functions, engages in disorderly or disruptive conduct in or [in] proximity to any restricted building or grounds," or "impedes or disrupts the orderly conduct of Government business or official functions," will be punished with a fine "or imprisonment for not more than 10 years, or both."[14]

This area might be where the president or someone else with Secret Service protection is visiting. Or "a building or grounds so restricted in conjunction with an event designated as a special event of national significance." That could be anything that Homeland Security construes it to be—including the two gang conventions, or a global summit such as the G-20 that likewise draws protesters, or even somebody booing at the speech of a political candidate. And this isn't seen as a violation of "the right of the people peaceably to assemble" as guaranteed by the First Amendment? But depending on who's defining a "National Special Security Event," you could be faced with a federal offense of between one and ten years in prison.[15]

Once Obama signs the bill, as he's expected to do, implementing its mandate may not be long in coming. In Chicago, Mayor Rahm Emanuel—Obama's former chief of staff—is getting ready for hosting the G8 and NATO summit meetings in 2012. This will create "unanticipated or extraordinary support and security needs," so Emanuel gave himself the power to marshal and deputize the FBI, DEA, ATF, and Department of Justice, along with state and county police and any "other law enforcement agencies" deemed necessary. Besides which, the city can permanently install new surveillance apparatus and enter into agreements with public or private entities concerning placement, installation, maintenance or use of video, audio, telecommunications, or other similar equipment. The location of any camera or antenna permanently installed . . . shall be determined pursuant to joint review and approval with the executive director of emergency management and communications.[16]

❖ ❖ ❖

In June 2011, way out in eastern North Dakota, police made the first arrests of American citizens with the help of a Predator, a spy drone "robot" aircraft developed by our military. The CIA uses these to spy on possible nuke sites in Iran and on Pakistani militants. Back in 2005, Congress first authorized Customs and Border Protection to use unarmed drones. Today, according to Michael C. Kostenik, a retired Air Force general who heads up an office supervising the drones, Predators are flown "in many areas around the country, not only for federal operators, but also for state and local law enforcement and emergency responders in times of crisis." The ex-police commissioner of New York, Howard Safir, figures drones could help in manhunts, like spotting a runaway criminal on a rooftop. But Jane Harman, who used to chair the House homeland security intelligence subcommittee, says nobody ever talked about using these to assist local police. "There is no question that this could become something that people will regret," Harman told the *L.A. Times*.[17] Like when those high-res cameras, heat sensors, and sophisticated radar end up targeting us inside our homes, Congresswoman?

AeroVironment Inc., our biggest supplier of small drones to the military, now has plans to shop a small chopper drone to about 18,000 state and local police departments around the country— once the FAA eases up its regulations, of course. The new drone, called Qube, buzzes like that angry bug in *Men in Black*. It fits in a car trunk, weighs 5 ½ pounds, and is remote-controlled by a tablet computer. Keep your eye on the robot-tech trade group, the Association for Unmanned Vehicle Systems International, which is already talking about 23,000 new jobs if only our airspace gets opened to commercial drones (though it's not specified whether these jobs will go to humans or robots).[18]

Is anyone wondering how come police today are uniformed with military helmets, visors, SWAT shields, shin guards, heavy vests, and ever-increasing firepower? Or why the cops who were pepper-spraying and mounting nighttime raids on the Occupy Wall Street sites have ninja turtle outfits along with choppers, special tanks, and sound blasting vehicles that were pioneered in Iraq? Other innovations from that war, such as wireless fingerprint scanners, are also being used by local PDs to check motorists. In Arizona and elsewhere, facial recognition software from our war zones is being utilized, and Raytheon Corporation just patented a new type of riot shield that puts out low-frequency sound waves that disrupt your respiratory tract and hinder your breathing!

Here's a mind-boggling statistic. I'm sure you're well aware of stun guns, which are also known as Conducted Energy Devices. One of these is the Taser, which is now widely employed by police forces across the country. "According to data collected by Amnesty International, at least 500 people in the United States have died since 2001 after being shocked with Tasers; either during their arrest or while in jail." This new brand of what's actually termed a nonlethal weapon has killed ninety-two people in California, sixty-five in Florida, and thirty-seven in Texas.[19]

There's something called the 1033 Program, whereby in 2011, over $500 million of surplus military gear ended up in the hands of American police forces . . . and orders for this year are up by 400 percent. Violent crime rates across the country have been declining since the early 1990s, but somehow SWAT teams are increasing. The West Hartford Police Department is now hosting a yearly Connecticut SWAT Challenge, in which dozens of sponsors display their wares—things like ThunderSledge tools to smash open chained doors and the black, bulletproof box-like trucks made by Lenco Armored Vehicles that can hold up to fifteen officers.[20] Not to be outdone, the cops in Cobb County, Georgia, have an amphibious tank, and the sheriff of Richland County, South Carolina, has an armored personnel carrier with a machine gun that he calls "The Peacemaker." Not to mention grants from Homeland Security that allow police departments to buy "BearCats" ("16,000-pound bullet-proof trucks equipped with battering rams, gun ports, tear-gas dispensers and radiation detectors").[21] And there's no listing of how $34 billion in grant money to local police and government agencies has been spent![22] By 2014, according to the Homeland Security Research Corp, its market for state and local agencies will reach some $19.2 billion.[23]

Just let those Occupiers go too far, and they'll find a Peacemaker pushing 'em towards a Pace-maker. That seems to be their sentiment of choice. You see, the powers-that-be are worried about these people's protest movements. A Washington lobbying outfit, Clark Lytle Geduldig & Cranford, came up with a secret plan on behalf of the American Bankers Association (ABA) looking to "undermine their [the protesters] credibility in a profound way," doing things like researching the activists' credit card histories and past criminal records, while keeping tabs on social media organizing efforts, the goal being to "create negative narratives of the [Occupy Wall Street] for high impact media placement to expose the backers of this movement." (Did you ever think it might be a smart thing for the activists *not* to have any visible leaders?) The lobbyists wanted $850,000 from the bankers to carry out their "opposition research" and prevent the Occupy Wall Street folks from having "very long-lasting political, policy, and financial impacts on the companies in the center of the bullseye." They'll even bring Santa Claus into the bargain, "when media reports cover the next round of bonuses and contrast it with stories of millions of Americans making do with less this holiday season." After somebody leaked this to MSNBC, the ABA admitted it received the "unsolicited" memo from the lobbyist and "chose not to act on it in any way."[24]

You can't say the same about the Police Executive Research

Forum, or PERF, which you have probably never heard of. It happens to be an international outfit with strong ties to Homeland Security and local law enforcement. They've also been holding conference calls with mayors and police chiefs around the country concerning the Occupy movement. Some reports are that as many as forty cities have gotten advice from PERF, after which the evictions of protesters took place soon thereafter.

PERF's honchos include Minneapolis' police chief Tim Dolan, who orchestrated the crackdown on "disrupters" at the Republican Convention in 2008; former Miami and Philly top-cop John Timoney, who dispersed the Free Trade Agreement of the Americas protest in 2003; and current board chair Charles Ramsey, who as D.C.'s main man coordinated the response to the World Bank and IMF protests.

PERF is also in the guidebook business. Their latest is called "Managing Major Events: Best Practices from the Field," a how-to for stopping "Anarchists" and "Eco Terrorists" with undercover teams to "grab the bad guys and remove them from the crowd." An earlier handbook called for "embedded media to control police messages." PERF-ect.[25]

But we shouldn't be surprised about "embedded media," a concept that was pioneered when the Iraq War began. It might raise a few eyebrows, though, to know that school bus drivers are being called into the War on Terror, and 20,000 mall security guards are being recruited to spot terrorists among shoppers. "If you see something, say something," as George Orwell said—whoops, that's actually a campaign slogan of Homeland Security, which is expanding its purview from transportation into hotels, sports stadiums, and Wal-Marts.[26]

They're getting some help, as are the local gendarmes, from at least seventy-two "fusion centers" around the country which share info from law enforcement and private companies to quietly spy on Americans. These are now operating in every state, fusing material from cops and citizens, immigration officers, and FBI agents. Between 2004 and 2009, about $426 million in Homeland Security grants went to fund the fusion centers, which also get probably an equal amount from state and local agencies.[27]

Has modern technology turned law enforcement into Big Brother? I recently read about a case going before the Supreme Court, *United States v. Jones*. Antoine Jones was a nightclub owner in D.C. who the feds suspected was dealing drugs. So they put a GPS device on his car in order to monitor the man around the clock. Sure enough, they ended up finding a lot of cocaine, and Jones was sentenced to life in prison. The U.S. Court of Appeals reversed the conviction, on grounds that the GPS affixed to his car was a warrantless search that violated Jones' Fourth Amendment rights against "unreasonable searches and seizure." Hear, hear! But the Obama administration asked the Supreme Court to review the decision, claiming there's no invasion of privacy when you're out to bust a drug trafficker, and so GPS tracking of vehicles ought to be allowed without any judicial permission. The Supreme Court will now decide "whether the Fourth Amendment's safeguards remain meaningful in the digital age," as writer David Cole says, "when widely available technological innovations—including GPS devices, cell phones, computer data-mining programs, and the like—make it possible to watch citizens more intimately and comprehensively than was remotely conceivable when the Bill of Rights was adopted."

Several federal judges around the country are already more than disturbed about this. Judge Diane P. Wood from Chicago wrote that surveillance using GPS devices "make the system that George Orwell depicted in his famous novel, *1984*, seem clumsy." Chief Judge Alex Kozinski of San Francisco has written that "*1984* may have come a bit later than predicted, but it's here at last."[28] Writer Cole raised questions like these:

> Should the fact that your cell phone company knows and records your location at any given moment mean that the government should be free to demand that information without satisfying Fourth Amendment requirements? Should the long-standing

police authority to search an individual upon arrest include reviewing all the texts and emails stored in his "smart phone?" Should customs officers' authority to search luggage without establishing any cause for suspicion at the border extend to laptop computers, which contain infinitely more private information than most of what could have been carried across the border when the "border search" doctrine was first created?[29]

I'm no stranger to the new surveillance technology. After I was elected governor in 1998, the state sent a big crew over to our house to install a hotline phone, supposedly in case somebody broke in. Call me naïve, but it took us a long time to figure out that we were being constantly monitored. But who was I going to complain to? The media would have just said I was being paranoid. Who do you go to about something like this, when you can't trust your own government—and you're *in it*! In fact, you're at the top of it! I feel now like I was way ahead of the times.

Here's one they hadn't yet come up with when I was in office. It's hidden software that can exist on your smart phone and that logs in every phone number, text message, and Google search, and reports these to the mobile phone carrier. The software is called Carrier IQ, which strikes me as somebody's bad joke of "carrying off" your supposed intelligence. When the Android operating system is running, Carrier IQ is always right there in the background without your knowledge. Guess how Carrier IQ identified itself on its website?—as "the world's leading provider of Mobile Service Intelligence solutions." You can learn more about all this in a YouTube video by Trevor Eckhart.[30]

The wave of the future may be merging surveillance with biometrics technology—using a person's facial features or iris patterns to determine their identity (supposedly, you can tell identical twins apart by scanning the eye's iris). These products are already being sold to police departments. One "success story is the MORIS device, a gadget attached to an iPhone that can run face recognition software, take digital fingerprints, and grab an iris scan at a traffic stop." The FBI has in the works a billion-dollar "Next Generation Identification" (NGI) system to "house iris scans, palm prints, measures of voice and gait, records of tattoos and scars, and photos searchable with facial recognition technology when it's complete in 2014. Most of this information is expected to come from local law enforcement." Other such databases exist at the Department of Defense, Justice, and Homeland Security.[31]

And if you really want to talk creepy, *Wired Magazine* has reported that the military has given research grants to several companies "to spruce up their drones" to do some TTL—"tagging, tracking, and locating" of humans. One company is already claiming "it can equip drones with facial recognition technology that lets them build a 3-D model of a face based on a 2-D image, which would then allow the drone to ID someone, even in a crowd."

According to Noah Schachtman's article,

> The Army also wants to identify potentially hostile behavior and intent, in order to uncover clandestine foes. Charles River Analytics is using its Army cash to build a so-called "Adversary Behavior Acquisition, Collection, Understanding, and Summarization (ABACUS)" tool. The system would integrate data from informants' tips, drone footage, and captured phone calls. Then it would apply "a human behavior modeling and simulation engine" that would spit out "intent-based threat assessments of individuals and groups."[32]

❖ ❖ ❖

"Never embarrass the Bureau," as J. Edgar Hoover used to say. Section 215 of the Patriot Act lets a secret national security court issue the FBI an order to go after "any tangible" things connected to an investigation.[33] In June 2011, it came out that the FBI had decided to give "significant new powers to its roughly 14,000 agents, allowing them more leeway to search databases, go through household trash, or use surveillance teams to scrutinize the lives of people who have attracted their attention." The Bureau can now even check out people and organizations "without firm evidence for suspecting criminal or terrorist activity." A whole new Domestic Investigations and Operations Guide is being prepared.[34] Unfortunately for us, I don't think it contains the phrase "probable cause."

Another newfound FBI strategy is called "domain awareness." Basically, that's another way of saying racial profiling. Turns out— surprise!—Muslims, African Americans, and Chinese are being targeted for investigation based upon their race or religion.[35] Well, not always. The FBI also targeted a dude who took part in a protest against Exxon Mobil, with three years of round-the-clock surveillance.

National Security Letters (NSLs), as they're called, can be issued by the FBI to libraries, phone companies, banks, Internet providers, and others, demanding information on somebody—and accompanied by a "gag order" that warns whoever receives the Letter to say nothing about it to anyone but a lawyer. About 50,000 of these are said to be sent out every year, so that email and phone contacts can be gathered. You still need a warrant to obtain the contents of these written and verbal communications, but that's rapidly becoming window dressing. The Obama administration has proposed expanding the definition of NSLs so that the websites you visit and the Google searches you make and the books you buy can always be tracked.[36]

It's getting pretty ridiculous, or maybe there are just too many employees with time to kill. There's a new program called SLATT, which offers online training for coffee shop owners and tattoo shop artists, among others, about how to spot potential terrorist activities. If customers at internet cafés pay for their coffee with cash, watch out! Another warning tells boat shop owners to be looking out for people wanting to become certified scuba divers. You can check out the actual flyers at http://publicintelligence.net.[37]

How far will we go in expanding the definition of a terrorist? FBI documents released under a Freedom-of-Information Act suit last December talk about animal rights activists being prosecuted under the Animal Enterprise Terrorism Act—for simply walking onto a farm and shooting video footage of what they considered cruelty to the domestic animals being bred there, and then "rescuing" one of them.[38] "The act was passed in 2006 at the request of the National Association for Biomedical Research, Fur Commission USA, GlaxoSmithKline, Pfizer, Wyeth, United Egg Producers, National Cattlemen's Association and many other corporations and business groups that have a financial stake in silencing animal rights activists." Not only "interfering with" the operations of an animal enterprise got criminalized, but so did installing a "reasonable fear" in those being protested, and causing a "loss of profits."[39]

Here's one that's chilling from the get-go but is the cover-up worse in terms of right to know? I'm talking about experiments carried out in the United States and Netherlands, where scientists in the lab created an extremely transmittable form of the avian bird flu virus, which is often lethal to humans but doesn't ordinarily spread. Most of the 600 cases so far—half of them deadly—originated in Asia since 1997. Now, our National Science Advisory Board for Biosecurity has requested two publications (*Science* and *Nature*) to censor what they planned to report, because "experimental details and mutation data . . . would enable replication of the experiments." Meaning, a terrorist-inspired pandemic. Well, why are they inventing an airborne H5N1 virus in the first place?![40] They've tweaked it genetically to make it more contagious! And what shocked the researchers was how easy it was![41]

As for Muslims—well, like the old recruitment adage says, Uncle Sam wants you! They're being called to account, against the First Amendment, for things they've said or put out over the Internet. In September 2011, a Pakistani resident legally living here got indicted by the Justice Department for uploading a YouTube video that was supposedly supporting terrorists—even though it didn't contain a word about violence. In the meantime, the CIA, which by statute only operates overseas (ha-ha!) is working with local police departments to do "human mapping" of various Muslim communities.

Informants known as "mosque crawlers" are busy keeping tabs on minister's sermons as well as cafés and bookstores.[42]

Let's look a bit deeper at the Internet, that bastion of free speech. To hear Hillary Clinton "talk the talk" at a Conference on Internet Freedom held at the Hague last December, America is in the forefront of protecting those rights. Our Secretary of State said boldly:

> When ideas are blocked, information deleted, conversations sti-
> fled, and people constrained in their choices, the Internet is di-
> minished for all of us. What we do today to preserve fundamental
> freedoms online will have a profound effect on the next genera-
> tion of users. . . . The United States wants the Internet to remain
> a space where economic, political, and social exchanges flourish.
> To do that, we need to protect people who exercise their rights
> online, and we also need to protect the Internet itself from plans
> that would undermine its fundamental characteristics.[43]

Except . . . except . . . few have done more in recent times to undermine those "fundamental characteristics" than Mrs. Clinton and the administration she's now serving in. I'm talking first and foremost about WikiLeaks. Now, it's understandable that Hillary would be more than a bit put out by some of the State Department cables released by Julian Assange and his team. After all, she's been exposed for ordering spying by our diplomats on their counterparts at the United Nations. She's gone after "credit card numbers, email addresses, phone, fax and pager numbers, and even frequent-flyer account numbers"—all actions that our government had condemned as illegal. And it turns out her State Department had pressured Spain to shut down independent investigations into the Bush administration's torture policies.

In retaliation, the United States went after WikiLeaks big time, in fact, what Australian diplomatic cables called "an 'unprecedent-ed' U.S. government criminal investigation . . . both in its scale and nature." The United States convened a grand Jury, mounted cyber attacks to stop WikiLeaks from being hosted in the USA, detained their supporters at airports, and grabbed their laptops without a warrant. "The White House warned government employees not to even look at [the] documents online—even though the world's largest newspapers were publishing them—and threatened that they would be breaking the law if they did."

It gets worse in the wake of WikiLeaks, justifying the group's founder Julian Assange calling the Internet "the most significant surveillance machine that we have ever seen."[44] Here's what Glenn Greenwald reported on the Salon.com website:

> The Obama Administration (following in the footsteps of Saudi Arabia) is seeking "a new federal law forcing Internet email, instant-messaging, and other communication providers offering encryption to build in backdoors for law enforcement surveillance." The Obama DOJ has insisted that it has the right to read opened emails with no warrants from a court. The Chairwoman of the Democratic Party, Rep Debbie Wasserman-Schultz, is sponsoring a bill under which "Internet providers would be forced to keep logs of their customers' activities for one year." The *Washington Post*'s Dana Priest and William Arkin reported in their "Top Secret America" series last year: "Every day, collection systems at the National Security Agency intercept and store 1.7 billion emails, phone calls and other types of communications."

The FBI has a request out to tech firms "to develop a program that would enable agents to sift through waves of 'publicly available' information." The goal "is to develop a sort of early warning system that provides real-time intelligence to improve 'the FBI's overall situational awareness.'" It's more than a bit curious that DARPA—the Defense Advanced Research Projects Agency which invented the Internet—is now working with the FBI and CIA in search of a program to monitor social media "chatter," like Twitter.

Meantime, Homeland Security is already busy checking out the social media websites and even has an operating procedure manual for doing so.[45] The assault on our privacy is, not surprisingly, being farmed out from government to private corporations. Homeland

Security outsourced their "social media monitoring program" to General Dynamics, the big military contractor, mainly scoping out keywords they say. It came out at a congressional hearing in February 2012 that "if you're the first person to tweet about a news story, or if you're a community activist who makes public Facebook posts—DHS will have your personal information."[46]

In December 2011, WikiLeaks released the Spy Files, nearly 300 documents that shed light on this "alliance," and caused Julian Assange to say: "What we are seeing is the militarization of cyberspace. It's like having a tank in your front garden." A few examples of what we now know:

- A brochure from SS8, a Milpitas, California, company, is pushing a product called Intellego that lets security forces "see what they see, in real time" including a "target's draft-only emails, attached files, pictures, and videos."
- Glimmerglass, based in Hayward, California, has equipment that allows government to "secretly tap into the undersea cables that convey all the data and phone traffic between continents."
- Another California outfit, Blue Coat of Sunnyvale, sells web filtering tools that let countries block dissident websites "to meet cultural and regulatory requirements."

Syria bought some Blue Coat machines from a reseller in Dubai, since because of U.S. sanctions the company can't sell these directly to the Syrians. But hey, it's all in the name of tracking down crooks and terrorists, right? The new moniker is "lawful interception."[47]

In late February, WikiLeaks started publishing the Global Intelligence Files—over five million emails gleaned from Stratfor, a Texas-based private intel outfit that fronts as a publisher while offering "confidential intelligence services" to Homeland Security, the Defense Intelligence Agency, the Marine Corps, and also big corporations such as Dow Chemical, Lockheed Martin, Raytheon, and Northrop Grumman. Incidentally, Stratfor was also out to destroy WikiLeaks. These documents indicate there's a secret indictment waiting to be served on Assange under the 1917 Espionage Act.

Stratfor's Vice President for Intelligence is Fred Burton, who used to be Deputy Chief of the State Department's counter-terrorism division. They've channeled tips to Israel's Mossad spy outfit and gave "a complimentary membership" to the ex-head of Pakistan's intel service. They "did secret deals with dozens of media organizations and journalists—from Reuters to the Kiev Post." In 2009, Stratfor CEO George Friedman got together with Goldman Sachs' then-Managing Director Shea Morenz and came up with the notion to "utilize the intelligence" from its insider network to set up StratCap "to trade in a range of geopolitical instruments, particularly government bonds, currencies and the like." Morenz in 2011 invested "substantially" more than $4 million and joined the Stratfor board of directors.[48]

WikiLeaks won't comment on who leaked them all the Stratfor emails, which I'm sure we'll be hearing a lot more about. Some activist hackers who call themselves Anonymous are saying they're the leakers.[49] Anonymous already took some interesting steps after eighty-six senators signed off on the National Defense Authorization Act that I wrote about earlier. They did a massive dump of previously-undisclosed information about these guys, beginning with: "Robert J. Portman is a Republican Senator from the state of Ohio . . . we are truly disturbed by the ludicrous $272,853 he received from special interest groups supporting the NDAA bill that authorizes the indefinite detention of U.S. citizens on U.S. soil. Robert J. Portman, we plan to make an example of you."[50]

Finally, there's SOPA, the Stop Online Piracy Act, supposedly aimed at expanding what law enforcement and copyright holders can do to fight the "rogue" websites that are peddling their goods, most of them based overseas. Under the Act, if someone did streaming of copyrighted content without authorization, it would be a felony. "The bill attempts a radical restructuring of the laws governing the Internet," according to Gary Shapiro, CEO of the Consumer Electronics Association. The information tech magazine *eWeek* says, "The language of SOPA is so broad, the rules so unconnected to the reality of Internet technology and the penalties so disconnected from the alleged crimes that this bill could effectively kill e-commerce or even normal Internet use."[51] For example, one amendment lets anybody seek court action to restrain a website's activities. But the State Department has already been lobbying other countries for strict new laws like SOPA. "They have even offered to fund enforcement and literally draft the laws that sacrifice free speech for greater copyright protection for Hollywood."[52] It hasn't passed Congress yet, but don't look for SOPA to go away any time soon.

Is this called "no more WikiLeaks ever again" because the security state would now have the power to censor and shut down the Internet? More than a million people have signed an online petition in protest of the SOPA legislation.[53] But, unbelievably, the entertainment industry seemed oblivious. Or maybe not, since the *L.A. Times* has reported that "the recording industry is pushing California's lawmakers to approve legislation that would allow warrantless searches of companies that press copies of compact discs and DVDs." The bill has no "standard for suspecting that counterfeiting is occurring" and would "give law enforcement officials the power to enter manufacturing plants without notice or court orders." In the meantime, one state is talking about making it a criminal act to share your Netflix password with your friends or family, because that's taking away from Netflix revenues.[54]

One last example of your Corporate Police State at Work: You may have heard about "fracking," short for hydraulic fracturing, whereby chemicals are injected into the earth at high pressure to bring up oil and gas. The documentary *Gasland* points out the dangers, which a growing number of environmental activists are fighting. (Filmmaker Josh Fox got led out in handcuffs after trying to film a House Science Committee hearing on fracking in January 2012.) At an industry conference in Houston, the communications director for Range Resources (Matt Pitzarella) explained how "we have several former psy ops folks that work for us . . . very much having that understanding of psy ops in the Army and in the Middle East has applied very helpfully here for us in Pennsylvania." Another speaker suggested his colleagues "download the U.S. Army-Marine Corps Counterinsurgency Manual, because we are dealing with an insurgency here." Psy ops and military manuals to put down citizen dissent. . . .

One of our founders, Benjamin Franklin, had this to say: "Those who would give up essential liberty to purchase a little temporary safety, deserve neither liberty nor safety." Is this the un-pretty pass that we've reached? Is our Constitution still a living document? You be the judge.

NOTES

1. Grabell, Michael. "Europe Bans X-Ray Body Scanners Used at U.S. Airports." *ProPublica*, November 15, 2011.

2. "Fear Pays: Chertoff, Ex-Security Officials Slammed For Cashing in on Government Experience." November 23, 2010, www.huffingtonpost.com.

3. Bill Gibbons: Friedersdorf, Conor. "Mission Creep: This Tennessee Highway Is Now Patrolled by TSA." October 2011, www.theatlantic.com. Also: Bennett, Brian. "TSA Screenings aren't just for airports anymore." December 20, 2011, www.latimes.com.

4. TSA and Homeland Security programs: Murray, Nancy and Kade Crockford. "A Nation of 'Suspects.'" Truthout and ACLU Massachusetts, September 29, 2011.

5. Salisburgy, Stephan. "How to Fund an American Police State: Real Money for an Imaginary War." TomDispatch, March 5, 2012.

6. "The military does not want new powers . . .": "Hobbling the Fight Against Terrorism." Editorial in the *New York Times*, December 8, 2011.

7. Lindsay Graham: Taibbi, Matt. "Indefinite Detention of American Citizens: Coming Soon to Battlefield USA." December 9, 2011, www.rollingstone.com.

8. Coleen Rowley quote: "Obama Should Veto Empire over Republic,"

www.commondreams.org, December 3, 2011.

9. "Corrupted, compliant politicians . . .": Ibid.

10. NDAA and Internet: Smith, Dave. "NDAA Bill Aims to Suppress Internet Freedom." December 16, 2011, www.ibtimes.com.

11. Ron Paul: Easley, Jonathan. "Rep. Paul says defense bill assures 'descent into totalitarianism.'" December 26, 2011, http://thehill.com.

12. National Defense Authorization Act: McAuliff, Michael. "Indefinite Military Detention Measure Passes on Bill of Rights Day." December 15, 2011, www.huffingtonpost.com; Taibbi, Matt. "Coming Soon: The Indefinite Detention of American Citizens." *Rolling Stone*, December 10, 2011; Rowley, Coleen. "Bringing the 'War on Terror' Home." December 4, 2011, http://consortiumnews.com; Wolf, Naomi. "How Congress has signed its own arrest warrants in the NDAA Citizen Arrest Bill.", December 14, 2011, http://wp.me/p1B8zG-hY; "Senate Votes to Let Military Detain Americans Indefinitely, White House Threatens Veto." November 29, 2011, www.huffingtonpost.com; McGovern, Ram. "Are Americans in Line for Guantanamo?" *Consortium News*, December 3, 2011.

13. Wyden on Patriot Act: Murray, Nancy and Kade Crockford. "A Nation of 'Suspects.'" Truthout and ACLU Massachusetts, September 29, 2011.

14. DB, Devon. "The Criminalization of Protest: Say Goodbye to Free Speech in America." March 9, 2012, www.globalresearch.ca.

15. Carter, Tom. "U.S. Congress passes authoritarian anti-protest law." March 3, 2012, www.wsws.org.

16. Harcourt, Bernard. "Outlawing dissent: Rahm Emanuel's new regime." January 19, 2012, www.guardian.co.uk.

17. Bennett, Brian. "Spy drones aiding police." *Los Angeles Times*, December 11, 2011.

18. Hennigan, W. J. "Opening Home Skies to Drones." *Los Angeles Times*, November 27, 2011.

19. Trimel, Susanne. "Police Taser Death Toll Reaches 500 in U.S." Amnesty International, February 28, 2012.

20. Connecticut SWAT Challenge: Becker, Andrew and G. W. Schulz. "Cops Ready for War." Center for Investigative Reporting, December 21, 2011, www.readersupportednews.org.

21. 1033 Program: Johnson, Robert. "Pentagon Offers U.S. Police Full Military Hardware." *Business Insider*, December 6, 2011.

22. $34 billion in grants: Elliott, Justin. "How the Feds Fueled the

Militarization of Police." *Salon*, December 26, 2011.

23. Homeland Security budget for states/localities: Becker, Andrew and G. W. Schulz. "Cops Ready for War." Center for Investigative Reporting, December 21, 2011.

24. "Exclusive: Lobbying Firm's Memo Spells Out Plan to Undermine Occupy Wall Street." November 19, 2011, MSNBC's Open Channel blog; Jilani, Zaid. "Washington Lobbyists Crafted $850,000 Secret Plan for Bank Lobbyists to Undermine Occupy Wall Street." Citing *Up! With Chris Hayes*, November 21, 2011, www.nationofchange.org.

25. PERF: Parrish, Geov. "Private cop organization, linked to DHS, helped plan raids on OWS nationwide." *Booman Tribune*, November 19, 2011, www.alternet.org.

26. School bus drivers, mall security guards: Murray, Nancy and Kade Crockford. "A Nation of 'Suspects.'" Truthout and ACLU Massachusetts, September 29, 2011.

27. $426 million: "How to Fund an American Police State. . . ." Cited above.

28. Federal judges' concern: Liptak, Adam. "Court Case Asked If 'Big Brother' Is Spelled GPS." *New York Times*, September 11, 2011.

29. Cole, David. "Keeping Watch on the Detectives." *New York Review of Books*, December 22, 2011.

30. Carrier IQ: www.huffingtonpost.com/2011/11/30/carrier-iq-trevor-eckhart_n_1120727.html.

31. Geneva, Tana. "7 Privacy Threats the Constitution Can't Protect You Against." February 4, 2012, www.alternet.org.

32. "7 Privacy Threats. . . ."

33. Savage, Charlie. "Public Said to be Misled on Use of the Patrioit Act." *New York Times*, September 22, 2011.

34. Savage, Charlie. "F.B.I. Agents Get Leeway to Push Privacy Bounds." *New York Times*, June 13, 2011.

35. Savage, Charlie. "F.B.I. Scrutinized for Amassing Data on Ethnic and Religious Groups." *New York Times*, October 21, 2011 (citing ACLU release of internal FBI documents).

36. National Security Letters: Shipler, David K. "Our Vanished Civil Liberties." *The Nation*, September 19, 2011.

37. Huff, Edwin A. "FBI Warning: Cash-Paying Customers May Be Terrorists." *Natural News*, February 8, 2012.

38. Kuipers, Dean. "FBI tracking videotapers as terrorists?" December

29, 2011, www.latimes.com.

39. Potter, Will. "Animal Enterprise Terrorism Act Threatens Activism." *Jurist*, February 2, 2012.

40. Grady, Denise and William J. Broad. "Journals Asked to Cut Details of Flu Studies." *New York Times*, December 21, 2011.

41. Grady, Denise and Donald G, McNeil, Jr. "Debate Persists on Deadly Flu Made Airborne." *New York Times*, December 27, 2011.

42. Muslims: Ibid.

43. "Conference on Internet Freedom, Remarks: Hillary Rodham Clinton," December 8, 2011, www.state.gov.

44. "Julian Assange: Internet Has Become 'Surveillance Machine.'" *Agence France-Presse*, November 28, 2011.

45. Heyes, J. D. "FBI in the Process of Creating a System for Monitoring all Conversations on Social Networking Sites." March 13, 2012, www.nationofchange.org.

46. Ungerleider, Neal. "Department of Homeland Security Tells Congress Why It's Monitoring Facebook, Twitter, Blogs." February 16, 2012, www.fastcompany.com.

47. WikiLeaks' Spy Files: Chatterjee, Pratap. "The New Cyber-Industrial Complex Spying on Us." *Guardian UK*, December 4, 2011.

48. WikiLeaks press release, February 27, 2012.

49. Anonymous as leaker: Hastings, Michael. "WikiLeaks Stratfor Emails: A Secret Indictment Against Julian Assange?" www.rollingstone.com.

50. "Anonymous Retaliates: Massive Information Dump Released on Senators Who Passed NDAA." December 27, 2011, http://freakoutnation.com.

51. Http://judiciary.house.gov/hearings/pdf/112HR3261.pdf.

52. State Department lobbying for SOPA: Greenwald, Glenn. "Hillary Clinton and Internet Freedom." December 9, 2011, www.salon.com.

53. Online petition: Carr, David. "The Danger of an Attack On Piracy Online." *New York Times*, January 2, 2012.

54. Sirota, David. "Fears of a corporate police state." June 5, 2011, www.salon.com.

CHAPTER SIXTEEN

THIRD PARTIES IN AMERICA

I used to hold out a lot of hope for a third-party movement in America, having had some success that way myself. Before getting into the personal part a little, let me do a quick historical review of how third parties came into being and generally faded from sight almost as quickly.

First, it's good to keep in mind that new parties have sprung up whenever there is a crisis in the country. With Andrew Jackson, the people were demanding more representation. The Republican Party came about through the North-South crisis. The Populist and Grange parties came out of an economic crisis in the rural Midwest, which led to William Jennings Bryan, who really did represent the farmers and was destroyed by the big money interests. "You shall not crucify mankind upon a cross of gold," Bryan famously said in 1896. However, they could, and did, and they still are.

A capsule history of third parties might go like this: The Liberty Party, founded in 1840, "died" in 1852. Dedicated to the abolition of slavery, it suffered from a lack of organization but also of media coverage. The Democrats and the Whigs largely ignored the issue of slavery as much as they could, and so newspapers of the day barely covered any news about the Liberty Party. Their best results were in New England and New York.

The Free Soil Party, founded in 1848, "died" in 1854—but essentially turned into the Republican Party when John Fremont ran in

1856. It was originally dedicated to not extending slavery into the new territories recently acquired from Mexico. Also lacking in organization, the Free Soil Party performed best in two New England states (Vermont and Massachusetts) and also in Wisconsin.

The Know-Nothing Party (also called the American Party), founded in 1845, "died" in 1860. This was very much a reaction to large waves of European immigrants who'd come in search of a better economic situation. These new immigrants were largely Catholics, and the Know-Nothings were mainly Protestants. Their party split on North-South lines over the issue of slavery, but they did get some state legislators elected.

The Constitutional Union Party, founded in 1859, "died" in 1860. When the Know-Nothings splintered into northern and southern camps, the Southerners bolted to this one. "Few parties, major or minor, have ever been so intent on avoiding the issues," according to the book *Third Parties in America*.[1]

The Greenback Party, founded in 1874, "died" in 1884. This was one of the most effective third parties in our history. Farmers in rural America were being gouged by the railroad companies and finding it difficult to manage the cost of their produce shipments. So they organized into clubs called grangers and tried to push the government to regulate the rates of railroads. After first forming alliances with Democrats in 1876, they held a convention and adopted a platform which included "a United States note issued directly by the Government." Two years later, they garnered "over a million votes and fourteen congressional seats," with the strongest support in the Midwest. The lasting legacy of the Greenback Party— government-backed currency, government labor bureaus, and a shorter work week "are today regarded as common features of American industrial society."[2]

The People's Party, AKA the Populist Party, founded in 1891, "died" in 1908. The more things change, the more they stay the same. After the Civil War, as many settlers migrated westward, banks in the East offered what today might be called "predatory loans" and sent land values skyrocketing—until a depression in 1887 sent them tumbling again. But the monopolistic railroad outfits then "set arbitrary prices" that "made it impossible for a farmer to pay off his debt." The Populists' platform called for "government ownership of railroads, free coinage of silver and a graduated income tax." They won majorities in seven Midwest and Western states and rural areas across the South. But guess what? The Democrats co-opted the free silver idea and many Populists "found it easier to remain in the Democratic fold," thus bringing an end "to the . . . sequence of minor parties rooted in the hardships of the farmer and laborer."[3]

The Prohibition Party, founded in 1869, is still active today (they netted 643 votes in 2008, as the National Statesmen, a name adopted in 1980). Like the original name suggests, these folks revolved around issues of temperance and the prohibition of alcohol and other controlled substances. They're the longest running third party in American politics, with candidates in every presidential election since 1872. In fact, they were the first party to endorse "women's suffrage, direct election of senators, an income tax, and child labor laws."[4]

My favorite third-party candidate was Theodore Roosevelt. As a Republican, he'd been president from 1901 to 1909 and anointed William Howard Taft as his successor. But when Taft didn't continue down the same progressive path, and Roosevelt couldn't convince the Republican National Committee not to renominate him, Teddy bolted from the Republicans and set up the Progressive Party/Bull Moose Party. Here's what his platform declared in 1912: "To destroy this invisible Government, to dissolve the unholy alliance between corrupt business, and corrupt politics is the first task of the statesmanship of the day."[5] The platform "echoed earlier Greenback and Populist" ones—"the direct election of Senators, direct primaries, women's suffrage, publication of campaign expenditures, regulation of interstate industry, a minimum wage, unemployment insurance, and old-age pensions." Roosevelt won 27 percent of the vote, to this day the best a third party candidate has ever done. But Woodrow Wilson co-opted a number of their ideas for the Democrats, and "the Progressive Party machinery, hamstrung by infighting and a lack of money and patronage, decayed."[6]

The Socialist Labor Party (SLP), created in 1876, "died" in 2008. This was a "by-product" of "an economic transition" that left "in many Americans the feeling that they had been left behind." They saw collective ownership over the means of production as the solution, and they were strong in the West and among immigrants. They also didn't want the country to enter World War I without the government holding a plebiscite of the people. That, not surprisingly, led to the Espionage Act of 1917, which allowed various government agencies to go after the SLP and its leaders. Cops and vigilantes were soon derailing their activities. Even though they hung in there and had a brief surge of popularity during the Depression, they've had next to zero impact on "election outcomes . . . or on . . . public policy."[7]

The Socialist Party of Eugene Debs and Norman Thomas came out of a split with the SLP, and many of their proposals became a part of mainstream Democratic politics, like labor laws, Social Security, and Medicare. Much of what became Franklin D. Roosevelt's social policies began with the Socialists. They were also involved in civil rights issues with A. Philip Randolph and Bayard Rustin before the major parties got involved, and had a lot of influence on Dr. Martin Luther King, Jr. Of course, since they wanted redistribution of wealth in some way—basically by taking money away from the rich and powerful—they got no positive play in the media, then or now. They were derided as a bunch of dirty commies, but in actuality were trying to create a more fair society. Not by government giveaways but by taking some of the ill-gotten gains from the rich, who *owned* the government.

In my home state, in the 1920s, arose the populist Minnesota Farmer-Labor Party, which existed independently until it was absorbed by the Democratic Party in 1944. The original platform called for protecting farmers and union workers, along with the public owning railroads, utilities, and natural resources. Between 1921 and 1941, they managed to elect four U.S. senators, eight U.S. representatives, and three governors. Hubert Humphrey orchestrated the merger into the Democratic Farmer-Labor Party, which exists to this day on the Minnesota ballot[8].

Robert LaFollette, a fellow I greatly admire, had tried to reform the Republicans from within. He bolted from the GOP in 1924 after he failed to get nominated to the national ticket, and his followers formed the Conference for Progressive Political Action (CPAA). La-Follette had championed the rights of Native Americans and African Americans, at the same time opposing the entry of U.S. forces into World War I. The Socialist Party sometimes worked with La-Follette, and he was also, according to the book *The American Radical*, "the most important and recognized leader of the opposition to the growing dominance of corporations over government." The CPAA actually got LaFollette's name on the ballot in every state except Louisiana, and he netted 17 percent of the national vote in the 1924 presidential election.[9]

Henry Wallace, who'd been FDR's vice president, got dropped from the national ticket in 1944 in favor of Harry Truman. Wallace and Truman didn't see eye to eye about the Cold War and foreign policy. Wallace preferred resolving things through the newly formed United Nations, while Truman felt military strength was more important. So to protest Truman's policies, Wallace made an unsuccessful run for president in 1948 and netted 2.4 percent of the vote.

Strom Thurmond and the Dixiecrats were the polar opposite of Wallace in 1948: a states' rights party that wanted to continue segregation of black from white. Thurmond did take four states in the south, but the Truman campaign somewhat co-opted the more "palatable" aspects of the Dixiecrat message and Truman took six states. The Dixiecrats "died" in 1951. The next year, Eisenhower and Stevenson both worked hard to win back Dixiecrats to their gangs.[10]

Incensed by John F. Kennedy's policies aimed at desegregation of the South, George Wallace formed the American Independent Party (AIP) in an effort to "send Washington a message that the nation's blacks had pushed too far too fast."[11] Supporters managed to get Wallace on the ballot in all fifty states in 1968, and he went on to win five southern states and 13.8 percent of the national vote. On May 16, 1972, Wallace was shot and paralyzed, and the AIP soon splintered into being irrelevant. Wallace was famous for pithy and often offensive campaign rhetoric that revolved around phrases like "law and order," a phrase that Nixon's Republican gang co-opted in their campaign rhetoric toward a "Southern Strategy" to realign most southern voters with them.

In 1980, something new and different happened. John B. Anderson, a moderate Republican Congressman from Illinois, decided to go independent after he failed to get the nomination—and ended up getting six million votes! I draw comparison to what we might be seeing today with Ron Paul's presidential candidacy, as a maverick Republican Congressman from Texas. Like Paul, Anderson wasn't afraid to raise break-the-mold issues. He'd introduced legislation (and made it the signature of his run) calling for a 50-cent-a-gallon tax on gasoline simultaneous with a 50 percent reduction in social security taxes. This would have put us well on the road to better fuel efficiency—long before global warming was being talked about—and would also have benefited the middle class. Anderson told it like it was, and still is: The idea that you could lower taxes, raise defense spending, and have a balanced budget was a pipe dream.

In the primaries, he was a serious contender for the Republican nomination, which eventually went to Ronald Reagan. Anderson then ran as an independent, and not only found enough support to get on the ballot in every state but also raised enough money to make a strong bid. The League of Women Voters said he met the qualification threshold of higher than 15 percent in the polls, so he could be allowed into the debates against Reagan and then-President Jimmy

Carter. But Carter said he wouldn't appear on the same stage with Anderson, who did pretty well one-on-one against Reagan. The next time, Reagan debated Carter alone and, in the end, a lot of Anderson supporters decided to vote for Reagan. But Anderson still had the sixth best showing of any third party or independent candidate of the twentieth century.[12] Ever since, he's been calling for some way to change the two-party gridlock on our political system.

It seems that about every dozen years or so, people get fed up enough with the two gangs for a new third party or, lately, independent candidate to appear on the horizon. In 1992, along came Ross Perot, the billionaire businessman from Texas. At one point, he was ahead of both Bill Clinton and then-President George H. W. Bush in the polls. He might well have gone on to victory, but suddenly Perot dropped out of the race because he claimed Republican operatives had tried to disrupt his daughter's wedding! When he came back in that October, he'd lost two crucial months. I suspect that Perot never actually wanted to win; he only wanted to make a statement. And as the momentum for him built up that summer, he got scared that he might pull it off. As it was, he was allowed into the presidential debates, and Perot captured 19 percent of the popular vote. Only Teddy Roosevelt ever did better.

I admired Perot at the time. In a classic case of being co-opted by one of the gangs (in this case, for a "good cause"), one of Perot's key campaign issues was to reduce the federal deficit. After Clinton went on to become president, he incorporated reduction of the deficit as an administration policy—and he balanced it too, until George W. Bush plunged the deficit into the toilet. Republicans also "stole" from Ross Perot. Their 1994 "Contract with America" included support for term limits, a line-item veto, and a balanced budget amendment. It was no accident that, when the Republicans took the midterm election in '94, two-thirds of the people who'd voted for Perot voted for *them*.

In 1995, Perot had established the Texas Reform Party, and the next year, our Independent Party of Minnesota affiliated with them because we saw a chance to go national. By the time different affiliates from third parties around the country came together for the presidential election of '96, Dick Lamm had joined the movement. He'd been a three-time governor of Colorado. He was a very bright guy and a savvy politician. Some of us wanted Dick to be the Reform Party's nominee that year. But at the eleventh hour, the Perot forces undercut Lamm and put the Texas billionaire up again as the candidate. Our group from Minnesota and a lot of others then started to question what was really happening. Apparently, Perot and his crowd didn't want to have a legitimate third-party movement. Maybe it was all about Perot's ego. And, of course, his money. . . .

He did get 8 percent of the popular vote in '96, which was still respectable for a third party candidate. But that time, the gangs had seen the light about letting him into the debates. When Perot scared the pants off the two gangs in '92, that had entitled him to almost $30 million of our tax dollars—just like the "big boys"—if he needed it for another campaign. But in '96, Congress changed the rules for the debates. The League of Women Voters got dumped, and a new Federal Debate Commission was created—appointed by the former heads of the Republican and Democratic national parties (gangs). Two of the appointees to the Commission had *been* the former heads of the gangs. Do you think our forefathers would rubber-stamp that baby?

Clinton was running for reelection against Bob Dole, who didn't want Perot allowed in the debates because that might cut in on Dole's conservative base. Clinton was so far ahead in the polls that debates could only bring his numbers down. So he and Dole made a backroom deal. They'd keep Perot out if Clinton could say how many debates and where they'd be held. They took their plan to the Federal Election Commission, which naturally gave it the go-ahead. That year, only two debates took place—guaranteed to have a small audience because they were on the same nights as the World Series.

The two gangs keep any independent or third-party candidates from having too much clout, through a variety of methods. First, they exercise control over who can get onto a state ballot. That is usually determined by a Secretary of State—who is a member of one of the gangs. Another way to squelch a third party is through FECA. That's the Federal Election Commission Act, passed back in 1974, a so-called "reform" that actually freezes out third-party challengers. I call this a FECAL matter because this law made it *legal* to protect the two gangs from a third-party upset, by allocating huge sums of federal money only to candidates of the Democrats or Republicans until after an election is over. And an independent can only get it after November, if he already appeared on the ballot in at least ten states and took 5 percent or more of the popular vote. As the book *Third Parties in America* says, "The FECA is a major party protection act."[13]

So what can be summarized about third parties?

1. They usually bubble up to the national level due to some sort of political instability or perceived crisis.
2. They usually congeal around one issue or a set of related issues. "Minor parties often advocate policies not embraced by the major parties. . . . Often these new positions can be accommodated with relatively little discomfort to the [major] party."[14]
3. Third parties usually have a brief shelf life.
4. Third parties are usually personality-driven or issue-driven.
5. Third parties are usually regionally based and/or with regional appeal.
6. Third parties usually suffer from a lack of media coverage or too much media coverage that borders on mainstream ridicule.
7. Third-party candidates usually do not participate in televised presidential debates (though Perot in 1992 was a notable exception to this "rule").
8. Third parties usually suffer from the double-edged sword that is public perception; voters don't support a "fringe character" or a candidate likely to not win a major election.

9. Third parties usually suffer from a lack of financial resources; they've never appeared to have the same fundraising/donor-cultivation abilities of the Democrats or the Republicans.

❖ ❖ ❖

A little more personal history might be relevant: When I first ran for office, to become mayor of my then-hometown of Brooklyn Park, the heads of the Minnesota Republican Party and Democratic Party *co-signed* a letter sent to every resident in the mail, stating that they endorsed my opponent. They called me the most dangerous man in the city. All I was, was a citizen. But thinking about it, maybe they were being accurate, because I'd been a Navy SEAL and then a pro wrestler, which makes me a pretty tough guy.

We were the Independence Party before we affiliated with the Reform Party because we really believed a national third party was starting out of Texas and Ross Perot. So we became the Reform Party of Minnesota. Put it this way, a third gang was formed temporarily. I've written some in my earlier books about what happened between me and Ross Perot and the Reform Party. It left a bitter taste in my mouth, that's for sure. But don't take my word for it, here's what author Micah L. Sifry had to say in his 2002 book, *Spoiling for a Fight: Third-Party Politics in America*:

> If it weren't for Jesse Ventura's establishment-shocking victory in the Minnesota governor's race on November 3, 1998, the Reform Party might well have been declared dead by the mainstream media well in advance of the 2000 election. Ventura was almost the political inverse of Perot. Ventura was sane, funny, self-deprecating, and grounded in the reality of working people's lives, not a secluded kooky billionaire surrounded by sycophants. He was a patriot, like Perot, but not an antiforeigner demagogue. He was also a real libertarian who never tried to buy a politician or get a government subsidy, unlike Perot, who was a big donor to Richard Nixon and other Washington insiders.[15]

Couldn't have said it better myself. Of course, like the author went on to point out, Perot was quick to take credit for my upset, calling it "a major victory for the Reform Party." The truth was, Perot hadn't done squat to help my campaign, nor had any of the other Reformers. They wouldn't even give me a donation, not to mention a loan. I'd voted for Perot twice in presidential elections, in '92 and again in '96, and when I ran for governor I needed his help. In Minnesota, there's a system where people check off some money on their tax returns that goes into a general fund for distribution to candidates running for office. I was supposed to get more than $325,000 to finance my campaign, a smaller percentage than my two opponents. But to get the funds, first you had to take out a loan from a bank which, after the election, the government would repay as long as you got at least 5 percent of the vote.

But the powers-that-be in Minnesota were doing their best to stymie me. So I flew to Atlanta with some of my people for a meeting with Perot. We figured he must know a bank in Texas that could grant the loan (he probably even owned some banks!). But he wouldn't even look us in the eye. I knew he wasn't going to lift a finger to help us—and I also knew that his version of the Reform Party was bogus.

The head of the Minnesota Banking Association at the time happened to be Bill Cooper, who was also chairman of the Republican Party. You do the math. A half-dozen banks turned me down, and there was only a month to go before the election. That's when the Franklin Avenue Bank came through, thanks to a member of our Reform Party on the Minneapolis City Council, who talked to their vice president one day over a backyard fence. That loan paid for the advertising that, after the debates, helped me win the election.

A poll taken by Rebloodlican gang member Frank Luntz at the time showed that nearly a third of registered voters would have considered voting for me if I'd run for president in 2000. But I'd made a four-year obligation to the people of Minnesota, and I just didn't believe that, for your own personal political gain, you start suddenly campaigning for another job. So my team began pushing for a viable third-party candidate, and we made clear we didn't mean Ross Perot.

Originally, the 1999 Reform Party convention was scheduled to be held in Minnesota, but basically to snub me, they moved it to Dearborn, Michigan. Then I came out and supported a non-Perot guy, Jack Gargan, for National Reform Party chair. I couldn't make it to the convention because of a thunderstorm, but I did address the delegates by phone and thanked Perot for a job well done. When he spoke the next day, for almost forty minutes, he never once mentioned my name or the fact that I was the party's top-ranking public official. Jack Gargan told the convention, "If you don't realize that Governor Ventura's victory is our ticket to party survival and build on that victory, then don't vote for me."[16] They saw the light; Jack won.

But that was about the peak of it. I tried like hell to recruit a good man to lead the Reform Party national ticket in 2000. John McCain had just started to take on George W. Bush that year when he came to see me in Minneapolis. At the time, he was a moderate and a veteran, and I was supporting him. I told McCain that if he'd quit the Republican Party, I'd break my promise to Minnesota and run on the ticket with him. But he said he couldn't do that. If he and I had run together, I think there's a strong chance we could have won as independents. I also talked to Colin Powell, Lowell Weicker, and even Donald Trump. They all ultimately said no. I might have considered running with General Powell as well. Unfortunately— or maybe as fate would have it—he'd already hitched his wagon to Bush's star. As Secretary of State, his speech about Iraq's supposed weapons of mass destruction was the deciding factor in pushing us into a war based on lies. Needless to say, I imagine General Powell regrets that today.

Anyway, Pat Buchanan ended up being the Reform Party's man of the hour. To me, he carried way too much of a religious agenda, and I'm a firm believer in separating church and state. After the Perot crowd attacked me publicly following a controversial interview I did for *Playboy*—even calling on me to drop out of the party—I gave them what they wanted. I called a press conference on the front steps of the governor's mansion, brought the key members of my team together from the third-party movement in Minnesota, and said, "The national Reform Party is hopelessly dysfunctional." I quit and aligned myself with Angus King, the governor of Maine who belonged to no party, and said I was going to change our state party's name back to Independence.

Pat Buchanan ended up getting just 422,368 votes nationwide in 2000, which comes out to a meager 0.43 percent. As the book *Spoiling for a Fight* says, "For all intents and purposes, the Reform Party experiment was dead."[17] Basically, Buchanan hijacked the Reform Party, and I'm sure he had plenty of help from Rebloodlican operatives. His candidacy was a great way to destroy momentum for a third party. The Reform Party self-destructed, and it was a darn shame.

Ralph Nader ended up running in the 2000s, and after the Supreme Court handed Bush the election over Al Gore, a lot of pundits said it was all Nader's fault for taking votes away from Gore. Baloney! This isn't about picking the winner of a horse race. People voted for Nader because they wanted him to become president. Don't free elections mean voting your heart and your conscience, no matter what? Besides, like other independents before him, Nader brought up a lot of topics that the two gangs wouldn't touch with a ten-foot pole.

Since that time, and since deciding not to run again for governor in 2002, I've been doing a great deal of thinking about third parties. My position is that the only way a third party can survive is to become as bad as the two that we already have, which just adds another entity we have to try to squash eventually. Instead of being a two-headed monster, we'll simply create a three-headed monster, a hydra. The way to take our government back is to defang and disarm what we've got now and make them no different than any other special interest group, with no more power. We've got a ferocious animal running amuck in our neighborhoods, and we need to turn it into a house cat or dog!

I'd make only one exception to the rule in 2012, and that's if Ron Paul decides to make a third-party run.

NOTES

1. "Few parties, major or minor . . .": Rosenstone, Steven J., Roy L. Behr, and Edward H. Lazarus *Third Parties in America: Citizen Response to Major Party Failure.* Princeton University Press, 1984: p. 59.

2. Greenback Party: Ibid, pp. 63–66.

3. People's/Populist Party: Ibid, pp. 68–75.

4. Prohibition Party: Ibid, pp. 75–78.

5. Teddy Roosevelt, "To destroy this invisible Government . . .": Cassidy, John. "Obama Spech Reax: Turning Point or Hot Air?" *New Yorker,* December 7, 2011.

6. Progressive Party/Bull Moose Party: *Third Parties in America*, pp. 85–87.

7. Socialist Labor Party: Ibid, pp. 90–92.

8. Minnesota Farmer-Labor Party: http://dfl.org/about/history.

9. Robert LaFollette: Joe, Mari. *The American Radical.* New York: Routledge, 1984. See also J. David Gillespie's *Politics at the Periphery* (University of South Carolina Press, 1993).

10. Strom Thurmond and the Dixiecrats: *Third Parties in America*, pp. 107–110.

11. Wallace "send Washington a message . . .": *Politics at the Periphery,* p. 107.

12. Www.nmpolitics.net/index/2011/07/a-case-for-a-third-party-candidate/.

13. "The FECA is a major party protection act": *Third Parties in America,* p. 26.

14. "Minor parties often advocate policies . . .": Ibid, p. 43.

15. "If it weren't for Jesse Ventura's establishment-shocking victory . . .": Sifry, Michah L. *Spoiling for a Fight: Third-Party Politics in America.* New York, Routledge, 2002: pp. 116–117.

16. Jack Gargan quote: Ibid, p. 122.

17. Buchanan vote total/ "For all intents and purposes . . .": Ibid, p. 142.

CHAPTER SEVENTEEN

RON PAUL: A MAN FOR THIS SEASON

There *is* one presidential candidate I happen to like a lot, and that's Ron Paul. He's a veteran of thirty-five years in the U.S. Congress who's already run for president twice (1988 as the Libertarian Party's candidate and 2008 as a Republican). We've interviewed him on multiple occasions for my TV show. The great thing about him is that whatever question you ask, he'll do his best to give an honest answer. There's generally no relationship today between elected officials and the public—but Ron Paul will at least talk to you, which is why so many young people also think so highly of him. When he had a counter-convention in St. Paul, where I spoke a few years ago, we didn't have any more security than you do for any Target Center event. Ron Paul isn't afraid, and in my view, he's a true man of the people.

So I came out publicly last December and endorsed him hands-down as my choice for president. That's because I want somebody who's going to change the direction of the country, a leader who will follow the Constitution and who believes in states' rights.

And somebody who will shock the status quo.

At the end of 2007, on the 234th anniversary of the Boston Tea Party, Paul showed up in Freeport, Texas, where organizers of a nationwide fundraiser had some barrels waiting for him to dump into the Brazos River. He passed by the ones that said "United

Nations" and "I. R. S." and threw one marked "Iraq War" into the water. Under the slogan "Liberty is brewing," in a single day the new Tea Party raised over six million bucks. This was before the "movement" really came together two years later and got co-opted by the billionaires. Paul's campaign literature justifiably calls him "Godfather of the Tea Party." But, like the man says, "I think parties are pretty irrelevant. Have you ever noticed that we change parties sometimes, but the policies never change?"[1]

He's accused Newt Gingrich of "serial hypocrisy," and that's one thing that can't be said about Paul. He's always been a straight shooter. My sincere hope is that, once he gets passed over by the Rebloodlican gang—and no matter how well he did in the primaries, he *will* be—he'll pull a John Anderson and bolt from the fold. If Paul runs as an independent or with the Libertarian Party, he'll absolutely get my vote. (I might even consider joining him on the ticket, if he asked me to.)

I've been quoting from our "paper of record," the *New York Times*, a lot in this book, along with my critique of their coverage in the chapter on media. This next one really pissed me off: an editorial they did called "Mr. Paul's Discredited Campaign." It began: "Ron Paul long ago disqualified himself for the presidency by peddling claptrap proposals like abolishing the Federal Reserve, returning to the gold standard, cutting a third of the federal budget and all foreign aid, and opposing the Civil Rights Act of 1964."[2] For one thing, much of that was a long time ago, since he's been elected to ten terms in the U.S. House of Representatives since 1976.

And tell me who else has stood up as strongly to the money powers? Congressman Paul gathered bipartisan support to get a bill passed that, for the first time, brought about an audit of the Federal Reserve—and revealed the trillions in taxpayer money doled out secretly to the banks as their reward for screwing over the American people. He'd earlier written a book called *End the Fed*. During his years in the Congress, Paul has often been the lone naysayer on legislation that he doesn't think is constitutional, leading some in Congress to call him Dr. No. His wife thinks they've got the spelling wrong—he's Dr. Know.[3] (Contrast this to Gingrich who, when asked how he planned to address the Federal Reserve, said: "Well, let's see, 'Sir' Ma'am.'"[4] Not cute, Newt.)

Here's one of the *New York Times'* op-ed columnists, Ross Douthat, on Paul:

> In both the 2008 and 2012 campaigns, Paul has been the only figure willing to point out the deep continuities in American politics—the way social spending grows and overseas commitments multiply no matter which party is in power, the revolving doors that connect K Street to Congress and Wall Street to the White House, the long list of dubious policies and programs that both sides tacitly support. In both election cycles, his honest extremism has sometimes cut closer to the heart of our national predicament than the calculating partisanship of his more grounded rivals. He sometimes rants, but he rarely spins—and he's one of the few figures on the national stage who says "a plague on both your houses!" and actually means it.[5]

Ron Paul is also the only presidential candidate—Republican or Democrat—who says we spend far too much on the military and have no business invading other countries. He believes that the Department of Defense should do just that: defensive, not offensive (literally and figuratively) foreign wars. Think of how much money pulling out of these messes would save. But aside from Rick Perry, who flew C-130s in the Air Force, Paul is the only candidate who actually did military service. He was a flight surgeon in the Air Force and then part of its National Guard in the '60s. The last great military leader we had as president, Dwight D. Eisenhower, was also the president who warned us about the military-industrial complex and called for cutting the Pentagon budget. Seems it's always the chicken hawks who want to spend more money. Throughout our history, the majority of our ex-presidents—thirty-one altogether out of forty-seven—have been part of our country's military at some point. But presuming neither Perry nor Paul ends up a candidate, this will be the first time in sixty-eight years that a presidential race has been between two non-veterans . . . and one of those will be commander-in-chief in charge of overseeing our war in Afghanistan and who knows what else.

Who do you think had by far the most donations of any candidate from our men and women in uniform? Between September 2011 and January 2012, Paul received $95,000 in individual donations from current and former members of the military. Obama came in second, with around $72,000.[6] Last year's total for Paul was ten times more than Romney raised and 100 times more than Gingrich (Newt used college deferments to avoid the draft during Vietnam, but now "promises he would strike foes at the slightest provocation").[7] Toward the end of February, several hundred troops held a rally outside the White House in support of Paul. One of the signs read, "Don't let anybody make you think that God chose America to be a policeman of the whole world."[8]

And Paul is the one his nutty opponents are calling crazy! He says that we shouldn't have invaded Iraq and that we sure as hell shouldn't invade Iran. He seems to appreciate that young men actually get killed in these wars that sound so good when politicians spout off in their speeches and debates and declare "mission accomplished." Not only does Paul find our warmongering ways to be draining the country dry—and has called for the immediate removal of our troops not only from Iraq but also from Afghanistan and military bases around the world—he isn't afraid to come right out and talk about "blowback." By that, he means that what's been called "our nation's invade-bomb-and-occupy first, ask-questions later doctrine" results in *more* likely terrorist retaliation, not less.[9] As Paul says succinctly, "We have an empire. We can't afford it. . . . We thought Obama might help us and get us out of some of these messes. But now we're in more countries than ever—we can't even keep track of how many places our troops are!"[10] (Today we have military personnel in 156 countries and bases in sixty-three countries. In 2010 alone, the U.S. spent $728 billion on the military. That's about 45 percent of the world's $1.6 trillion total, six times more than number two spender China.[11])

Here's another "crazy" Ron Paul idea: "To me, foreign aid is taking money from poor people in this country and giving it to rich people in poor countries, and it becomes weapons of war."[12] He's been accused of being anti-Israel, but here's what he actually has said:

> Stop and consider America's policy. We give $3 billion a year to Israel in loans, and we give $12 billion or more in assistance to Israel's self-declared enemies. Some of these are countries that say they will drive Israel into the sea. . . . We should be their friend and their trading partner. They are a democracy and we share many values with them. But we should not be their master. We should not dictate where their borders will be nor should we have veto power over their foreign policy . . . our aid in the region is out of balance and it is wrong. Foreign aid does not help Israel. It is a net disadvantage.[13]

Paul isn't afraid to bring up the still-taboo subject of Cuba either. When I was governor in 2002, I went there on a trade mission that the Bush Administration tried to stop. Otto Reich, who was Bush's State Department top dog for the Western Hemisphere, even came out publicly saying he hoped my group wasn't going to Cuba to sample the sex trade! I demanded an apology from the administration, but of course, it was never forthcoming. Anyway, I even had an audience with Fidel Castro, which you can read about in my book *Don't Start the Revolution Without Me!* And I sure came away believing it was way past time to lift our economic embargo and open up relations again with our neighbor ninety miles to the south.

Ten years later, you still had Newt Gingrich saying at a debate in Florida that U.S. policy "should be aggressively to overthrow the regime and to do everything we can to support those Cubans who want freedom." Was that a sound bite from fifty years ago, Newt? Addressing Cubans citizens, Rick Santorum called for sanctions to continue until they had "gotten rid of these tyrants who have controlled you for these 50-plus years." He also said, in all seriousness, that if Cuba were China in terms of where it was situated, he'd be just as against it.

The only voice of sanity has been Ron Paul, who put it like this:

> I think it's time to quit this isolation business of not talking to people. We talked to the Soviets. We talk to the Chinese. And we opened up trade, and we're not killing each other now. We fought with the Vietnamese for a long time. We finally gave up, started talking to them, now we trade with them. I don't know why the Cuban people should be so intimidating. I think we're living in the dark ages when we can't even talk to the Cuban people. I think it's not 1962 anymore. And we don't have to use force and intimidation and overthrow of governments. I just don't think that's going to work.[14]

Ron Paul also had the guts to say, in a debate back in 2008, that the 9/11 attacks were the Muslim world's response to our military's machinations around the world. When Rudy Giuliani demanded he take that back, Paul refused.[15] Paul has also asserted that, after 9/11, "immediately before there was any assessment there was glee in the [Bush] administration because now we can invade Iraq."[16]

Anyway, we're supposedly outta there now, almost nine years later, and look at the results:

- About $1 trillion of U.S. taxpayers' money spent or approved.
- Nine billion dollars of taxpayers' money lost and unaccounted for.
- Number of U.S. troops killed: 4,487.
- Number of U.S. troops wounded: 32,226.
- Number of U.S. troops returning with serious mental health problems: 30 percent within their first few months back

home. (The Iraq and Afghanistan Veterans of America group has estimated that nearly *one in three* deployed over there suffer from PTSD, depression, or traumatic brain injury. Altogether, we deployed 1.5 million to Iraq, so you do the math.)[17]

- Number of Iraqi "insurgents" killed: 55,000 (rough estimate).
- Number of Iraqi civilians killed: more than 100,000 (according to a secret U.S. government report released by WikiLeaks). Some estimates put the figure at more than 600,000.[18]

Hell of a liberation. . . . And this doesn't take into account how the Pentagon can't seem to locate documents explaining whatever it spent $1.7 billion on out of money from the frozen assets of Saddam Hussein supposedly being held by the New York Federal Reserve on behalf of Iraq's people. The DoD just can't find the spreadsheets after conducting "multiple electronic database searches" along with looking through a hundred boxes of files. A report by the Pentagon's Special Inspector General for Iraq Reconstruction concludes this is just a problem of "record management." Also unexplained is what ever happened to over $100 million in cash that was being kept at Saddam's old palace in Baghdad during the course of the war.[19]

❖ ❖ ❖

Young people most of all like Ron Paul, just like they did Howard Dean. He doesn't play the game, and he says what he thinks. Paul enjoys a huge amount of popularity among young voters despite the fact that, at seventy-six, he's by far the oldest candidate out there. I guess the youth haven't been brainwashed yet by the gangster media. We don't really know how much the Democrip-leaning ones are for Paul, because they don't get polled about him, but a Gallup poll taken among Rebloodlican-leaning voters last January found that 31 percent between the ages of eighteen to thirty-four preferred Paul as the candidate, compared to 26 percent for

Romney.[20] Early on, Paul came in a close third in the Iowa caucuses thanks to their support (the only age group Romney won was sixty-five-and-older, the exit polling said).

Then look at what happened with Maine's 2012 caucuses in February. The chairman of that state's Rebloodlican party is Charles Webster, who spent months cooking up "voter fraud" to dissuade thousands of out-of-state students from going to the polls. These young people spend most of their year attending colleges in Maine, and the state's Rebloodlican Secretary of State, Charles E. Summers, Jr., investigated Webster's so-called "evidence"—and found it to be completely bogus. It goes against federal law too. As if this wasn't bad enough, Webster declared Mitt Romney the winner of the Maine Caucuses, even though three different counties hadn't yet had their votes counted. Paul, it was claimed, "lost" by 194 votes to Romney.

The corporate media would have you believe that Paul's popularity with young people is all about smoking weed—because Paul supports legislation that would allow any state that chooses to legalize marijuana. Come on, that's an easy stereotype. The war on drugs, he's rightly said, is "a total failure," adding that "it undermines our civil liberties. It magnifies the problems on the borders. We spent—over the last 40 years, $1 trillion on this war. And believe me, the kids can still get the drugs. It hasn't worked."[21]

The fact is, Paul's stands against crony capitalism and our imperial wars, and what's happening simultaneously to our civil liberties, are what a lot of younger people admire. He also is a staunch opponent of the death penalty ("rich white people don't get the death penalty very often," Paul points out). On the immigration issue, he rejects the idea of "barbed-wire fences and guns on our border." As for abolishing the Federal Reserve, "What's wrong with the idea of taking away the power, from a secret group of individuals, to print money at will."

The thing that's ultimately so appealing about Paul is that he's managed to keep his integrity and stay *outside* the party-line bullshit. Here's what a twenty-two-year-old computer programmer in Seattle, Andrew Pilloud, said about Paul: "The fundamental emotional response to Paul is the same as Obama in 2008. He is the candidate for change. I personally think he's more likely to bring around change than Obama was. Once he gets into the White House he's going to do less compromising of his principles." Another fellow, twenty-one-year-old Carlos Alfaro of Arizona State University, said: "I think because [students] were so involved [in the 2008 election], they were also really involved in seeing what went wrong. They felt that betrayal." Now he's a Paul supporter. So is Justin Clements, a twenty-one-year-old finance major at the University of Washington. He thinks Paul's economic platform "really resonates with the youth. [Paul] is saying, look, we need to take control of our future, because it's been squandered and gambled by previous generations."

Some other students take it a step further. "What Ron Paul's campaign has really shown us is that the two-party system isn't sustainable for much longer," according to Ryan Neal, a twenty-four-year-old from Columbia University. Added Pilloud, "We have two parties that both stand for different factions of the elite." And here is Stephen Silvestri, a twenty-four-year-old New York waiter who's behind Paul and said: "I'm just really sick of Republicans and Democrats. They're part of the same money-grubbing game."[22]

On February 18, 2011, while bigwig Missouri and Kansas Rebloodlicans were feasting on steak at conventions not far away, Paul had a rally that drew a couple thousand to Kansas City's Union Station, including a few who snuck away from the fancier banquet. They stood and chanted while Paul talked about how our country went off track. "We've slipped away from a true Republic," he said. "Now we're slipping into a fascist system where it's a combination of government and big business and authoritarian rule and the suppression of the individual rights of each and every American citizen." More than once he slammed Obama for signing a law that could put anybody suspected of association with al-Qaeda or similar "terrorism" to be put in military custody. Name me any other candidate willing to go out on these kinds of limbs.[23]

The powers-that-be are actually pretty terrified of Ron Paul, and justifiably so. For two years running, by a big margin, he'd come out on top in a straw poll of those attending the yearly Conservative Political Action Conference (CPAC). In this election year, the organizers didn't want to take the chance that Paul might do it again. They switched away from paper ballots to electronic voting, which you could do from a computer or hand-held device. The American Conservative Union's current president, Al Cardenas, was upfront about the reason. "In the past," he said, "to his credit, about 80, 90, 100 percent of people who were there and liked Ron Paul voted, and probably a very small percentage of those who liked others bothered to vote." By shifting to the quicker voting method rather than manual counting, and letting members vote whenever they wanted during the conference, the hope was that another candidate besides Paul would carry the banner. To his credit, Paul didn't bother to attend.[24]

I can't leave out the fact that Paul was a real comrade-in-arms with my lawsuit against the Transportation Security Administration (TSA) that does the screening at our airports. Late in 2010, he introduced the American Traveler Dignity Act in Congress, talking frankly about how "the real problem is that the American people have been too submissive." Paul also said: "Can you think how silly the whole thing is? The pilot has a gun in the cockpit, and he's managing this aircraft, which is a missile, and we make him go through this groping X-ray exercise, having people feeling their underwear. It's absurd, and it's time we wake up."

Paul went on to make some powerful points, about what's happened over the decade since about 3,000 people died on 9/11. "Since that time . . . we have also lost 6,000 of our military personnel going over there and trying to rectify this problem. We have lost 400,000 people on our government-run highways. We have lost 150,000 people from homicides. . . . We're not dealing with it the right way . . . groping people at the airport doesn't solve our problems." The lock on the door and the gun inside the cockpit were "the greatest boon to our safety." Let the private sector, preferably the airlines themselves, provide for the security for their property, is the way Paul sees it.[25]

Here's the thing about Paul: It's about the issue, not the gang ideology. He and the American Civil Liberties Union have worked together in the past. "In 2009, the ACLU sued the Transportation Security Administration on behalf of a staffer for Ron Paul's nonprofit organization, Campaign for Liberty, who was briefly detained in an airport after hesitating to explain why he was carrying a box of cash."[26] He pointed to Dennis Kucinich, the liberal Ohio congressman, as being an ally on civil liberties and foreign policy.

Paul also has a unique strategy in terms of getting delegate support at the convention. It's perfectly within the rules set up by the system. His people are focusing on the states with caucuses instead of "winner-take-all" or proportional primaries—states like Iowa, Colorado, Nevada, Minnesota, and Maine. The rules vary from state to state, but after each precinct votes, they select delegates to go to county conventions, which in turn choose a smaller number for the state levels. It's those county and state level conventions that end up picking the national convention delegates. Who they're going to support doesn't have to be announced ahead of time. What Paul's campaign has done is get his precinct-level people to volunteer to be county convention delegates, in hopes they will outnumber the other guys when push comes to shove. At the national level, a winning candidate needs to have 1,144 out of the 2,286 delegates attending the convention. Let's say neither Romney or Santorum can hit the magic number. That's when Paul's quiet army of caucus delegates becomes important. He could end up "winning" a state's delegate count even though he didn't top the popular vote. "Modern conventions are supposed to be highly organized, tightly controlled displays of popular unity," as one forecaster put it. "At the very least a successful Paul delegate strategy could shatter that prospect."[27] And *that* is democracy in action. Nah-nah-nah-nah-nah.

I'm not saying I agree with Ron Paul down the line on everything—but why should I have to? Right now, he's about it among politicians willing to speak truth to power. So I have to agree with what's on the T-shirts among his volunteer workers: "Ron Paul Rocks America." And with the pro-Paul pop songs they play over the loudspeakers at his rallies: "Ron Paul! Start a Revolution! / And break down illegal institutions."

To sum it up, Chuck Baldwin, who Paul endorsed as an independent running in '08, says this about him:

> Dr. Paul knows the Constitution. He has studied it. He has read what America's Founding Fathers and framers have written about the Constitution. He has studied the enlightenment philosophers, theologians, and teachers—you know, the same ones that Thomas Jefferson and James Madison studied. He knows that the reason America is in the mess it is in today is because the Constitution has been abandoned. And he also knows that the only way to fix it (politically) is to return to constitutional governance.
>
> Therefore, when Dr. Paul talks about drugs, foreign policy, military adventurism, or even social issues, he does so from a constitutional point of reference. And the Constitution is clear when it comes to these matters. Domestic drug laws are the exclusive responsibility of the states—as is virtually every other law enforcement matter. Foreign entanglements, empire building, turning our military personnel into the world's policemen, etc., are all anathema to constitutional government. And the longer our political leaders continue to ignore the Constitution, the more America will continue to side down this slippery slope in which we now find ourselves.[28]

NOTES

1. Sanneh, Kelefa. "Party Crasher." *New Yorker*, February 27, 2012.

2. "Mr. Paul's Discredited Campaign." Editorial in the *New York Times*, December 28, 2011.

3. Paul's wife on Dr. No: Zemike, Kate. "Ron Paul, G.O.P. Loner, Comes in From Cold." *New York Times*, December 13, 2010 .

4. Gingrich on Federal Reserve: Bai, Matt. "Glory Days." *New York Times Magazine*, January 1, 2012.

5. Douthat, Ross. "Pariahs and Prophets." *New York Times*, January 1, 2012.

6. Larotonda, Matthew. "Veterans for Ron Paul Rally at White House." February 20, 2012, http://abcnews.gocom/blogs/politics.

7. Paul donations from servicemen; Gingrich and Vietnam: Egan, Timothy. "Ron Paul, the Soldier's Choice." *New York Times*, December 23, 2011.

8. Larotonda, Matthew. "Veterans for Ron Paul Rally at White House." February 20, 2012, http://abcnews.gocom/blogs/politics.

9. Sirota, David. "Why Do Young Voters Love Ron Paul?" *Salon*, November 28, 2011.

10. Paul on Obama: Sanneh, Kelefa. "Party Crasher." *New Yorker*, February 27, 2012.

11. Military expenditures: Stockholm International Peace Research Institute, cited in "The Invincible Military-Industrial Complex," www.readersupportednews.org.

12. Paul on foreign aid: at Western Republican Presidential Debate, video at www.realpolitics.com, October 18, 2011.

13. Paul on Israel: interview with Newsmax's Doug Wead, www.newsmax.com, December 7, 2011.

14. Ron Paul and candidates on Cuba: Martin, Roland. "The Hypocrisy of America's Cuba Policy." www.cnn.com/2012/01/28/opinion.

15. Zemike, Kate. "Ron Paul, G.O.P. Loner, Comes in from Cold." *New York Times*, December 13, 2010"

16. Montopoli, Brian. "Ron Paul: 9/11 Prompted 'Glee' in Bush Administration." CBS News, December 10, 2011.

17. Iraq and Afghanistan Veterans figures: Froomkin, Dan. "How Many U.S. Casualties in Iraq? Guess Again." December 30, 2011, www.readersupportednews.org.

18. Figures: "Iraq War Facts, Results & Statistics at November 30, 2011." http://usliberals.about.com/od/homelandsecuritl/a/IraqNumbers.htm.

19. Javers, Eamon. "Pentagon Unable to Account for Missing Iraqi Millions." CNBC News, January 31, 2012.

20. Gallup Poll: Thompson, Claire. "Why Ron Paul, elderly libertarian crank, turns young voters on." February 14, 2012, http://grist.org.

21. Paul on drugs: Republican debate, November 2011.

22. Student quotes about Paul: Ibid .

23. Liebe, David A. "Paul says U.S. 'slipping into a fascist system.'" *Associated Press*, February 19, 2012.

24. "CPAC Straw Poll Changes Hurt Ron Paul's Hat-Trick Chances." February 9, 2012, www.huffingtonpost.com.

25. "Ron Paul to TSA": www.RonPaul.com, November 17, 2010, concerning HR 6416.

26. Paul and ACLU: Sanneh, Kelefa. "Party Crasher." *New Yorker*, February 27, 2012.

27. Harris, Paul. "Ron Paul Quetly Amassing an Army of Delegates." *Guardian UK*, February 24, 2012.

28. Baldwin, Chuck. "What Ron Paul's Detractors Reveal." February 23, 2012, www.newswithviews.com.

CHAPTER EIGHTEEN

WHERE DO WE GO FROM HERE?
A CALL FOR A NO-PARTY SYSTEM

Our country's distrust of government has reached its highest level ever. In December 2011, *USA Today* came out with an analysis of voter registration statistics, state by state. Where voters get registered by party affiliation, Democrats were on the downswing in twenty-five of the twenty-eight states—all told by 800,000 people. Republicans declined in twenty-one states, by about 350,000 people.

But Independents were on the increase in eighteen states, gaining 325,000 people. States with big increases along independent lines were Florida, North Carolina, Colorado, and Florida. The elections director in North Carolina said that he thinks the winner in 2012 will be "whoever is attractive to the unaffiliated voter."[1]

George Washington, mind you, set the example—he was elected as an Independent before any parties existed. Besides Washington, two other presidents—John Tyler and Andrew Johnson—switched to Independent while in office.

At the state level, we've already seen a shift. In governor's races in recent years, independent and third-party candidates have won in Connecticut, Maine, Alaska, and Rhode Island (as well as Minnesota, of course). In 2010, independent candidates also beat out major party nominees in races for the Senate in Colorado and Florida.

And you've gotta know there's something "in the wind" when the very strategist in charge of Bush's campaign ads in 2000 and 2004, Mark McKinnon, now says he's interested in "anything that disrupts the current system."[2]

Given the dissatisfaction sweeping the nation, one of the strongest manifestations of democracy activism has been the recall movement. Right now, only nineteen states allow recalls of elected officials through petition drives. But in 2011, at least 150 officials in seventeen different states faced recall votes. That total included thirty mayors and eleven state legislators (nine in Wisconsin—where Scott Walker is now the third governor in U.S. history looking at a recall vote). This is a sure sign that more and more voters are ready to "throw the bums out."[3]

Besides the recalls, there are other signs of a shift. Bernie Sanders, the Independent U.S. Senator from Vermont, has called for a constitutional amendment to overturn the Supreme Court ruling that declared corporations to be persons and opened wide the door for no restrictions on secret campaign spending. What had happened was "a complete undermining of democracy," in Sanders' terms, and a century-long ban on corporate donations needed to be enforced. You'd need a two-thirds majority in the two houses of Congress and ratification by three-quarters of the fifty states to make the amendment happen. And I, for one, am enthused about it.[4] It was also heartening to see that the Montana Supreme Court went against the *Citizens United* ruling, by putting back in place the state's century-long ban on corporate direct spending on candidates or committees.[5]

Most promising of all, the citizenry is coming together around this. In January 2011, petitions with more than 750,000 signatures were delivered to Congress calling for the constitutional amendment to reverse this decision. In January 2012, over 350 protest events were held around the nation.[6] In February, fifty grassroots organizations sent letters to the House and Senate Judiciary committees demanding hearings on the need to change this.

Right now, we'd also need a constitutional amendment to get rid of the Electoral College, an action that a Gallup poll showed 62 percent of Americans are in favor of doing. For the first time, Republican voters joined Democrats and Independents in saying that the popular vote ought to decide presidential elections.[7] The Electoral College was created during the Constitutional Convention in 1787, intended to bring some stability to the thirteen states where communication and travel were slow. It was a horse-and-buggy idea that has long outlived its time.

The Electoral College is not only antiquated, it's undemocratic. The most powerful elected official we have is the only one *not* required to have the most votes to win! Supposedly, in our democracy, every voter should have equal representation, but that's hardly the case. Campaigning for president pretty much now goes on in a few big swing states. If you happen to live in Ohio or Florida, where the race is bound to be close, you're disproportionately important. A little rural town in Podunk, Ohio, becomes more important than a big city like, well, Minneapolis; not to mention that these swing states are where the most venal corruption takes place (the Supreme Court stealing Florida for Bush in 2000, and the electronic voting machines stealing Ohio for Bush in 2004). The 2000 election actually marked the fourth time in our history that the man who won the most votes lost the presidential election—starting with Andrew Jackson in 1824 (lost to John Quincy Adams), then Samuel Tilden in 1876 (lost to Rutherford B. Hayes), Grover Cleveland in 1888 (lost to Benjamin Harrison), and Al Gore in 2000 (to George W. Bush).

Look, in Article II of the constitution the founders guaranteed that if a state thinks it should give its electors to the national winner of the popular vote, they've got every right to do so. And states representing 132 votes in the Electoral College have gone forward to enact national popular vote legislation, pledging that whichever candidate comes in first among the people nationwide will get all their electors. (You only need 270 total in the Electoral College to win an election.)

This is part of a National Popular Vote movement whereby the Electoral College would continue to exist but could be superseded without going through trying to amend the Constitution. Through an interstate compact, participating states agree ahead of time to automatically give their electoral votes to whomever takes the *national* popular vote—*not* who gains the majority in their own state. So far, eight state legislatures have passed laws endorsing this, along with the District of Columbia. The latest to sign on was California. (See www.nationalpopularvote.com for more.) The Heritage Foundation says (oh no!) this would "diminish the influence of smaller states and rural areas" and "encourage voter fraud" and "radicalize American politics."[8] Excuse me, but didn't the Rebloodlicans, who are supported by the Heritage Foundation, already do that? Isn't the crux of the matter whether every person's vote should count for something?

Some new and, I think, very creative ideas are being proposed. In August 2011, the chairman and CEO of Starbucks, Howard Schultz, sent out a long email to everyone in his company. He wrote of being frustrated about "the lack of cooperation and irresponsibility among elected officials as they have put partisan agendas before the people's agenda." The response to the boss's email astonished him with its support. Schultz then called on people to basically go on strike against all the politicians—and stop making contributions to their campaigns. "It's a sad state of affairs that the only thing they'll listen to is money," he said, but given that fact, it was time to force Washington's hand with a boycott.[9]

The new means of communication can begin to allow candidates to bypass party and big donations. That's what Howard Dean got going back in 2004, and Obama followed up to some degree in '08. Now there's a for-profit political startup called Ruck.us, founded by two sons of politicians (Ray Glendening and Nathan Daschle) who believe "the two parties have simply failed to keep pace with today's world." Their idea is to Internet-connect people around collective action, beyond whatever party or political ideas they have. So you go to their website, sign up, and pick out what issues matter to you. You end up with a "Ruck," meaning the 50, 100, or 250 folks who have similar viewpoints. Then you're linked up to a communication feed to find out what your Ruck is talking about and what actions they're involved in.

Daschle the younger has said: "Ruck.us takes the core features of political engagement—matching like-minded people, and then allowing them to exchange information and take collective action—and rebuilds them. Political parties have held a monopoly on these features for the last 200 years. Thanks to social media technology, that's no longer the case. It is not a third party, it's 'anti-party.' It challenges the deeper premise of whether parties are even necessary in the 21st century." So far, Students First, LiveStrong, and Rock the Vote have partnered with Ruck.us for reaching out to their own audiences.[10]

Until you scratch the surface, another Internet-based effort toward a third choice for president seems interesting. That's Americans Elect, which as of November 2011 had raised $22 million toward having several rounds of Internet voting and then holding a nonpartisan nominating convention online in June—with any registered voter able to take part. These "delegates" will end up nominating a presidential ticket that includes one Rebloodlican and one Democrip, with the goal of being on the ballot in every state. Pretty ambitious but, as of Christmas 2011, the nonprofit group had already gotten onto the ballot in a dozen states—including California and the swing states of Nevada, Colorado, Ohio, Michigan, and Florida—and they'd collected signatures in seventeen more states that allow this process before an election.

The *New York Times*' Thomas Friedman, a big horn-tooter for globalization in the past, has come out and said excitedly:

> What Amazon.com did to books, what the blogosphere did to newspapers, what the iPod did to music, what drugstore.com did to pharmacies, Americans Elect plans to do to the two-party duopoly that has dominated American political life—remove the barriers to real competition, flatten the incumbents and let the people in.

Okay, all well and good, even though I don't even do email. The problem is, Americans Elect is one of those "social welfare" groups that don't have to divulge anything about their donors, thanks to the Supreme Court's *Citizens United* decision. Those who've dug into it, though, have learned that they've gotten some prime real estate for offices in New York and D.C. "financed with some serious hedge-fund money." The group's board chair, Peter Ackerman, is an investment banker who's pumped in more than a million of his own wealth after being a switch-hitter donator over the years to both existing gangs. Ackerman has also sat on a Cato Institute board that wanted to privatize social security. He used to be Director of Capital Markets at Drexel Burnham Lambert, the outfit made infamous by Michael Milken. Other funders have been reported as hailing from Lakeside Capital Partners, the Mt. Vernon Group investment fund, and the Promotion Marketing Association.

American Elect's bylaws state that any ticket chosen by the Internet "convention" must then get approval from the group's Candidate Certification Committee (CCC)—to make sure that the ticket has (gang) members "responsive to the vast majority of citizens while remaining independent of special interests and the partisan interests of either major political party." The board members appoint the CCC. Recently, Americans Elect loosened the rules to allow a majority vote of the "delegates" to override their decision. But beware of Greeks bearing gifts, is one way to look at this whole business.[11] My question is, why the secrecy? Americans Elect has said it's needed because "its underwriters fear retaliation for challenging the political status quo."[12] Except, those underwriters may be among the hidden undertakers for American democracy. The group's top strategist, Douglas Schoen, has advised the Democrips on the side to keep a distance from the "dangerously out of touch" Occupy Wall Streeters.[13]

When it comes to parties, the true Libertarian Party (not to be confused with the Tea Party, whose end result would be feudalism!) is the party most aligned with our Constitution. The Constitution is still the greatest document ever written for the benefit of mankind, which has held the republic together better than anything the world has known. If followed fully to its principles of free trade, a small, transparent, and compassionate government, maximum personal liberty, and non-intervention in foreign conflicts, our country would still be the most prosperous and least indebted nation on earth.

So let's go back again to a time when democracy was alive and well. Here's John Adams:

> There is nothing which I dread so much as a division of the republic into two great parties, each arranged under its leader, and concerting measures in opposition to each other. This, in my humble apprehension, is to be dreaded as the greatest political evil under our Constitution.[14]

Remember, John Adams is a guy who defended the British in court after the Boston Massacre, because that's how much he believed in the system he was trying to create. That wasn't a popular thing. The equivalent today was Dick Cheney going after the lawyers who are defending the Gitmo detainees. Cheney would call Adams a traitor for defending these enemies of our nation. But if our nation is going to stand for anything, then you *do* defend your enemies.

Do you ever find it ironic that a country that espouses freedom of choice offers only two real choices in our presidential politics? What if we were instructed to make our selection between two cars or two shirts or two sizes for our families? There are only a handful of two-party democracies on our entire planet (besides ours, Japan, Jamaica, and Malta qualify, with Spain and England dominated by a pair but not utterly beholden); most of the other democracies all have multiple parties. But if there's one thing our own Crips and Bloods agree on, as we've seen earlier in this book, it's to keep themselves the only game in town no matter what. We just had a major election a few years ago that was run on the concept of change we can believe in. Sorry, I don't believe. Where is it? Both parties tell you they're gonna give you something different, but in the end it's all about *them*.

So my proposal is: a NO PARTY system. Allow me to quote George Washington once again for a little back-up:

> However [political parties] may now and then answer popular ends, they are likely in the course of time and things, to become potent engines, by which cunning, ambitious, and unprincipled men will be enabled to subvert the power of the people and to usurp for themselves the reins of government.[15]

Parties could still exist. The founders acknowledged that, but only to the point of being no different than any other entity or endorser. If a certain candidate gets backed by the Democratic Party, fine—but you *don't put the affiliation next to the name on the ballot.*

Make all our elections nonpartisan. That way, the public has to learn who you *are*, if you follow me. Let candidates inform voters based on their positions, not these ridiculous stereotypes like "I'm a Republican and therefore I stand up for family values," or "I'm a Democrat and so I'm fighting for the working man." It's up to you, the voter, to know which candidate has which endorsements. Then, if you're a Crip or a Blood, you have every right to vote that way. But at least the gang's colors, or emblem, would not be on the official ballot. You wouldn't stand there in the booth and pull the lever for a whole column of candidates from one party. You'd have to be more involved in the process!

Look at what's happening: I mean, how can each member of an entire political party so consistently vote exactly the same way on every kind of issue? It's impossible for that many "free thinking" humans to vote alike, unless they're controlled by something other than their own minds. Such monolithic behavior ought to be a tip-off to fraud and betrayal.

Without the two gangs pumping millions into local races, wouldn't congressional elections be more local and more about qualifications than who's got the dough-re-me? Eliminate parties, and no longer would committee assignments in Congress be parceled out because of seniority or "party loyalty." There'd be no more majority and minority.

Today, with redistricting, less than 10 percent of all federal elections are even competitive. Because the parties control the districts, they know who's going to win ahead of time. It's all within the two gangs. Did you ever think about what a difference it might make if our representatives in Congress didn't sit together by party affiliation—but had to sit geographically or maybe even alphabetically? There's a new group called No Labels that wants to do away with partisan seating, among its twelve-point action plan.[16]

Why do you need groups within the Senate and the House? You pass laws by a majority vote, first in the Senate and then the House. It is what it is. If the measure gets more votes, it passes; otherwise, it fails. But no one is given the title of being a Democrat or Republican anymore. When they get up, they speak as John Smith, Senator from Wyoming, or wherever. Eliminate the gang connotation. They will still probably be loosely part of the gang, but you're taking a huge step in helping to destroy the stranglehold on power that the gangs control, by forcing them to run without a party.

Just think! No more dumb polls telling us how the different gangs view the different issues.

You don't necessarily need campaign finance limits, though you could go with structured limits on donations. I would say equally to be looked at is full open disclosure of where every penny contributed comes from. You'd no longer have hidden money that could be contributed to the gang, which can then do things that are unaccounted for. This way, you put the entire onus onto the campaign committee of a particular candidate. This is how you beat what the Supreme Court did. Corporations can give, but the candidate must run with open disclosure. He or she is completely responsible, and nobody else. So if somebody accepts $50 million from the oil companies, he or she has to disclose that completely. Then the public would know—well, guess who's gonna have this guy's ear? And you could say, okay I'm going to vote for someone else whom they haven't paid off.

Now if they end up paying off *all* the candidates, then you're stuck with who you're stuck with. But we get back to the personal responsibility of the voter, and until that responsibility is exercised, we're barking up a tree. You're still gonna get the knuckleheads who get in the booth and say, I'm just gonna vote for whatever name I like the best. Fine, but at least you're not voting over which gang you like the best. (Even if you picked people randomly, that'd be more honest.)

Another situation that should be dealt with is these party caucus staffs paid for by our general tax dollars. I'm an independent and always have been. Why should a portion of my taxes go to pay for these gangs to have secretaries and other expenses? Do we pay the General Motors lobbyist group? Well, yeah, we did in the bailout, along with Chrysler. But that's not a general policy. If we don't pay special interest groups to have their lobbyists at the Capitol, why do we pay *these* gangs to do the same thing?

For the presidential election, you'd obviously need to have multiple primaries of some sort. Maybe you'd start with regional primaries. You'd have to break the regions up based on population, because naturally the Eastern seaboard has more people than the mass of the Midwest, for example. But you could have two candidates coming out of each of eight regions of the country, then a national primary with sixteen candidates from the regions, and out of that you take the top four vote-getters to be on the national ballot. You could even have one of the four candidates endorsed by *both* parties (although the odds of that are slim to none, because for a strong portion of the Republicans, there's the litmus test of being anti-abortion).

But no more would you see the corporations dominate at the two party conventions, where they don't really care who wins because they've paid off both! Right now, the candidate has to subject himself to the gang, because if he or she opposes the gang, they won't endorse him or her in the next election. This makes the gang the power broker of who your choices are. The candidates have to swear allegiance to the gang first, the people second. As it stands, there are cases where the Bloods do something or the Crips do something, cases where they combine together, and cases where they pretend to work separately.

Gang politics are a lot like pro wrestling when you think about it, where it's portrayed that the opponents are such adversaries. But ultimately, behind the scenes, it all comes down to good-old-boy clubs—just like the Senate, where it's a matter of how do we pull the wool over the eyes of the people and keep our cushy jobs. These guys are all multimillionaires coming out of office. (I was working for $60,000 a year, take home, when I was governor.)

No answer or solution is perfect. Everything can be abused, but ultimately this brings it closer to the people. Nonpartisan elections are not some innovative new concept—I participated in one! In the city of Brooklyn Park, you might go in with ten candidates in the primary for mayor, and then the top two vote-getters go forward into the general election in the fall.

So I see this as a step towards winning back our country. The country isn't generally stolen by major events but in essence by small incremental things that chip away at the foundation and the base and cause it to crumble. This is a great way where we could throw a huge trough of cement back on the base and restore some of the solidarity of the crumbling republic. Is it the whole answer? Shit no, nothing ever is. Not when it's as big as the federal government. But it's something that could change course to where things might take a different turn.

What the hell, explain to me how this would be worse than what we've got? We're in a war today against the merger of corporate and state power (fascism, as Mussolini defined it). The government still wants us to believe that you, the individual, have the say so. That's the big lie. How much of the pie is actually left for us? The answer is very little.

There are already some potentially good steps in the direction I'm pointing at. California voters have passed Proposition 14, which in primary elections puts candidates for every state and national office except president on the same ballot and lets a voter choose any one of them—no matter the party. Then the two candidates with the most votes face off in the November election, even if they're both from the same party. It's called a "nonpartisan blanket primary," and, a nickname I like, the "jungle primary." Louisiana and Washington State, along with Alaska, have this in place as well. There's not even any voter party registration in Washington, and no signature requirements to get on the ballot. (There's a Prefers No New Taxes Party as well as a Prefers Salmon Yoga Party—for real!—depending upon which lotus flower you're sitting on.)[17]

Instant Runoff Voting (IRV) is a parallel deal that's been around awhile. In fact, in Australia, IRV has been used for elections to their House of Representatives since 1919. Ireland uses IRV to elect its president and London for its mayor. Even here in the United States, Minneapolis, St. Paul, San Francisco, Oakland, and Portland, Maine, have it in place for mayoral elections. And the Motion Picture Academy uses it to bring us the Best Picture Oscar every year.

Sometimes it's called Ranked Choice Voting, and here's how it works: It's one person, one vote, but out of however many candidates are on the ballot, you rank them in order of your top three choices. Every ballot is counted for first choices first. If one candidate gets over half of those votes, he or she gets elected. If that doesn't happen, the last place candidate loses out and you go to another round. Should your candidate be in the next round, well and good, otherwise you pick among who's left. It keeps on going that way until somebody emerges victorious.[18]

When this process was used for the first time in a mayoral election in Portland, Maine, in November 2011—actually the first time their mayor hadn't been an appointed politician—it was an extremely competitive election. Fifteen candidates were in the running, and voter turnout was about 50 percent higher than had been predicted.

In my view, IRV, by allowing multiple candidates, could possibly stop the parties from being the only two games in town. It won't eliminate money as a force, but the change that's needed is to break the grip of the two gangs!

The group No Labels aims at a grassroots movement for independents. Its first convention took place in New York at the end of 2010, attended by New York Mayor Michael Bloomberg, Florida Governor Charlie Crist, and some other names among congress people. Their goal, they say, is a nonpartisan consensus on the big issues—a step, at least, in the right direction.[19]

But I'm more excited about the Occupy Wall Street movement that seems to scare the crap out of Bloomberg. I love this one: The protesters have even figured out how to turn high-tech tactics back on the cops. In New York, a fellow named Tim Pool acquired his own Parrot AR surveillance drone that he calls the "occucopter." "It is a lightweight four-rotor helicopter that you can buy cheaply on Amazon and control with your iPhone. It has an onboard camera so that you can view everything on your phone that it points at. Pool has modified the software to stream live video to the internet so that we can watch the action as it unfolds." He's looking to police-proof the device by "trying to get a stable live feed so you can have 50 people controlling it in series." And even having another device so that the occucopter could be remote-controlled from England![20]

When the Rebloodlican Governors Association met in Florida last November, one of their chief strategists, Frank Luntz, said flat-out that he was "so scared of this anti-Wall Street effort, I'm frightened to death. They're having an impact on what the American people think of capitalism." Heaven forfend! Except, he should have substituted "plutocratic corporatism." Anyway, Luntz's advice was to replace the word capitalism in their speeches with "economic freedom" or "free market" and call the middle class "hardworking taxpayers." Don't talk about jobs, say "careers." Don't call it "government spending," call it "waste." Finally, be sure and tell the occupiers "I get it . . . I get that you want to fix the system."[21]

I'm afraid all those people "get" is how to learn George Orwell's "doublespeak"!

Wall Street can put Occupy down all it wants. One big hedge fund manager said, "Most people view it as a ragtag group looking for sex, drugs and rock 'n' roll." A veteran bank executive said: "It's not a middle-class uprising. It's fringe groups. It's people who have the time to do this." Jaime Dimon, the CEO of JPMorgan Chase, said: "Most of our clients like us. If you have any great ideas . . . you guys can write them up and send them to me. We'll take them into consideration."[22]

Well, right off! That kind of "considerate" attitude is just what has so many of the 99 percent closer to storming the Bastille than anytime certainly in my lifetime. Not only students but also unions are getting involved, and even a few courageous cops have crossed the barricade line. Now there's InterOccupy, "an elaborate website with multiple weekly phone calls during which occupiers trade ideas, coordinate multistate actions, and plan for the future." Folks from about 150 occupations around the United States have taken part in these, and led to shutting down ports on the West Coast for one.[23]

It was heartening to see, in January 2012, the OWS movement join with the National Prison Divestment Campaign for actions in thirteen cities. The divestment refers to the private prison industry and the role of big financial institutions like Wells Fargo and Bank of America. Yep, the same people involved in totally screwing our economy are busy investing in putting more Americans behind bars. Wells Fargo, as it happens, owns three-and-a-half million shares in GEO Group, after the Corrections Corporation of America (see chapter five), the biggest private prison operator in the country. At one of the actions, it got revealed that the detaining of immigrants is a gold mine for these companies. "Since the Department of Homeland Security took over immigration enforcement in 2003, the number of immigrants detained each year has almost doubled to 390,000. Today, nearly 50 percent of all federally detained immigrants are housed in private prisons."[24]

Also, let's hear it for the New Noncorporatized Media! I'm talking about the coming together of WikiLeaks and Anonymous, which will not only reveal more hacked truths that government doesn't want us to know about—but force the mass media to pay attention or get seen for the spineless gang supporters they really are.

Thousands of people are starting to realize that what politicians want us to do is sign up for their propaganda packages, which only reflect the will of their lobbyist paymasters. To get our unconditional endorsement, they talk down to us, scare us, lie to us with claptrap solutions to the nation's problems. And until now, their manipulations have worked quite effectively, especially in conjunction with the de-balling of the media.

Are we really only card-carrying reds, blues, greens, teas, mavericks, liberals, traitors, terrorists, communists? I'm sorry, but any form of unquestioning allegiance is nothing more than life on autopilot. We are constantly asked to cancel our individual thinking, questioning, and demanding by the very people who are supposed to be encouraging it!

Contributing to the national dumb down is the appeal to laziness and accepting screeds of prejudice, bombast, and manipulation as neatly packaged thought. Why should politicians be accountable to a populace whom they've lulled into passivity? They just go on shilling for their true Masters of the Universe—the oil companies, banks, military contractors, pharmaceutical and insurance giants, and so on. If you can't lug a bag of cash down K Street, you're shit outta luck.

I found this summation by Allison Stanger, author of *One Nation Under Contract*, to sum up the situation pretty clearly:

> Money's conquest of American politics has therefore rendered impotent the well-worn prescriptions of the left and the right, which now deliver only scapegoats rather than solutions. This is because the terms of political engagement have shifted dramatically over

the past two decades. In the twentieth century, big government was by definition bureaucratic government. Today, government can be 'big' in terms of spending while handing all its work over to contractors. In the twentieth century, business and government were adversaries. Today, the wall between the two that may have once existed has become a revolving door and both share common interests. Neither liberal nor conservative visions of good government can be realized so long as government itself is for sale.[25]

Here's another idea that's recently surfaced. Force the Federal Communications Commission to stop TV broadcast outlets from charging for campaign ads. That would go a long way toward ending this Super PAC bullshit. Way back in the Communications Act of 1934, Congress under FDR established the general requirement that broadcasters must act in the "public interest, convenience and necessity." That idea of the media as public trustee is something that actually got upheld by the Supreme Court. So let's Occupy the FCC![26]

It's going to take a whole lot of detailed nuanced thinking and action to get us out of this mess. First, we must make politicians understand that we aren't going to rubber stamp their actions anymore based on lies. And if they try to make suckers out of us, they must understand that we're going to turn them out on their heads (if not a rail or a pole). We won't be dumbed down, manipulated, or sold out anymore. Those days are coming to an end. It's our turn, We the People, E Pluribus Unum! Let's Panic the Party Animals and the Plutocrats! Let's take our country back!

Just get up off the ground, that's all I ask. Get up there with that lady that's up on top of this Capitol dome, that lady that stands for liberty. Take a look at this country through her eyes if you really want to see something. And you won't just see scenery; you'll see the whole parade of what Man's carved out for himself, after centuries of fighting. Fighting for something better than just jungle law, fighting so's he can stand on his own two feet, free and decent, like he was created, no matter what his race, color, or creed. That's what you'd see. There's no place out there for graft, or greed, or lies, or compromise with human liberties. . . . Great principles don't get lost once they come to light. They're right here; you just have to see them again!

—Jefferson Smith, in the movie
Mr. Smith Goes to Washington (1939)

NOTES

1. Wolf, Richard. "Voters Leaving Republican, Democratic Parties in Droves." *USA Today*, December 25, 2011.

2. Mark McKinnon: Stevenson, Richard W. "Group Clears a Path for a Third-Party Bid." *New York Times*, December 18, 2011.

3. Spivak, Joshua. "2011: The Year of the Recall Election." *Los Angeles Times*, December 29, 2011.

4. "Bernie Sanders Proposes 'Saving American Democracy Amendment.'" From the senator's office, December 8, 2011.

5. Gouras, Matt. "Citizens United Lose in Montana." *Great Falls Tribune*, January 2, 2012.

6. Quigley, Bill. "How to Cut Corporate Power." *Common Dreams*, February 6, 2012.

7. Camia, Catalina. "Gallup Poll: Americans want to scrap Electoral College." *USA Today*, October 24, 2011.

8. National Popular Vote/Heritage Foundation: von Spakovsky, Hans. "Protecting the Electoral College from the National Popular Vote Scheme." October 18, 2011.

9. Howard Schultz' idea: Nocera, Joe. "Boycott Campaign Donations!" *New York Times*, August 13, 2011.

10. Empson, Rip. "Political Sons Launch Ruck.us: A Social Engagement Platform Based on Issues, Not Parties." September 26, 2011, http://techcrunch.com; Tafel, Rich. "Crash the Parties." September 20, 2011, www.huffingtonpost.com.

11. Americans Elect: Elliott, Justin. "The slick shtick of Americans Elect." December 9, 2011, www.salon.com; Wood, Daniel B. "2012: The Year of the Third-Party Candidate?" *Christian Science Monitor*, December 25, 2011.

12. Underwriters: Marcus, Ruth. "Americans Elect: A Wild Card for the Internet Age." December 29, 2011, www.nationofchange.org.

13. Douglas Schoen: "The 1 Percent President." February 18, 2012, www.fair.org.

14. John Adams on parties: "Letter to Jonathan Jackson (2 October 1780)" in *The Works of John Adams*, vol. 9, p. 511.

15. George Washington on parties: Quoted in "What If There Were No Political Parties?" by Chris Slavens (March 17, 2010 at www.theepochtimes.com).

16. www.nolabels.org.

17. "Nonpartisan blanket primary."

18. www.instantrunoff.com.

19. No Labels: Bai, Matt. "In a Culture of Independence, Bloomberg Could Skip the Party." *New York Times*, December 14, 2010.

20. Sharkey, Noel and Sarah Knuckey. "OWS Fights Back Against Police Surveillance by Launching 'Occucopter' Citizen Drone." December 22, 2011, www.alternet.org.

21. Moody, Chris. "How Republicans are being taught ot talk about Occupy Wall Street." *The Ticket*, December 1, 2011.

22. Quotes from hedge fund, banker, and Dimon: Schwartz, Nelson D. and Eric Dash. "In Private, Wall St. Bankers Dismiss Protesters as Unsophisticated." *New York Times*, October 15, 2011.

23. Elliott, Justin. "Occupations in winter." December 26, 2011, www.salon.com.

24. Khalek, Rania. "Occupy Joins the Fight Against Private Prisons." February 17, 2012, www.truth-out.org.

25. *"One Nation Under Contract*—Six Questions for Allison Stanger." www.harpers.org.

26. Cole, Juan. "How the FCC Can Take the Money Out of Politics," February 24, 2012, www.nationofchange.org.

ACKNOWLEDGMENTS

Thanks to Randy Foote, Professor of Political Science at Roxbury Community College, for his editorial assistance. Also our appreciation in this regard is extended to Audrey Peterson and to the 2011 team of interns at Skyhorse (under supervision of the astute editor Jason Katzman).